OUT OF THE SPOTLIGHT

George Green

Printed in the United States of America

First Printing, 2015

ISBN 978-0-9915272-6-7

www.georgegreen.net

Twenty years from now you will be more disappointed by the things that you didn't do than by the ones you did do. So, throw off the bowlines, sail away from safe harbor, catch the trade winds in your sails. Explore, dream, discover.

Mark Twain

Table of Contents

Spotlight Interviews

Gone But Not Forgotten

Acknowledgements

Where have the years gone to? I left KABC Radio on May 1st, 1996. I spent almost thirty-eight years with the station, seventeen of them as President and General Manager. I was in an intense spotlight in my role as the General Manager. Then, the Walt Disney Company bought the company and fired many of the radio managers. I was one of them. Three days' notice and my Spotlight went out. A year later I decided to write this book because I realized that there were others, like me, whose spotlights had also gone out. But then they, like me, went on to another spotlight.

Thus, in 1997 I started writing this book including interviews with major celebrities from many walks of life. I put the book aside in 2009 to pay attention to some other interests of mine. Then, because of my age and concern that there was a lot of unfinished business in my life, I decided to complete the projects I'd started many years before, one of these being *Out Of The Spotlight*.

I needed some help. My son, Randy Green, came to my rescue! His knowledge of the internet enabled him to find three important members of my production and creative staff. He found an Illustrator in Indonesia. Nidhom is his name, and he has helped me to finish my five children's books, and created the sketches for *Out Of The Spotlight* with his outstanding skills.

Also on the staff is the talented book-designer, Xenia Janicijevic Jovic, from Serbia.

She contributed her valuable thoughts and ideas to all of my seven books, and put them together perfectly.

A big thank you must also go to Rabbi Jerry Cutler and Jerry Pollin, two friends of mine who recommended many of the people I have interviewed for this book.

But the person who I must tip my hat to is a lady named Carly van Heeden. She lives in South Africa and as my editor, and friend, is really the live-blood of all my books. Her energy and enthusiasm toward what I do, along with her editing talent, brings to life everything that I write.

And finally, my son, Randy. Acting as the producer of my books, he also acts as the glue behind my production team. He is bright, experienced and above everything else I might say; he knows how to deal with his father... *ME!*

Out Of The Spotlight is not a small book; almost three-hundred pages, forty-five interviews with the most interesting people I have ever known in my whole life!

Each of them has a story to tell and, in a respect, I must acknowledge each of them, because without their honesty and their stories about themselves, *Out Of The Spotlight* could not have been written.

So, my hat is off in a salute to each of them for the amazing and interesting life-stories that they've shared in this book. For all of you who have taken the time to buy and read *Out Of The Spotlight... I THANK YOU!*

GEORGE GREEN

About Out of the Spotlight

This book was written with the purpose of helping others to understand that when our primary spotlights are removed, or dimmed-out, there is another light burning, waiting for us to stand beneath it. But we have to create it ourselves.

Included is a compilation of interviews with men and women who once stood proudly beneath their bright lights. Some made a personal decision to walk away from these lights, while others were asked to leave.

What did they do? How did they respond? Who did they become? And finally, how did they keep their very own self-charged spotlights burning?

Introduction to George Green

American born George Green has worked in the entertainment industry all his life.

Upon compiling this book in 2015, George is eighty-four-years-old. Even at this age, there isn't much that can hold him back from doing what he loves to do most. Whether this be spending time on his boat with his family, skiing in the mountains, playing bridge, competing in golf tournaments, working with guide and service dogs, putting together a legacy of music left to him by his father, or writing his series of children's stories; one would swear George is still in his early fifties.

Aside from being a well-known leader in his former career he is also a father, grandfather, and friend to many. George has a certain tenacity that cannot be matched, and even though he was dealt a foul hand in his earlier years, he bounced back with more to offer to life around him than ever before.

At a young age, George joined the air-force and served in Germany for one and a half years. On returning he attended UCLA where he studied to become a school-teacher, graduating in 1955. After graduating he found a job with NBC as a Paige where he handed out free 'audience' tickets to folks walking by the studio. In those days a live audience really was a 'live' audience! In 1957 he moved on to work, for a short time, selling radio spots in Palm Springs.

In 1959 he joined KABC TV in Los Angeles as a junior TV salesman, and then moved on to KABC Radio in early 1960. Shortly after arriving at KABC Radio, Ben Hoberman, the manager of New York's WABC, came to Los Angeles and turned KABC from a solely music-orientated station into an 'All Talk' station; the first in the nation. At KABC George worked as a sales-person from 1960 to 1965. In 1965 he was promoted to general sales manager. He was again promoted to the top position of President and General Manager in 1979, and held that position until he left the station in May, 1996. With George as their guide, KABC Radio soon made industry history by introducing various programming and marketing innovations that literally propelled KABC into becoming one of The United States' top revenue and profit producers.

During his time at the station George wrote, recorded and aired over two-thousand editorials, which were broadcast to over one-million listeners per week. His devotion and outstanding efforts earned him numerous awards, too, including the 'Executive of the Year Award' from Southern California's 'Executive Magazine' in 1987. It appeared at this time that George was irreplaceable.

However, after thirty-eight years of giving it his all, George was called to a breakfast meeting in the spring of 1996. The Walt Disney Company had purchased Capital Cities in 1995; Capital Cities being the company that owned the KABC media empire at the time. In this meeting with the KABC company's new president, George was asked, "When would you like to retire?"

George replied, "In two or three years from now, perhaps." By this time George was sixty-five-years-old.

But at that same meeting, George was told, "Your replacement will be here on Monday."

George's termination at KABC was the start of a ripple of terminations over the year that followed. Ultimately the Walt Disney Company let go of and replaced numerous staff members during that next year; all of them left in a state of confusion, unhappy about the life-changing choice that had so abruptly and unexpectedly been made for them.

George spent the next few months feeling unnerved, saddened, outraged; a mixture of emotions filled his being as he tried to comprehend what had happened to him and his fellow colleagues. But he quickly realized that life goes on; there are always new mountains to climb, new successes to find. He had to go forward, not backward.

"Looking back gets us nowhere. Things can never be what they were. There can always only be what will be." He started fresh, under his own steam, under his own spotlight at the ripe-old age of sixty-five. But perhaps no one can tell the story better from for this point on, than George himself.

Opening by George Green

In the spring of 1996, a thirty-eight-year career in radio broadcasting that had given me influence, prestige, fame and financial independence, ended suddenly without warning.

I was president of KABC Talk Radio in Los Angeles, a station I had worked for since 1960, when it pioneered the All-Talk radio format. KABC was one of the most famous stations in America, and a legend in Los Angeles. It had been my whole life and it was a great life.

Then, over breakfast it disappeared forever. The Walt Disney Company bought KABC, and almost immediately started making changes in top management at the KABC Radio network. On 'May Day', at breakfast with the new president of KABC Radio, I was told I was being replaced after having been with the company for thirty-eight years.

Everything I depended on was gone. I was sixty-five-years-old with little other direction. I knew I had to go on but didn't know how. I had never failed at anything before. I was out of the 'bright' spotlight that was on me when I was with KABC.

When I left I was full of two emotions; rage and revenge. I wanted to start my own business with a suite of offices, and even hire my old secretary whose position at KABC was also terminated. I wanted to expand this business in media marketing and talent management. But Mim, my late wife, suggested I convert one of our spare bedrooms into an office and expand later, if I still wanted to. She was always ahead of me in displaying her sensitivity to a situation, while offering down-to-earth, sensible advice. I did what she suggested. I opened George Green Enterprises.

At the same time I decided to gather a little advice by asking the experts; those who had perhaps gone through a similar experience, whether forcibly or on their own. I knew many celebrities through working in radio, so I began with them. Before I knew it I had interviewed as many as fifty individuals; some of America's top-achievers.

I wanted to find out if my thoughts were correct; that there were two, main, different emotions that take place when a person leaves their primary job in life. I wanted to know; if someone retires because they want to, are there always negative feelings or a desire to seek revenge... or continuous feelings of looking back at 'what was'? I ultimately discovered that these feelings of rage, revenge and sadness, really only come when one is laid-off or fired.

Through the stories of those I had the privilege to interview, I saw how I could rebuild my life. I then also realized how their stories could help others, too. During this time came the saddest day of my life. I lost my wife, Mim Green. She died February 6th, 2006.

Like so many other widowers, I met Myrna Odwak and she and I have been living together for more than nine years. Yes, we can love more than one person in a lifetime and Mim, before dying, recommended that I do exactly what I did. She knew I would not want to live alone. My life with Myrna has been a joy.

Back to *Out Of The Spotlight*. When I decided to write the book I was going through a transitional period in my life. As mentioned, I suspected that there were a lot of people, from all walks of life, who were experiencing the same emotions and finding the same answers that I found; that we all had to get used to not being in the intense spotlight we were under while growing our business, getting better at our jobs, or successfully raising a family, after semi-retirement or retiring entirely from 'the business'.

It was 1997 when I started. For a number of reasons, I spent a lot of time and money writing the first part of Out Of The Spotlight. But then I put it aside, like so many other projects I'd started (too many to discuss here).

Here it is, 2015. I am eighty-four-years-old, attempting to finish this important book that I started writing in 1997. It is important to me because it was my first attempt at writing, at being on the creative side, and more importantly trying to find my own identification. Back then I was always introduced as; "Oh, you know George. He was the general manager of KABC Radio. You must have listened to his editorials."

I just wanted to be introduced as 'George'. Now, at the age of eighty-four, the word 'mortality' has special meaning.

When we were thirty, forty, fifty or even sixty, life seemed to be a never-ending thing. I don't think that way anymore. Life is short. I am beginning to see the light at the end of that tunnel.

My life is different now. So many of my friends are no longer with us. But being an older citizen is not so bad, as long as one has their health. I remember my mother and father always told me that 'health is wealth'. How right they were! So, I take every day as it comes, enjoying the world as it is.

Fortunately I am financially comfortable thanks to my thirty-eight years at KABC Radio. My health is good and I'm grateful that I've lived this long. But, no matter what, I still do not want it to end. I live in a house in a suburb of Palm Springs. The weather is great for someone like me who loves to play golf. That is my main sport. I'm grateful to still be able to play the game with a reasonable handicap.

Yup! Life is good and I hope it continues. I found love, new friendships, new business opportunities and equally importantly; I have been successful in my life. I also finally have my own identification; just plain-old George Green! Yeah!

I do not want to stop thinking, or having great ideas of what should be done in this world. I do not want to stop enjoying every day of my life, hoping it will not end. But reality has stopped me from thinking too far ahead. I know there is an end and I know that someday, maybe not too soon, the spotlight that I am under now, no matter how dim it may be, will be out.

So, because of these thoughts about how long we will live, I thought I would enter a new phase of my life; starting a project... and finishing it!

Aside from Out Of The Spotlight, four years ago I started writing a book with my son-in-law's sister, Maria Giacchino. I had been telling children's stories to my kids for fifty years. All the children's stories were about animals who couldn't do what they were expected to do, but they had other strengths that, when discovered, would carry them through their lives.

I wanted to write a story about a lion who couldn't roar. I wanted to write a story about a dog who couldn't bark, a story about a cat who couldn't meow... and so on.

Maria Giacchino and I wrote the first book, The Lion Who Couldn't Roar. Maria was great at writing poetry and she wrote most of that book. With good illustrations, the book was published and hundreds of copies were sold. At the time I was certainly proud of the book, but deep down I knew that although the story was mine, the words were written by Maria.

In September 2013 I became very philosophical about life. I knew I was living in one of the last chapters of the Life of George Green. Hopefully there are many more to come, but I thought of the shortness of life and decided to finish writing my children's books, and also to finish Out Of The Spotlight.

I started on four more children's books and, lo and behold, I finished writing them!

Softy, The Bird Who Couldn't Fly. Toby, The Laughing Hyena Who Lost His Sense Of Humor. Fred, The Dog Who Couldn't Bark. And Fluffy, The Cat Who Couldn't Meow.

I was blessed with three wonderful children, each of them having their own talents for living their lives. Randy, my youngest son, is the tech in our family and he took on the job of producing the books. We found a wonderful illustrator in Indonesia, a fantastic editor in South Africa and a book designer in Serbia.

My, oh my... technology today makes working with these people easy!

Carly van Heerden, my editor, and I are working together as I write this introduction to *Out Of The Spotlight*, putting together some finishing touches. More than fifteen of the first fifty people I interviewed have passed away. I decided, before I join that deceased list, I wanted to finish my book.

So, here it is ladies and gentlemen; the finished product...

OUT OF THE SPOTLIGHT

Spotlight Interviews

Ed Ames

Downsized as a singer by Rock n' Roll

Edmund Dantes Urick (Ed Ames) was born in July, 1927, in Maiden, Massachusetts, to Ukrainian Jewish parents. He grew up in a less-fortunate environment with four brothers and four sisters. He attended Boston Latin School where he studied classical and opera music, as well as literature. During high school, Ed and three of his brothers formed a quartet called 'The Ames Brothers'. They released their first major hit in the 1950s, 'Rag Mop'. In the early 1960s the band separated. However, Ed chose to pursue a career in acting and studied at the Herbert Berghoff School.

After playing the role of Chief Bromden in the Broadway production of 'One Flew Over The Cuckoo's Nest', talent scouts from 20th Century Fox spotted him and soon he was playing the role of the Cherokee tribesman, Mingo, in the television series Daniel Boone, alongside Fess Parker. Ed's career as a singer and an actor bloomed during the 1960s.

However, his spotlight began to dim towards the end of the sixties as rock n' roll began to take over. Show business didn't care much for artists, and his audience suddenly shrank. He was still able to perform in television and as a concert performer, but soon these concerts began to disappear.

One of Ed's lowest moments was when he was replaced in a Vegas show by a football star, Joe Namath. Suddenly the calls stopped. Ed felt robbed of his dignity. He chose to go back to UCLA where he became somewhat of a bridge between generations, and studied theater and cinema arts.

Ed's advice for coming out of personal depression and moving into another spotlight is to call on your courage. He wanted to continue as a performer but would not be *wedded to the necessity of performing to a point that he didn't feel worthwhile as a man, or as a human being, if he wasn't on the stage.'* So, he advises against continuing in the performance industry if it means that the performer will be downsized and inevitably forgotten. Instead, he suggests pursuing other things; in his case it was writing and directing.

"I think you should do something that demands your talent and your attention, and your energies."

Ed Ames has an inspiring, self-fulfilled attitude. "When I do a good job, I don't need the audience to tell me!"

Interview with Ed Ames

George Green: During the fifties, the Ames Brothers were King of the Hill and you had a marvelous career. Tell me about the highlights of your show-business career, when that spotlight was bright.

Ed Ames: Suddenly my opinions became important although they shouldn't have been, I mean; any more than a plumber if you come down to it! A bright plumber is as bright as a show business personality. When I sang with my brothers we had a lot of hit records. The money wasn't anything like it is now. Of course, the dollar wasn't the same. We were just kids who had come to New York and they said, "Come here, guys," and we were on a record.

George Green: The spotlight was still pretty bright at the time you were doing television; you were in Las Vegas...

Ed Ames: Yes, I did television and also a lot of musical shows.

George Green: At what point did you think that the spotlight was not as bright; you knew that things were changing?

Ed Ames: The business changed so much. Suddenly it became a rock n' roll world. Other people, along with myself, felt less interest in my records. The audience got smaller. The marketing changed. Suddenly record companies and record stores, and record distributors, were more interested in the 'rock' thing. By the mid-eighties there was very little demand for people like myself or Andy Williams, or Tony Bennett or anybody like that. It didn't affect me as much as some because my life was not completely tied up in the record business. I did acting on television, on the stage; I did concerts.

George Green: What was your feeling at the time?

Ed Ames: Well, you have to adjust. I was scheduled to do a show. At the last minute they decided they wanted to do something less formal. Joe Namath who was a great football star, he was my substitute, went in and I was gone. I realized then that things weren't the same. That bothered me a lot.

George Green: How did your 'close people' respond? Were they supportive?

Ed Ames: Some were and some were not. I didn't go 'kerplunk' and fall to the bottom of the well. The guys who had been my buddies and friends, and had worked with me and for me, they suddenly became unavailable. I think that is something that probably happens universally. I don't like it. I have a terrible thing about people who don't call back. It offends me. Even if I don't know the person well, or it's someone I don't care about that much, give me the respect of a call back.

George Green: The company I worked for, for thirty-eight years; I was angry at the way they did some things and I was hurt. Did you ever have that feeling?

Ed Ames: Yes, certainly. I feel it robs you of your dignity. It's an insult and it was ungracious, humiliating, cruel and I didn't like it. My friends in 'the business' would call back, if at all, a week later or they would have their secretary call and make apologies. It distressed me and angered me.

George Green: How did your activities change? Did you have a plan in mind?

Ed Ames: I went back to college and got two degrees. It was something I wanted to do; in Fine Arts at UCLA. The younger kids knew who I was. They would walk up beside me on campus and start talking with me. They would say, "I'm having trouble with my Dad. He doesn't understand." I was sort of a bridge between the generations. In fact I went to an agent friend of mine who got a writer with me, and we actually conceived a television series based upon that.

George Green: So you seemed to cope pretty well emotionally with the fact that a part of your life was not in the spotlight.

Ed Ames: I don't know. You have to call upon your courage and you have to have a philosophy. I did have a philosophy that carried me through. It's nothing earth shattering. I did have a general life plan that I wanted to continue for the rest of my life performing, but on the other hand I did not want to be so wedded to the necessity of performing that I didn't feel worthwhile as a man, or as a human being, if I wasn't on that stage. I never allowed myself to get into that frame of mind. So, one thing I did was to go back to college. I started writing. I studied directing while I was in college, too. Unfortunately I never went as far with that as I wanted to. I made up my mind that I wouldn't take jobs that I felt were demeaning. When I was a kid, I used to look at big stars and I didn't realize what the pressures were. I knew there would come a time and that's why I did start preparing myself for it. But my dream was to go on and work until I die with my boots on, but on my own terms. Or, if not, there are other things. I was not going to allow myself to be shattered. I know a lot of people in this business who hang on. I didn't want that to happen to me.

George Green: What would you advise other people going through a life transition, whether they have been downsized or they are getting older; when the cheering stops, what is your advice?

Ed Ames: You can beat your head against the wall and then become verbose, frustrated; fall apart. Or, you can find something else to do.

George Green: Climb another mountain.

Ed Ames: You climb another mountain; a different mountain. I reached a point in my life when I started giving back, too. I did a lot of charity things. I don't give it away easily. The talent you have given for a lifetime; I don't like to give it away, but I will give it away for the things that I love. That is what I consider 'pay back'. I went back to school and that's a wonderful thing to do, for anybody. Why should you sit around and have the 'empty-nest syndrome'?

George Green: One thing about show people; the desire to hear the applause is constant until the day you die.

Ed Ames: I'm not like that. I love it, I'm not kidding, but I don't need it. A lot of people in our business need it. I'm trying to improve myself. It's a different approach.

George Green: So the bottom line is 'keep busy'.

Ed Ames: I think that's it.

George Green: Are there things, or anything else that has given you as much of a rush as you had when that spotlight was so bright?

Ed Ames: I don't think so. But the opportunities, the challenges, took all your courage and energy to meet them, and when you were successful in doing that... I mean... those are highs!

Pat Boone

Pat ~ "A lot of people think there are two Pat Boones; they literally do!"

Charles Eugene 'Pat' Boone was born in June, 1934, in Jacksonville, Florida. As a toddler his family moved across to Nashville, Tennessee, where he spent his childhood and then attended David Lipscomb High School. After high school he went on to study at Lipscomb University and North Texas State College. In 1953, Pat married Shirley Lee Foley. Both her parents were well-known singers. Together Pat and Shirley chose to settle in Leonia, New Jersey, and Pat continued to study at Columbia University, School Of General Studies, in New York. He graduated from there in 1958 with a Bachelor of Science degree.

However, during this time he discovered his passion for performing and his career as a singer began. His entrance into the spotlight was 'too much, too soon'. TV, radio, movies and chart-topping records hurled this college student into an intense international spotlight. Since then Pat is said to have sold over forty-five-million albums, many of which were cover versions of songs by other artists. He's had over thirty-eight of his songs featured on the top-forty list over time, and has appeared in over twelve Hollywood movies, some of which include 'The Pied Piper of Cleveland', 'Mardi Gras', 'The Cross And The Switchblade', 'Roger And Me', and 'Precious Moments' to name but a few.

Growing up with a strong Christian faith, Pat turned to gospel singing in the late 1960s.

He and his family took to touring. Being a performer at heart, he had his own way of doing things, ways that were not always understood by the public. For example, when he arrived at the American Music Awards dressed in black leather after releasing an album of heavy-metal covers, he was misunderstood and dismissed from Gospel America. After later explaining the reasons for his actions, he was welcomed back. But Pat was often hurt by his critics. "A lot of people think there are two Pat Boones. They literally do," he says.

Pat pursued his passion for writing, too, and wrote a number of gospel/Christian-related books, some of which have gone on to become best-sellers. He claims to live by the wise-words of George M. Cohan; "Always leave them wanting more!"

Pat Boone currently lives in Beverley hills, Los Angeles, with his one and only wife, Shirley. They have four daughters who have also found success in life.

Interview with Pat Boone

George Green: Can you describe your feelings when you first entered that spotlight in the early fifties? How intense was that light?

Pat Boone: Well, it was intense and it was quick. I was in college at North Texas State. Randy Wood of Dot Records called me. I flew to Chicago. I recorded an early rock and roll pop version of a hit by a group called 'The Charms'. We made us a hit single only to find that Frank Sinatra recorded it, so did Doris Day, so did The Lancers, so did about three pop groups who were all well-known, and I was unknown. So, Randy Wood put me on planes and sent me to twenty cities in eighteen days. I was constantly on TV and radio. Each city had me on a crazy pressured merry-go-round of appearances and meetings. I went back to Denton, Texas, to see my wife after this eighteen day ordeal, thinking, *'If this is the entertainment business, I don't want this.'* My impression was that 'this is way too much work.' The next record, 'Ain't That A Shame', went right to number one on the pop chart. Things were happening so fast. From then on, for the next five years, I was virtually never off the charts. I starred in my own TV show, and I made some movies. 'Love Letters In The Sand' was the biggest seller. It went all over the world. I was learning how fabulous the record business could be. You make a record in a studio in Chicago, and you find that people all over the world are hearing and enjoying what you did.

George Green: How did you feel about that?

Pat Boone: It was phenomenal! I fell in love with the record business. DJs are playing my record. I pull up to a traffic light, I see a car full of kids and the windows are down and it's hot, and they're just jumping up and down and singing at the top of their lungs to my record of 'Ain't That A Shame'. I wanted to say, "Huh, kids, that's me, huh, huh, it's me." I didn't, but I sat looking at that car full of kids jumping up and down and enjoying my record. Something just melted like a time capsule inside of me. I thought, *'I like this, I want more of this.'* I got plenty over the next four years because I was never off the charts. I got used to being in the limelight and enjoyed it.

George Green: Did you think it was going to go on forever?

Pat Boone: Each record I thought might be, virtually, my last. I was in college all this time and I thought God was giving a terrific way of working my way through school. I was going to be a school teacher. I just wanted to be in the lives of young people and be a good influence. I saw this as a weird set of circumstances, allowing me to get through college with a wife and kids. When I graduated in 1958 we had four children. I had a multi-million dollar movie contract. When I took my last exam at Columbia I stopped in Central Park, lay on my back, looking up at the sky and I thought, *'I have to make a decision. Am I going to apply for a teaching job or shall I see where these contracts lead me first? If I do fulfill the contracts, then that's three or four years of good income.'*

George Green: You were going to become financially secure for your family.

Pat Boone: I felt I would have at least a nest egg. I did have a deal with a licensing company for all kinds of Pat Boone products, so I arranged for all of the proceeds from the merchandising and endorsements to go into trust funds for my daughters, toward their education and marriages. Eventually that did pay for college and weddings, and some extras.

George Green: When did you suddenly look up and say, "It's been a great ride and now the real world..."

Pat Boone: When the Beetles took! My record sales were diminishing and drying up. At that point a little entrepreneurial light came on. I was supporting a Dutch painter, a great portrait painter. I was his only sole source of support. I brought him over from Holland. Now I had no record royalties to speak of, and I'm paying for this painter. I put the two together; had him paint portraits of the Beetles, got the license from Brian Epstein and made more money selling Beetles pictures that year! A few years ago I went to Liverpool, to the Cavern which is now a Beetles shrine, and there was original prints hanging in the Cavern as tributes to them. In my career I have worn many hats. I had some pangs from time to time, of regret that I didn't make a certain move here or there that might have kept the career going. I didn't establish a reputation for a certain kind of music. I was always the Jack-Of-All-Trades. I did a little of this, and a little of that. To me; the perks, the advantages, privileges, all these things always seemed excessive. I hadn't earned them and I always felt embarrassed if someone wanted to take me to the head of the line. I always used to say, "I'll wait, I'll wait." I really didn't want any special privilege. So, when that began to dry up I felt fine with that. Still, I got more than the average person, but my attitude has been that 'you put me on an island with no prospects of ever getting off that island and I will be like Swiss Family Robinson. I will start creating something out of it.'

George Green: Did you ever have any disappointments, as far as friendships or people you thought were your best friends, suddenly turned out not to be?

Pat Boone: No, haven't had that. I have never had excessive expectations of other people, either. I am aware of everybody's pressures, the things that come to bear on our decisions. When it would seem to me that somebody had given me short shrift, I would say, "Well, I guess they got a lot of other things that are pulling on them." I'm aware of just what pulls at me all the time. I drop the ball. I, inadvertently, sometimes don't give somebody the attention I would like to. It's just that I am so pressed that I can't. So, I figure that other people are the same way. The only people who have hurt me are critics, like with this new album for people who were into heavy metal, not ever going to be into heavy metal, wouldn't like the original records if they heard them because it isn't their taste. I'm doing my 'mildly exciting' versions of heavy metal classics.

George Green: About the album; you look at the headlines, you are on every single television show, I don't recall the intensity of the spotlight beating like it is today?

Pat Boone: It seems like ten times greater than it ever was. Of course, there is the misunderstanding; people thinking I had really sold out and dived head first into heavy metal and I'm just going to be a different person. They don't get the fact that I was joking and spoofing this whole idea of the metal thing, and that I'd done a very good album. If they took the time to listen to it, they would realize that it is not out of character for Pat Boone.

George Green: When you did it, did you anticipate what would happen?

Pat Boone: All I felt was that they would get a big laugh; that the audience would appreciate it and laugh at the idea of me coming out as a heavy metal guy. If Alice Cooper did what Dick Clark asked, coming out in white bucks and looking like Pat Boone, everyone would have gotten the joke. But at the last minute he backed out. I think he put on white bucks, looked down and got seasick or nauseous! When I came out in the leathers, the earrings, the choker and the glasses and all of that, flexing my pecks and the tattoos... for sure I thought we would get a laugh. And we did! It was just fun. I did not have any idea that it was going to be the most talked about part of the AMA, and that it was going to have repercussion after repercussion after repercussion.

George Green: And at this moment it hasn't stopped, has it?

Pat Boone: No, in fact it is still reverberating on, because I still have about four-hundred requests for interviews from radio stations and newspapers backed up. I don't regret that at all. I would do it again. But, I would urge Alice to do his half and come out as me!

George Green: What advice would you give anybody adjusting to a fading spotlight?

Pat Boone: Keep doing what you did in the beginning. Enjoy what you do. Do it for the enjoyment, not the money, not the reward, not necessarily the public acceptance. If you keep getting up at bat enough times, you are going to get at least a single. You might get a double, you might hit a triple. And, once in a while, you might even get a real lucky break and hit the pitch just right and knock a homer. But the thing is, you got to get up for the love of the game. If you love the game, it is its own reward. And if you get good at it and if you get another chance to play on a winning team, great. But keep doing it for the sheer love of what made you that entertainer in the first place.

Abbe Lane

Your life is not over just because your acting career is

Abigail Francine Lassman (stage name; Abbe Lane) was born in December, 1932, in Brooklyn, New York.

Abbe started performing on stage at the very young age of four-years-old. She was only thirteen-years-old when she performed in a major Broadway show for George Abbot. Abbe had to lie about her age and wear high-heels to get the role!

She then went on to do a number of Broadway shows. At the age of fifteen she was cast in a show for Michael Todd (husband of Elizabeth Taylor). There she met her first husband, Xavier Cugat, a famous Latin band-leader. He asked her to audition for his band, which she did and he hired her. Being so young, her mother travelled with her and Xavier for the first year. At the age of sixteen Abbe's alternative was to marry Xavier, which she did despite the vast age gap.

As she became more successful and began featuring in international films, television and in performances such 'Surprising Suzie', 'Donatella' and 'The Bachelor' to name but a few, Xavier became less of a celebrity. This resulted in some jealousy and an unstable, abusive partnership. Abbe finally escaped him by choosing to catch a flight at a different time. She forfeited every luxury, including their estates, just to get her 'freedom' and 'sanity' back. This is the focus of Abbe's book, 'Where Is Love', which she wrote later on in life, once she'd married Perry Leff. She met Perry only a week after her divorce with Xavier was finalized, in 1964. Together Abbe and Perry had two sons. Abbe also took on the role of mother to Perry's two sons, from his previous marriage.

Abbe became best-known for her top-selling record 'Be Mine Tonight' in 1958. During the same year she starred alongside Tony Randall in 'My Captain'. She also became seen as one of the 'sexiest' woman entertainers of her time. In her later years, Abbe continued to appear in television shows such as 'The Brady Bunch', 'The Flying Nun' and 'Vega$', among others, and on stage in Las Vegas. She also featured in Steven Spielberg's 'The Twilight Zone'.

Abbe received her own star on the Hollywood Walk Of Fame for her unique contributions to television. She, Perry and family live happily today at their home in Los Angeles, California.

Interview with Abbe Lane

George Green: Would you mind giving me some of the highlights of your show business career, and even touch on the good times and maybe the bad ones.

Abbe Lane: I started when I was a child, as a child performer, when I was four-years-old. When I was fifteen I met Cugat. I was appearing in a Broadway show for Michael Todd. He saw me in the show and asked me to sing with his band, which was a big push because it was a Latin band and I'm not of Latin American origin. The jump from going from Broadway stage into singing with a Latin band was really a shock. My mother came with me because she was not going to let a fifteen-year-old girl travel by herself. The whole adjustment to the Latin music and learning to speak Spanish; that was the first major change I made. I dyed my hair black, and became a Latin bombshell. Subsequently, because my mother could not travel with me anymore, my Dad was objecting, I married him at fifteen. He had been married many times before I became the star of the Cugat show.

George Green: Why did you marry him?

Abbe Lane: I had gotten a taste of being featured in an orchestra. I imagined I was going to be in movies. I thought it was a glamorous life and really didn't know what marriage would be all about. I just thought it would be going from my parents' home to someone else who would love and protect me. Unfortunately, that turned out not to be the case. As I said, my mother could not travel with me anymore and the only way to stay with the band was to be married. He, obviously, loved young women. All his former wives had been vocalists but they all had been much younger, except his first wife. We started to travel the world and I started to gain a lot of popularity. We made our first tour in Europe in 1955, and I was an enormous success with the orchestra. I got so many motion picture offers in Italy while I was there, and in Spain. It just dazzled me. I could not believe what was happening. So, I returned to Italy after the tour was over and started to make films. Cugat allowed me to return based upon the premise that I would get him to write all the music for the films, if they were musicals, and that I would still go out in between films and perform. It was a tradeoff. I made twenty-two films in Italy and I had enormous success there. It seemed like I was born to do that. Then we would come back to the United States. Then I was signed to a contract when I was about nineteen, to 'Universal', much against my ex-husband's wishes. I made some films at Universal, but he saw to it that MCA got me out of the contract because he didn't want to lose his star. So, I made only about six or seven films in the United States. That part of my career lasted for about ten years. Because the personal problems were so tremendous, I wasn't able to continue with him. He was very abusive. It became intolerable. I was only twenty-six and I just felt I couldn't put one foot in front of the other anymore. We worked twelve months a year. I was a work horse and a slave.

George Green: After the marriage is over; you're decimated emotionally...

Abbe Lane: Emotionally and financially.

George Green: How did you handle that transition?

Abbe Lane: At that time, in 1964, the only grounds for divorce was adultery, and neither side had claims for that. So, I was forced to relinquish all the money I had earned, and the apartment and the car and everything he had supposedly given me. Emotionally, I was so drained from his threats. He kept my music and finally the lawyer that obtained the divorce for me was able to secure the current music that I had, because without my music I couldn't work. He wouldn't release my gowns. So, we got my music and my gowns so I could work. Then three of the agents who handled Cugat for twenty-five years came to me and said, "We were only booking him for the last five or six years because of you, and we want to represent you." So, even though I was totally alone in the world, except for my parents, they promised that they could get me Las Vegas and things. I would have to prove that I could be a star on my own, which I got the opportunity to do quite quickly. I was called to California about ten days after my divorce, to do the Jack Benny TV show. Then I met Perry, my husband. I was very, very vulnerable at that point, and frightened. But we fell in love and offers started coming in from Europe again, and Las Vegas was a huge success. It was kind of beginning again.

George Green: What were your plans if you hadn't met Perry Leff?

Abbe Lane: I had no plans except to work and try make money because I was taking care of my entire family, and I had myself to take care of. He had taken all of the money that I worked for all those years.

George Green: How many years did you spend at all the hotels in Las Vegas?

Abbe Lane: I would say from the time I was sixteen until my last engagement, about two and a half or three years ago. I could still play Vegas if I wanted to. The offers come in all the time.

George Green: The years when the spotlight was the most intense on you were both Cugat and Vegas. Is that right?

Abbe Lane: About five years ago Spielberg called and asked me if I wanted to do the movie, 'The Twilight Zone'. I did that because it was Spielberg and I enjoyed working with him. I go back to Italy probably twice or three times a year and do a TV special. But I haven't actively pursued anything here in the last few years.

George Green: You had some moments where you were not... where that spotlight started to dim on you, didn't it?

Abbe Lane: Yes, of course. Unless you pursue it all the time... my children started to go to school and I didn't want to be away from them long periods of time. Of course my career started to diminish because I refused engagements.

George Green: How did you handle that transition from super stardom to ordinary housewife, writing, raising children?

Abbe Lane: The book tour reaffirmed that people do know Abbe Lane. A generation, say from forty up, would have heard the name. But my personal life is so good and I found so much contentment in that aspect, I have and had no regrets. I wasn't obsessed, as many performers are, with living in the past. Of course, everyone likes to be recognized and be admired, especially a woman, but I always knew that when I got married to Perry I would be making a choice, because I intended to have children and I didn't want to wind up one of these older women with no kids, no family and just scrap books... and just being faceless. I mean, that to me is not a life.

George Green: You never had these down moments that most performers go through.

Abbe Lane: Not really down. There's moments of longing when you see something come up and it reminds you of something that you may have done, or would like to have done, and you think, *'I could have done that or maybe I should have done that.'* But it's fleeting. You don't go from being a star into being an unknown, overnight. It's a very gradual thing. Many other stars of great magnitude are not being offered roles. I mean, there is just a point in time when you just... it ends. I am involved in charity. I was president of SHARE, that was two years ago. S.H.A.R.E ladies and I did the show for two years, producing it. I danced for eight years in the show and I'm still on the board.

George Green: Are you finding success in your writings?

Abbe Lane: Yes, I'm finding success. It was amazing to me that I could write and not only have a book published, but have it so accepted. In fact, the book is optioned to be made into a Broadway musical.

George Green: How do you compare the spotlights of being an author; is it more of a mature spotlight?

Abbe Lane: I think it's a very respected spotlight.

George Green: I had as long a ride as any executive ever had with ABC. Now I'm writing books. I'm on top of two books. I'm a Gemini. You never do one at a time! It's something that I've never done and it's a challenge, and a mountain that's not singing for you - but it's something else. Is that part of the motivation for writing?

Abbe Lane: I never went to college and I always felt intimidated. It was a great challenge to me. I'm now writing a straight novel, a great challenge because I'm hitting upon an area that I, myself, didn't know existed... that I could do.

George Green: It's another mountain to climb.

Abbe Lane: It is another mountain to climb. I don't know of a greater finale to a career.

George Green: How important is family and peace of mind?

Abbe Lane: I think, for a woman, it's vital. I think for a woman it's essential that you build a life away from show business, because you know at some point in time it's going to end.

George Green: What else would you advise young or old performers when they're going through a transition?

Abbe Lane: If it's diminishing because of circumstances, the roles are not out there, obviously they should still try as hard as they can. But if age is starting to be a factor, and the fact that they never quite achieved great stardom, I would think that they have to turn within themselves. People have other forms of artistic expression. I know I've been praised for my talents of decorating our homes, and I can sculpt. Then I found out that I could write! No, I couldn't do brain surgery tomorrow morning at nine o'clock... but the advice would be to turn within yourself and see if there is something that is unexplored that you could do.

George Green: Find other mountains.

Abbe Lane: Right, because you never know until you try.

Arte Johnson

Very interesting... but stupid!

Arthur Stanton Eric 'Arte' Johnson was born in January, 1929, in Benton Harbor, Michigan. After high school he attended the University of Illinois at Urbana Champaign Illinois. There he worked with the Campus radio station and the theater guild, and finally graduated in 1949.

Arte tried his hand in the advertising industry but found no success there. One day he walked into an audition for the Broadway show 'Gentleman Prefer Blondes' and, much to everyone's surprise, was cast in the show. This was the start of his career as a performer. He then went on to star in another off-Broadway show called 'The Shoestring Review' at the President Theatre in New York. Consequently, Arte soon moved on to work in film and television.

Aside from the roles he played in television shows like 'It's Always Jan', 'Sally', 'Hennessey', 'Alfred Hitchcock Presents', 'Bringing Up Buddy', 'The Twilight Zone', 'Bewitched', and 'The Jack Benny Program' to name but a few, he also landed a few roles in major motion pictures like 'The Subterranean', 'The President's Analyst', 'Love At First Bite', and 'The

Thirteen Ghosts of Scooby Doo', among others.

But most folks who have heard the name 'Arte Johnson' link him to a show in which his spotlight burned super-bright. 'Rowan and Martin's Laugh In' was a television show that ran from1967 to 1973. In the show Arte portrayed a number of characters, including Wolfgang, a German soldier, and Tyrone a 'dirty-old-man'. He then coined the catch phrase for the show, "Very interesting, but stupid!" which he'd heard in a World War II film. Arte and his brother Coslough 'Cos' Johnson earned an Emmy Award for their contributions to the show.

However, although Arte became as well-known as he was, it all came to an abrupt end one day in 1972 when management at NBC decided to start doing things differently. He no longer had the freedom to perform spontaneously, and as a result he left. He never heard from them again, and even though he found 'odd jobs' here and there, including voice-acting roles for various children's shows and films like 'The Smurfs', 'Top Cat', 'Animaniacs', and 'Yo Yogi!' he never really put his heart back into television or film. He went back to Broadway for some time, though, which he refers to as 'completing his circle', as Broadway was indeed his major beginning.

Arte always had a sincere interest in and love for books and reading. Therefore, he chose to also channel most of his energies into this hobby, becoming a collector as well as an audiobook narrator.

In 1997 he was diagnosed with non-Hodgkin's lymphoma but was treated successfully. He recalls the ups and downs, the rejections without justification, and the emotional confusion he often felt throughout his career in television and film. However, by keeping his own inner spotlight shining on a hobby he loved very much, he was able to enjoy life to its fullest and overcome most obstacles.

Today Arte lives happily with his beautiful wife, Gisela, in Southern California. The advice he gives is, 'never get caught up in a career to the point where it becomes the sum total of your life.'

Interview with Arte Johnson

George Green: Tell me about all the good stuff.

Arte Johnson: I came out of New York as a stage performer and was brought out here by a major agency, but there was no work. So, I went to work in a clothing store in 1958 to '59 in Beverly Hills, and had a great clientele. I had a boss and I was a former client of his; I had been buying my clothes from him for a long time. He kept saying to people as they came into his store, "Why is this guy working here?" I had been on Broadway! Then someone came in one day and told me that somebody at MGM was desperately looking for me. I couldn't figure that out. I asked why they didn't speak to my agent. They told me that nobody knows who my agent was. It happened to be one of the best known agencies. I went over there and I discovered that the man who was representing me said that this project had no room for me. It was lying on top of his desk. I picked it up and looked right at it. If I was a blind man I would have said, "Let's get Arte Johnson over here to do this thing." This 'Jack' looked at me and baldly said, "There is nothing in there for you." I took the script and threw it at him, across the room, and I ran out ranting into the legal department and asked for my release immediately. I got the release, and wound up doing a movie. It wasn't a great successful movie, but at least it took me back into the business as opposed to being a clothing salesman.

The picture was 'The Subterranean', which was not a big success but it was one of Arthur Fried's last strokes of musical movies, and had a marvelous cast and incredible score that was a great thing. So, I was back in show business in a sense, and I finally had this opportunity to go in and talk to somebody about a show called 'Laugh In'. It was just by accident that I got involved with some people who were involved in the project. When I went in to see the guy, it was a guy who I knew from New York. He had seen me working in the various small clubs around town. It was pleasant. I did a musical act that had comedy in it. It was clever more than comedy; a little abstract. It was very New York; chic kind of act. That's how I got into 'Laugh In' because he knew what I did prior to that. The impact of 'Laugh In' was something that was beyond anything I had anticipated in my lifetime. I admit I had a problem handling it. I was newly married and constantly being surrounded by people. Having a total lack of privacy was something I had never really anticipated, and was not quite ready for. That kind of adulation and that kind of reception was beyond belief; going to New York and having to have a body guard. At the height of that show it was impossible. There had to be someone there to keep people from pushing you into walls. This went on for four years. 'Very interesting,' became a catch phrase which stunned me. I came up with the phrase. Everything I contributed to the show, all the aspects of the show, the characters I brought to the show, were all mine. I had been working on them in various phases for years. It was nothing new to me. And, it was easy. It was like falling off a log. I didn't have to prepare or study. I did it intuitively. Everything was instinctive.

George Green: What happened in 1972?

Arte Johnson: In 1972 they got into a situation where they suddenly decided they could save money by not shooting the show as free-form, as they had done it prior. They started scripting what I call the 'ad libs'. I didn't work on that level. I had a terrible time working on that level. One thing led to another. There was a lot of anger and a lot of hostility and whatnot; me to them. I said, "That is not the way I do it. I wouldn't enjoy doing it like that." It didn't have the spontaneity that I was used to. I just asked for my release from the show. I left the show in '72. The show continued on for a little bit longer, not much longer.

George Green: Did you think, when you left the show, that life was going to continue on and you would get another gig?

Arte Johnson: I did. I was positive I would get another gig. I was positive that since I had been the creation of NBC, I was positive that NBC was going to find me a slot. To this day, I don't know why, they didn't find a slot for me. To this day, every subsequent director or leader of NBC has never returned a telephone call. In twenty-five years I have never had a call from NBC. At first I had no idea what transpired. I had no idea what happened. I did a quiz show for them. I did a couple of quiz shows for them. The new head came in and promises were made, statements were made and then telephone calls were unanswered, meetings were cancelled and that was the end of it. I get no response from any telephone calls. You get used to that. You recognize that it's just a game. This is the way they play the game and you're on the receiving end. So what do you do? What choices do you have? I was very fortunate I kept working. I had a tremendous residual benefit having done 'Laugh In'. People recognize me for that. Douglas Kramer, Lenny Goldberg, Aaron Spelling used me on those constant comedy shows that they had; 'Love American Style', 'Fantasy Island'. I was a working actor with no great thing happening. There was no great career moves being afforded to me. There was no planning; nothing. It was just haywire. It was out of control. I did a movie with OJ Simpson, believe it or not. I spent eight weeks with him doing this movie for television.

George Green: Did anyone stay in contact with you?

Arte Johnson: We stayed relatively friendly but none of them were in a position of making any kind of decision that would aid a career, because they were all interested in their own careers. I understand that. I am very pragmatic about the business. I think loyalty is a very minimal factor in this whole society. The only place I'm seeing loyalty is on the current level where you have a bunch of kids coming out of USC or UCLA who went to school together and they are giving each other jobs. I see it. I guess, if we had come out of that same kind of back grounding, we would have done the same thing. But when we came up, there were no educational practices that compacted all of this talent and said, "Okay, now we're going to teach courses in track motion photography." I went to the University of Illinois; we didn't have a drama department. We didn't have any of those things. I got my degree in radio. We had a radio station but it was nothing. How could you compare it to what's going on now? Kids going to film school are not only learning but they're dealing with talent because they're shooting these projects, and when they make it they move their friends into the spot. I see it constantly.

George Green: The lady that you married, you're still married to her?

Arte Johnson: Oh yes, twenty-five years (2009).

George Green: From 1972 she has been very supportive, obviously, and she's been your best friend?

Arte Johnson: I never had a problem. I had a roof over my head, I have always had a very good business manager. I never wound up in a position where I had to... I did soap operas at ABC. The funny thing is, over the course of my career, I quit 'Laugh In' on my own. Sometimes I have had jobs where I have done quiz shows, I have done soap operas and in each case, for some reason down the line, I have been dumped on every one of these things.

George Green: How did you accept that kind of rejection?

Arte Johnson: I started looking at it and I started laughing, and I said, "I built one of the loveliest characters." I did 'General Hospital'. I did a marvelous little character that had tremendous attitude. There was so much depth to him as a character. One day a new producer came in and then I was out for the next two years.

George Green: You have had twenty-five years to adjust.

Arte Johnson: Well, I'll tell you something; most of my friends, my friends come from other areas of show business. My friends are in politics in Washington, DC. I am loaded with guys on both sides of the isle. I am very heavy into corporate. I've been book collecting all my life. I can walk into book stores and they know me when I walk in. They know that I'm a collector. I've had other interests.

George Green: What emotional issues did you have to deal with, and what techniques did you use to cope with the emotions of that transition?

Arte Johnson: The emotion thing was the acceptance of the fact that you were rejected. First of all you experience guilt all on your own. You assume your own guilt. You say, "What did I do wrong?" Then you suddenly come to the conclusion that it had nothing to do with you. It's external. It was nothing that you did. It certainly wasn't your capabilities or your talent. I never questioned my talent at any time. I never felt that I was in over my head. I never got into things that were over my head. So when things happened and I fell apart, I just kept looking at them as if to say, "What part of me was not something they could handle or corporate. What didn't I afford them?" You start thinking on that level. People loved me, people wanted me and then I got a call one day telling me that I was not good enough to be on the show.

George Green: Do you think it's easier or harder today to make a career or life transition?

Arte Johnson: I think that today a career transition is exceptionally difficult, because you have so many instant stars created who really don't have the talent or the capability to sustain that. In the old days when a star was created, when a star came up, he had started some place down below. He wasn't an instant discovery. He did it by plodding and plugging. Today you have a generation of kids who all of a sudden… a little girl does a movie and her next movie she's making ten-million-dollars. How can you equate your lifestyle to that instant-made wealth and adulation? How can you cope with it? And then, as fast as it's turned on, it's turned off. What happens then? Where do you go? A musical group came out with a record, platinum. They bought big homes. They got big cars. Then suddenly there's no second album, there's no third album, and now what do they do? They have money. They have very little education. They have no social acumen. What do you do in those cases? Those are the people I have great pity for. They wind up overdosing. They wind up doing ridiculous things with their lives. It's a rarity that you'll find these people channeled into things that benefit society.

George Green: What did you not expect to happen?

Arte Johnson: I didn't think I would be caught up in that 'male' thing. I thought I was too level-headed. I discovered that I did get caught up in it and that the romance of it got me. I started believing the publicity. I never went haywire in terms of the financial aspect. I never lived beyond what I was. I never had the Cadillac or Rolls Royce. I never bought the seven-million-dollar home. I never did those crazy things. But, certain other aspects of it I did. There are things that I regret. I don't know how to explain it because they're not specific. They are within myself. There are certain things that just change. After you got through this period of time, you suddenly reach back and say, "I want to reconstruct this. This is all way out of line. This has no relevance." I was very fortunate. I had a good education. I saved my money. As I told you, I wasn't desperate to go out and get work. My home was paid for so I had a roof over my head. Still to this day, I drive a 1971 vehicle. My wife drives a 1967 vehicle. So, those things never really appealed to me. My emphasis was in the world of books. I would buy collector's items. We have antiques. Our tastes were very upscale.

George Green: What advice would you give others going through transitions such as the one you experienced?

Arte Johnson: My training for the transition started at the early part of my career. Being in show business is so different than a lot of other things, because as a performer you can work extensively for two weeks and then spend the next four months not doing a thing. You have to discover something in that interim period to occupy your time, because you cannot sit by the telephone and you can't keep knocking on doors because it is not relevant. You get them bored. You get bored. Two gentlemen, whom I have been very, very good friends with for years; one was an executive with an insurance company; one of them was in the banking business, they were both getting to that stage where they were thinking in terms of retirement. They were panic-stricken. They didn't know how they would occupy their time. I keep telling them, I said, "You will have to find charities who can utilize your intelligence and organization. You will have to find organizational things just to keep your mind going. You will have to leave and see what's going on." Most of the guys I know will sit down every morning and will read the New York Times, the Los Angeles Times, trying to keep on top of everything. Most of them have investment in the stock market. So, you do some research here and there. Then the other aspect of it is to constantly be inquisitive and be the kind of person that takes trips and goes out to see the world.

George Green: How often did you think of getting out of show business?

Arte Johnson: I was the guy who would go to the best parties and would wind up standing in the corner watching everything happen, and listening to the conversations because I had no contribution. My ego was never such that I was selling myself. I never knew anything about show business. My wife didn't know anything about show business. I've always had one dream. I always thought... *'I started out on Broadway. I would like to close the book by going back to Broadway.'* Well, this past summer we were on a cruise and one of the stops was in Cannes. We went for a nice walk. We went to an observation thing and we thought we would stop and have a nice little lunch at a little restaurant down the street. At the bottom of one hill was a guy, and he looked up at me and I looked down at him, and we started running for each other. It was like a bad commercial for Irish Spring soap! The two of us grabbed each other in the middle of this narrow street and we hugged and held onto each other. It was a chap I hadn't seen in forty years. When I started out in New York we were both young. It was a marvelous moment. He said that he needed me; this was 'Kismet'. We exchanged addresses, took pictures. We came back home and I get a fax from Hal; 'let's work together.' To make a long story short, I'm opening up on Broadway on the 17th of April in Candid. Hal pulled me into the show. I'm going to do all the ancillary parts, anything he wants me to do, but I don't want any responsibility. I told him I don't care what the critics say. I'm not doing this for my career. It's making the door come full circle. It has nothing to do with money. I'm closing the book. My wife says, "With your luck you're going to win a Tony Award, and they will want you to stay on, and on, and on." I told her one year, I'll give them the one year and at the end of the year I'm coming back home. I would like to go out in a blast of glory. I won an Emmy Award the first time I did 'Laugh In'.

George Green: Any last thoughts about transitions and how to make them successful?

Arte Johnson: Transitions stem from the fact that the individual, when he's involved initially, should have some channel that he sends some of his energy into; something that is away from what you are doing now. One of the great problems that most people who retire have is that they have no interest outside of the work that they have been doing all their lives. They fell apart because they had no hobbies. They had no external interests. Whatever it is, it has to be something beyond what you do. Too many people get caught up in their career and that is the sum total of their lives.

Katharine Ross

If it's not worth doing, it's not worth doing well

Katharine Juliet Ross was born in January, 1940, in Hollywood, California. She later moved to Walnut Creek, California, where she attended Las Lamos High School and graduated in 1957. As a youngster Katharine spent most of her time on horseback.

While studying at Santa Ross Junior College in 1957, Katharine was introduced to the acting world via the production of 'The King And I'. She never finished college; instead she chose to rather pursue a career in acting, and hence went on to San Francisco where she joined the Actor's Workshop in 1959. During this time she did some television work and was brought to Hollywood by Metro (now known as MGM). After some time she signed across to Universal Studios.

Her career as an actor flourished during this time. She became well-noted for her roles in films such as 'Butch-Cassidy And The Sun Dance kid', 'Tell Them Willie Boy Is Here', 'Shenandoah' and others. She was nominated for an Oscar for her role as Dustin Hoffman's girlfriend in the movie 'The Graduate', and although she didn't win it, she was presented with a Golden Globe Award for 'new star of the year', for the same role. She then won another Golden Globe Award for best supporting actress, for her role in 'Voyage

Of The Damned'. Also, for her role in Stepford Wives, Katharine won the Saturn Award for best actress.

Although she loved to act, there were times when the roles she was offered were not suited to her tastes and she'd refuse them. Such an incident led to the end of her relationship with Universal studios. Not fazed by this, Katharine went back to performing in playhouses in Los Angeles. However, she continued to act in films on occasion. Her most recent roles include Donnie's therapist in 'Donnie Darko', and Carly Schroeder's grandmother in 'Eye Of The Dolphin'.

Katharine also went on to become an author of a number of children's books, some of which include 'Bear Island', 'The Teeny Tiny Farm' and 'The Baby Animals' Party', to name but a few.

Katharine's personal life has been an up and down road, having been married five times. Her final marriage to Sam Elliot has been deemed as one of Hollywood's most successful. Together they had daughter, Cleo. Sam and Katharine still live together today, in their home in Malibu, California. In 2013 they took to the stage together in 'Love Letters' (nominated for the Pulitzer Prize for drama) as a benefit for the Malibu Playhouse.

Interview with Katharine Ross

George Green: Tell me how you got started and what happened in your early life?

Katharine Ross: I grew up in a middle-class kind of existence. My parents exposed me to a lot of stuff. They took me to the theater, the ballet and to see art. I guess I responded to that! The first thing that I wanted to be was a veterinarian. I was not a particularly good student per se. I kind of 'fell' into acting I think; it wasn't the plan I had, but I guess I was headed there all along. I started to go to college and took a speech class; it was kind of connected to a drama class. They did two plays a year. I found out I enjoyed it so I got involved. I was cast in my first television show in San Francisco; it was a one-day part. I read for that and got that; I got into the union because of that. I was hooked!

George Green: Were you aware of the rejections that might be coming to you?

Katharine Ross: Probably not. One thing led to another; an agent called me. I was in the right place at the right time. It was later on, then the rejection hurts more and you take it more to heart. But you can't dwell on it, you have to move on. 'Shenandoah' was my first movie. Like I said; right place, right time!

George Green: This was big time because you were on the set with one of the great actors of all time, Jimmy Stewart.

Katharine Ross: I've never forgotten it. You learn from everybody.

George Green: You did 'The Graduate' with Dustin Hoffman before 'Sundance', didn't you?

Katharine Ross: Yes.

George Green: 'Shenandoah' happens; you've got a real rush - how did you feel about that?

Katharine Ross: I was brought up that it's kind of impolite to talk about yourself and things. Life goes on. It's not like, "Oh, wow, I've done this…"

George Green: You don't like to talk about your success?

Katharine Ross: It's nice to have but it's pretty fleeting.

George Green: Tell me about 'The Graduate'. Did you audition for that?

Katharine Ross: I did.

George Green: You must have had an emotional high when somebody said, "You're going to be working with Dustin Hoffman."

Katharine Ross: I didn't know who Dustin Hoffman was!

George Green: So you both shared the spotlight together?

Katharine Ross: Yes. I didn't work for eight months after 'The Graduate'. There wasn't really anything that I wanted to do. I was always opinionated about what kind of stuff I wanted to do.

George Green: Your career; was it always up, up, up, or were there down periods?

Katharine Ross: There's always lots of down periods.

George Green: Did you ever lose faith in yourself?

Katharine Ross: I'm not someone who dwells on the lows. I had other things that interested me. When you turn things down, you get a certain reputation that you don't want to work. I'm very stubborn! I think that in some ways, the only power you have is the power to say 'no'. You don't have to do anything you don't want to do.

George Green: That shows real confidence.

Katharine Ross: I just want to have some kind of belief in the project I'm working on.

George Green: What stimulated you in 'Donnie Darko'?

Katharine Ross: I thought it was a good script. I enjoyed it!

George Green: How important is working compared to family?

Katharine Ross: I think family is paramount.

George Green: What makes you absolutely ecstatic?

Katharine Ross: I don't know; a great day, communication with friends. I'm always looking for something interesting to do.

George Green: What advice would you give to young actors or actresses, or people that are going full-time to climb that ladder of success?

Katharine Ross: You've got to be passionate, and I think you have to be realistic if possible. There's always going to be somebody that says, "You can't do that." If you have the passion, you don't listen to that; you don't take it to heart and you move on. You've got to go forward.

George Green: You can't dwell on the past.

Katharine Ross: No. Today is the gift, that's why we call it the present. Now, if I was a young actor starting out at this time, I don't think I could do it; this whole 'celebrity craze'. I don't know how these people even have a life? I had a solid upbringing and it was very important that I had a life other than what I did. I don't think I could, now, withstand the scrutiny and attention that is lavished upon people. It's inhuman!

Monty Hall

Let's make a deal... for charity!

Monte Halparin (stage name; Monty Hall) was born in August, 1921, in Winnipeg, Canada. After attending St. John's High School he went on to study at the University of Manitoba where he graduated with a Bachelor of Science degree, having majored in chemistry and zoology.

Monty began his career in radio, in Winnipeg. In 1946 he moved to Toronto and discovered that his forte and talents lay in hosting game shows. It wasn't long before he became a well-known television celebrity. In 1947, Monty married Marilyn Plottel and together they had three children.

Aside from performing as a game show host, towards the end of the 1950s he was also cast as a performer on two children's shows known as 'Cowboy Theatre' and 'Fun In The Mornings'.

In the early 1960s, Monty moved to Southern California. There he developed and produced the acclaimed game show 'Let's Make A Deal', along with partner Stefan Hatos. This show began in 1963 and ran for many years on NBC. Stefan and Monty created their own production company, Hatos/Hall Productions, and a number of highly-entertaining game shows were born. Some of these include 'Split Second', 'Chain Letter', 'For The Money', 'It's Anybody's Guess' and 'The Joke's On Us', to name but a few.

2008 saw Good Morning America present a show of 'Let's Make A Deal' as a part of their Game Show Reunion Week. Monty was of course asked to host the show. In 2009 CBS announced that they would bring 'Let's Make A Deal' back to the screen, with the younger Wayne Brady as host.

Monty received accreditation as creative consultant and co-creator of the show. Hatos/Hall Productions were also credited as the co-production company alongside Fremantle Media. During 2010, Monty appeared alongside Wayne Brady on a few of the episodes. In March 2013, he made a special appearance in the name of Let's Make A Deal's Fiftieth Anniversary Celebration. Then, in October of 2013, Monty appeared on the show once more with his recently-won 2013 Daytime Emmy Award.

Monty Hall was given his own star on the Hollywood Walk of Fame in 1973, in recognition of his thirty-six years as a game show host. In 2000 he was given his own Golden Star on the Palm Springs Walk of Stars in California. Then, in 2002, he was also recognized on Canada's Walk of Fame.

Aside from the bright lights that come with stardom, Monty also played a very important humanitarian role, raising funds for children in Canada and around the world. He has raised over one-billion dollars for charity and works closely with 'Variety, The Children's Charity', an organization of men and women involved in show business who aim to better the lives of disadvantaged children. For this work, Monty was honored by the prestigious Order of Canada, a Canadian National Order originally established in 1976 as a fellowship that recognizes outstanding achievements and distinguished service by Canadians who go on to make a difference in Canada (and the world) through their contributions and actions.

So, not only was Monty loved by millions around the world for his game show hosting talents, he is also admired and respected for his work with the less fortunate.

Interview with Monty Hall

George Green: Go through a few minutes of that early start of Monty Hall.

Monty Hall: I came from a family that had a really rough beginning. I was very sick as a youngster. I was homeschooled by my mother, so I graduated high school at the age of fourteen. While my friends went off to college, I became a delivery boy. I raised enough money to go back for one semester. I dropped out after the first year of college. I went to work at the wholesale clothier. There was a young man who had inherited his father's business, across the road from the clothing store where I worked. He saw my father and said, "What is your son doing? Why isn't he at school?" My father explained we had no money. He told my father, "If he would like to go back to school, tell him to come and see me." I went to see him and he said, "I will finance you but you have to live by my rules. You have to keep an average of at least B+ or better. You must never tell anybody where the money came from. You have to promise to do this for somebody else someday." He put me through three years of college. I had a great college career. Then, my fifth year, I became president of the student body. I was working at the radio station and was making enough money that I did not need his help.

George Green: Was it the campus radio station?

Monty Hall: No, it was in the city; CKRZ.

George Green: What made you go there?

Monty Hall: I had been recruited. I was doing musical comedies in college. The director also directed radio drama. Then I worked for the Canadian Broadcasting Corporation. I went to school in the daytime and radio station at nights. This was before television. In 1946, the manager of the radio station calls me in and says, "Here is a map of Toronto. I think you should go there." I said, "Am I fired?" He said, "No, I think you have a lot of talent, you have to go to the big city." I packed up a little suitcase and started my career in 1946 in Toronto. At the same time television started in 1947. I had two or three different shows immediately. In 1954 the shows were cancelled. I jumped in the car and drove to New York where I spent months knocking on doors.

George Green: Everything was up; you were successful and then... nothing. Tell me about that emotional feeling.

Monty Hall: I am alone in an apartment. I have a wife and two babies back in Toronto and I am crying myself to bed every night. It is so cruel. You are in this big city and cannot get an appointment, but you are determined to keep on going. It was a tough time. Then I was reading a life magazine; a story about Sylvester Weaver. They talk about him being 'daring' and 'presumptuous'. I composed a telegram and sent it to him. I said, "I am an emcee trying to get into work. I cannot get an appointment. I am calling you because I am trying to do something that is 'daring' and 'presumptuous'." Monday morning I get a phone call. "This is Mr. Weaver's secretary. He would like to meet the man that composed that telegram." So, I went in to see him. He says, "I got only fifteen minutes. Tell me everything." I am blurting it all and spilling it all out. He turns to his assistant and says, "Get him to see every man he wants to see." The assistant looks at me and says, "Who do you want to see?" I said, "Everybody." I did not get one thing. I started commuting back and forth to Toronto. I would write a one-page letter which I would mimeograph and send to everybody I could not see. It was called 'A Memo From Monty'. I would say all the things that have happened to me in New York; a funny joke; a guy I met on the plane... I come to New York and start calling these people that I sent the memo to. I call Steve Krantz. The girl says, "He wants to talk to you." He gets on the phone, he says, "I did not get a memo from Monty this week." I said, "I stopped writing it because I did not think that anybody cared." He says, "No, I enjoy those things." He takes me out to lunch, he says, "I have a show; I am having trouble with the reading. I want you to look at it and tell me what you think I should do to fix that show." So, I write a thesis. Steve Krantz says, "You start working January as the emcee." I moved to New York and my career started May, 1956. I moved my family down to New York. The day that I brought them from the airport I get the call that 'your show is cancelled'. I have a wife and two babies and I am unemployed in a new country.

George Green: The spotlight just went out.

Monty Hall: You know what I did? We went down to Florida. We came back. I started knocking on doors again and it was an up and down time, but I had faith in myself. Then I got a call from Mark Warner of NBC network. Although my show was cancelled, he said, "I watched you and I like you. I am going to give you some work, a little show called 'Cowboy Theater'." All of a sudden I am working again. But the cowboy show finished 1957, so I go on the road doing industrial shows.

George Green: Infomercials?

Monty Hall: That is right. So, I did that then I come back and the same Steve Krantz called me and said, "I have a show and an idea. It is a show called 'Bingo At Home'." The show lasted just a few weeks because we had thousands of prizes to give away; we could not avoid it, so they cancelled the show. But I am at Channel 5 for a year and they liked me, so they let me do things like a Sunday morning children's show. Then they brought soccer teams from all over the world to play in a big league, but they could not find an announcer. I interview and tell them that I played soccer in Canada and I get that job. At the same time I am playing golf. I see my wife; she drives up and says, "You have to call Merrill Heatter at Heatter-Quigley, it is very important." So I call and he says, "We have a show called 'Video Village'. Jack Norris has left us. Get in your car and come into New York immediately." I drive into New York and I'm on the air, live the next morning. The Heatter-Quigley people say, "This guy just saved our lives and he was great." So I kept the job. In 1961 Merrill Heatter says, "CBS has empty studios on the West Coast. Are you going to come with us?" I said, "Are you kidding? I can live anywhere!" I leave my wife and kids in New York and I am commuting back and forth, and then I moved the family out to the West Coast. While I was in New York I tried to sell a show called 'First Impressions', a psychological game show. I have a meeting with Dave Levy of NBC and I convince him that he should make a pilot of this show, but I am moving to the West Coast so I have to hire somebody in New York to produce it for me. I hire Art Stark. But Art is on the East Coast. I made him my partner and now I am doing 'Video Village' at one network and producing 'First Impressions' on the other. We needed a producer because I was over at the other studio. That man's name was Steve Hatos. We came up with an idea called 'Let's Make A Deal'.

Author's note: *Monty refers to Stefan Hatos as 'Steve'.*

George Green: You and Steve came up with that idea.

Monty Hall: Yes, Steve and I together. He died fifteen years ago (1999) but we made a partnership. We do not have legal papers between us, but we remained partners. Now, how do you try out a show? Well, we would call clubs, a young lawyer's group, some people on the top of the supermarket, then we did it for the Latter Day Saints, and fourteen women, and they loved it. So, we say to ABC that 'we would like to do a run through for you'. They go crazy over it. I go into the back room where the ABC executives are, with my agents and Steve. I'm euphoric because I hear how they enjoyed the show. I walk into the room and all I see is glum faces. Steve says, "They do not like it." Steve and I went across the room to the Carriage House. I do not drink. I had a martini; that is how upset I was. So, we do it for NBC and I get the same tremendous reaction. I go backstage and again the guy turns it down. I found out that this man was about to leave NBC, so was not going to buy any shows. But his assistant went back to New York and said, "I liked it. We should do a pilot." We did the pilot in April, 1963. Well, a month has gone by I have not heard from anybody; April, May, June, July, August, September - do not hear a word. October, I get to call from Bob Aaron. He says, "We will put you in." We went on January 2nd, 1964, and the rest is history! We did it twelve and a half years. Then we did it in syndication. Then we came back off and on for thirty-six years. It starts again on October 5th, on CBS, starring Wayne Brady.

George Green: You own the show, too?

Monty Hall: Yes. Steve and I own the show. In the 1990s, I do not want to do the show anymore. So I get a call; Dick Clark calls me and says, "Do you want to partner up with me? I can sell the show." I said, "Fine!" He said, "Send me tapes; I want to study the show." He calls me a week later and says, "I cannot do this show, it's too tough. How do you do this show?" I said. "Okay, let's put on a hunt." We advertise and cannot find anybody. We keep auditioning. Finally we pick a guy called Bob Hilton. After about five or six weeks I get a call from a woman and she says, "Unless you take over the show immediately, we are cancelling." I do not want to go to Florida. I do not want to do the show again. I'm seventy-years-old, it is enough already! But I go down and I do the show. They could not get a rating. So I hear 'bang, bang', as they are tearing down the set, and we did not do the show again. Then came the big chance, 2003, NBC wants the show nighttime. We are trying to find an emcee. Nobody wants to do the show. Finally I get Billy Bush. They get me a director. He does not want to listen to anything I say; he was calling the wrong shots; he's out of it completely. It was the worst mess I have ever seen in my life.

George Green: So that was the end at that point?

Monty Hall: So that is the end. Then, this past year, 2009, we get a call from CBS. They say, "Let's get to work." CBS says, "If Monty Hall is not going to do it, you better find us a host." They auditioned quite a few people. We cannot find anybody. We need a guy who shines right through, so they said, "There is one guy that we like. His name is Wayne Brady. We like him." We make a pilot, he tests great, they buy the show!

George Green: The humanitarian part of Monty Hall is interesting to the world as your 'Let's Make A Deal' persona. You give of yourself and you continue giving. The new spotlight on Monty Hall really shines brightly.

Monty Hall: There are three parts of my life. Number one is family. Number two; I like charity work. I have raised one-billion-dollars over sixty-five years. Number three is my career; 'Let's Make A Deal' made number two possible.

George Green: Your mother, she was your charitable inspiration?

Monty Hall: My inspiration for everything.

George Green: What kind of shows were you doing for charity?

Monty Hall: I was emceeing little banquets and so on, for the hospital. With the help of some people in the motion-picture business, I could go to small towns and they would open up the movie house on Sunday, charging no admission. I would take Marilyn, an accordion player, a tap-dancer and a film. We go to the theater. People would come in; it was free. I would start the first half of the picture then I would stop. I would come out and sing a couple of songs, the tap dancer would tap with the accordion player, and I would show a picture about the Variety Village we are building for handicapped children. People would put money in the bucket, and I would play the second half of the picture. I would raise eight-hundred-dollars, one-thousand-two-hundred-dollars on these weekends. That was my introduction to really hard fundraising.

George Green: You also had four hospitals named for you.

Monty Hall: And I have three honor doctorates for my charity work. I do not have an Emmy...

Author's note: *this interview was conducted prior to Monty Hall winning his Daytime Emmy Award in 2013.*

...One of the reasons is you have to nominate yourself. I felt it was beneath my dignity to nominate myself.

George Green: You have five-hundred awards from various charities.

Monty Hall: I have plenty of honors.

George Green: The humanitarian that you are is as important to you as your career.

Monty Hall: 'Let's Make A Deal' was good for my ego; good for my show business reputation; gave me the money to be able to do all the things that I do. It enabled me to help families, nieces and nephews, and people. The humanitarian side of it; you cannot describe or compare going to a hospital that you helped build, going through the children's ward and standing with the parents of a child, and the parents say, "Thank you for saving my child's life." You cannot compare that with a television award.

George Green: What advice would you give to others trying to climb that ladder of success but find themselves falling out of the spotlight. How do they get back into another one?

Monty Hall: First of all you have some talent. If you do not have the talent, you are wasting your time altogether. You must believe in yourself, that you have talent, then you have to have the courage and determination and guts to stick it out until that lucky day comes when the 'talent' intersects with the 'opportunity'. But the opportunity will never come if you do not stick it out.

George Green: You have to accept rejection, don't you?

Monty Hall: Rejection is the name of the business. It is called rejection, but if you quit you will never reach that lucky day. Believe in yourself, have courage.

George Green: What do you say to people who keep looking back and do not want to accept anything other than what was?

Monty Hall: You have to accept that. I took the next road. I took the next avenue and accepted the avenue.

George Green: Do not dwell on the past.

Monty Hall: You cannot. You and I have run into a lot of people like that, who are still dwelling on the past. The past was wonderful. The past was prologue to what is happening now.

George Green: That is why God put your eyes in front of you, in front of your head, instead of in the back of your head.

Monty Hall: Look forward to the next thing. When I lost a lot of shows, I always say 'there is another streetcar coming down the street'. You missed the streetcar. There is another one coming down the street. Let's work towards the next one. It is always the next one.

George Green: There is always another mountain to climb in your life isn't there?

Monty Hall: It is there! Climb it!

George Green: You have had a great life.

Monty Hall: A fantastic life; childhood illness where I almost died, walking the streets looking for work, being rejected. But through it all; number one — 'that girl'! When I went walking the streets looking for work, Marilyn was home with the kids. She knew she had to be strong so that I could stick it out there. She had to stick it out there.

Brief Update Interview with Monty Hall, April 2014

George Green: You've found some peace, I'm sure, in this world and you're still doing some charity stuff.

Monty Hall: I'm not doing it on the road anymore. I used to be on the road and go throughout all Philadelphia. I stopped that. I still do some of the charities locally, and then Palm Springs, but I'm not going on the road anymore. Don't forget I'm ninety-two now!

George Green: Ninety-two is a great year. It's okay to have two glasses of wine a day. You can get a little fat, and fat is better than being skinny.

Monty Hall: I like that!

George Green: How long have you been married to Marilyn?

Monty Hall: Sixty-six years.

George Green: You've done so much for mankind, for yourself, your friends, your neighbors. You've had a marvelous, marvelous life and I just wish you good health. May we both continue on for a long time.

Monty Hall: George, I don't play golf anymore, but next time we've got to get together.

Jean Heller

Two second-places do make a first

Jean Heller was educated at Michigan University, and attended the School of Journalism at Ohio State. Her dream was always to go to New York City and become a journalist there. She received an offer to go to the Boston Bureau but that wasn't where she wanted to be. Then, the Dean from Ohio State School of Journalism helped her to find a job in New York with AP (Associated Press). Jean worked in radio for some time where she learned a great deal, but still she wanted to work with newspapers.

Wanting to show her skills, she took initiative and wrote a story about guards on the train-line between Coney Island and Bronx. At first she never had permission to do so, but eventually received it. Pleased with her work, she was then asked to join the New York Bureau of AP.

She excelled in her position there and, after doing a story on the final voyage of the Queen Elizabeth II (QE II), was transferred to Washington. She joined a team and they started out slowly. It was then decided that Ray Stephens would lead this team. He was known as a wonder-man, and led them to earn second place for the Pulitzer Prize.

After that, Jean and the team went on to unravel more stories that made the news. They were successful in each of their endeavors, but perhaps the first major breakthrough for Jean, at the young age of twenty-five-years-old, was her releasing the 'Tuskegee story' to the world. The story itself made headlines in all major newspapers including the New York Times.

In brief, the Tuskegee story involved Jean unraveling the truth about the US Public Health department not providing syphilis victims in Montgomery with treatment. She learned that they were in fact using these victims as experiments. They wanted to know if the effects of syphilis were any different on black folks than they were on white folks. Jean went to Tuskegee and finally discovered this truth; that patients had been lied to, were refused medication and never made aware of their illness. They were instead being told they had 'bad blood'. Of course this was a horrific conclusion; folks being made to suffer for the purpose of a governmental experiment. She wrote the story, brought it home, and blew everyone away. For the story, she earned second place in the Pulitzer Prize again, behind the winning story that she felt was mishandled regarding Thomas Eagleton receiving electric shock treatment prior to his being named McGovern's running mate.

Jean continued to produce excellent stories and soon came across another story that, in all honesty, could have changed the world as we know it.

At the start of the first Gulf War, the Bush administration had greatly exaggerated the need for war, telling the world that the Iraqis were far more powerful, in far higher numbers, than they actually were. They said that Saudi Arabia needed the US to intervene and help them, claiming that there were 'a quarter of a million Iraqi troops and tanks on the Kuwaiti border, ready to go into Saudi Arabia.' Jean got onto the story and with the help of two satellite experts from the Soviet Union, they determined that there was no cause for alarm; there were no Iraqi troops at the borders, there was no sign of infiltration via tanks into the area at all. However, somehow the government managed to convince the world that war was necessary, based on photographs that were never released... highly classified... perhaps non-existent? Jean ran her stories anyway, which sadly were much like the sound of a pin dropping in a thunderstorm.

After this time, Jean was asked if she'd like to manage the St Petersburg Times in Florida. They were happy with the way she'd energized staff in Washington and wanted her to do the same in Florida. After marrying Ray Stephens, the leader of the team she first worked with at AP, together they moved to Florida and she started out in management. However, this wasn't her cup of tea and she yearned for more of challenge. She was promoted further until eventually she ran on the editorial board. This was fun for her to some degree, but not as challenging or rewarding as reporting. Finally, she simply asked for a position as reporter, and her wish was granted.

Shortly after the 9/11 tragedy in 2001, the Bush administration were again making claims that had no grounding. They stated that weapons of mass destruction had come into the picture. Jean investigated and again contacted one of the same men whom she'd worked with before, who'd helped her determine the lack of troops outside Saudi Arabia. They found out that the aluminum tubes that the administration was describing as part of the center used for enriching uranium for the weapons, were in fact of such low-grade that they could never possibly have been used for such a delicate job. These 'weapons of mass-destruction' were, in fact, just rocket launchers. Jean took her story to the major editor at the St. Petersburg Times. He refused to run it, saying he had his own story which obviously coincided with the claims made by the administration.

This was when Jean lost faith the industry; a story that again could have changed the world was rejected. One can only imagine the height of her frustration. Not only did this bring Jean to a new low, a very short while later Ray took a bad fall and died as result.

At first, after her story about the weapons had been discarded, she'd considered leaving the St. Petersburg Times. But after Ray passed-on, she realized that doing what she loved would be all that could see her through her difficult time. She stayed on as a journalist and appreciated the support she received from the friend's she'd made at the Times office.

After some time Jean and a good friend, David, decided to try their hand at a small company of their own. David had been a script editor, one who decided which scripts would be used by Disney, and of course Jean had her reporting and writing background. They opened a small online company with the aim of helping authors, screenplay writers and small businesses to better their works. Their work included reviewing written works, typing copy for websites and assisting small business to create websites of their own, among other things. It took off slowly. At first Jean was still working with the St. Petersburg Times, but when work for her company came in more frequently, she realized she might be able to earn a living this way.

After a two week vacation from the paper; during the second week of the vacation she dreaded going back to the Times. Arriving back at work, it was clear to see she didn't want to be in the industry anymore. Her boss suggested she leave. It was an emotional experience for her. She was not fired as such, and was still friends with everyone at the Times, but she had hoped to complete twenty years in the industry. By leaving when she did, she only completed nineteen.

It took Jean some time to adjust, but she eventually did. Today she lives at peace with everything she's been through and focuses on her own company, The Vision's Group, helping other writers, authors and businesses to become their best.

Many of us believe that Jean Heller should have won first place for the Pulitzer Prize for her Tuskegee story and, as importantly, her stories on the wars. The world should have heard her. Regardless, Jean will forever be noted as one of the greatest journalists, if not the greatest, of our time.

Interview with Jean Heller

George Green: Give me the background of Jean Heller. Tell me about yourself and what happened.

Jean Heller: I was educated in the University of Michigan and Ohio State. I was in graduate school at Ohio State, and I desperately wanted to go to New York City. That was my goal; to be a journalist in New York. UPI offered to send me to the Boston Bureau but I didn't want to go. I wanted to go to New York. The Dean of the School of Journalism at Ohio State called the general manager of AP in New York and said, "We're about to lose her to UPI. What can you do for her?" So they hired me and they put me in the radio Department at AP. Radio news at the time was considered the bottom of the food chain, but it was a good place to start because writing radio splits taught me how to write fast and think quickly. I did that for a while and really wanted to get out of it and start doing newspaper work. So I took it upon myself, without permission, I never thought I needed any special permission to do this; New York City had just started putting army guards on the subway trains to prevent crime. I wanted to ride all night with one of those guards. I just showed up on the subway train. That 'B' line, I think, is the longest, from Coney Island to the Bronx. I presented myself to a guard and pretty much set off a panic. "What is she doing here?" They eventually got permission for me to ride the train. I wrote the story for the New York Bureau of AP. They appreciated the initiative I took and moved me over to the bureau. I did some good work for them. They wanted to transfer me to Washington DC. They had just formed the special investigative reporting team and thought I would be good, because I was so aggressive. I didn't have any special training but they thought I would be a good match for the team. This was in spring of 1967. They had told me that I was going to be the one to cover the last voyage of the Queen Mary between New York and England. When the head of AP told me he wanted me to go to Washington, I asked, "What does that mean for the Queen Mary trip?" He laughed and said, "Okay, we'll wait to transfer you. You can do that trip, take your remaining two weeks' vacation at the far end, and when you come back, report to Washington." So that's what I did! I became part of this team that got off to a slow start. But they put a new guy in charge, Ray Stephens, a tremendous leader. The team took off! Under his first year of leadership we finished second as a team for the Pulitzer Prize.

George Green: That was a wonderful accomplishment.

Jean Heller: Yes! We were pretty proud of ourselves. This was well into the Vietnam War era and nobody really knew how screwed up military procurement really was. I found out that the Navy was paying millions and millions of dollars to a company called Comcraft which is better known for kitchen furniture. They were paying Comcraft to build rocket-launchers. The company was already under investigation for overcharging, by an obscene amount of money, the Navy. We were successful in getting the Navy to withdraw its contracts. We were also the ones who exposed the problems with the M-16 rifle. It was getting guys killed in Vietnam because it wasn't working right. There were a lot of stories that went into that package. We were very proud of it. I guess it was in 1972 when (I was still a member of that team) I broke the Tuskegee story which was the biggest story of my career, certainly up to that point. I had always said that if I got a byline on the front page of the New York Times I would retire. Since I was twenty-five-years old at the time, it was a little premature.

George Green: Why did you decide to do that one?

Jean Heller: I was in Miami Beach covering either a Republican or Democratic national convention, and a friend of mine had a friend who'd gotten a very strange letter in response to an inquiry. He showed her the letter and she didn't know what to do with it. She was on her way to a reassignment in Europe at the time. She said, "I know someone who might be able to look into this." She gave me a copy of the letter! Basically, the letter; a US Public Health Service employee in San Francisco had heard that the US Public Health Service was running a study, and had been for years and years, in which they were refusing treatment for syphilis to a group of very poor black farmers in Alabama. It started in 1932 and had been going on for forty years. They were refusing to treat these men so that they could 'autospy' them after they died and determine if the effects of untreated syphilis are different for blacks than they are for whites. That was the only purpose of the study. It seems ludicrous to consider risking anyone's life to answer a question like that. At the time the study started, penicillin didn't exist in 1932 and the treatment for syphilis was heavy metals. The treatment was as bad as the disease. Even after penicillin became available, these men were refused treatment on the grounds that the military needed all the penicillin, which was ridiculous.

We determined by compilation that of the three-hundred to four-hundred men who did have the disease, more than one-hundred of them died during the course of their untreated disease. How many of them passed it on to others, to their wives, their girlfriends? How many children were born with it? It's impossible to know that. One of the individuals who had the disease checked himself into a clinic in Montgomery, Alabama. The people running the study went to Montgomery and forced him to leave the clinic. They warned the clinic that they would be prosecuted if they accepted anymore syphilis victims from the study. So, the men were never told exactly what they had. They were told they had 'bad blood'. Every year the US Public Health Service doctors would come to town and they would do spinal taps in return for their participation. The men would get a hot meal, certificates of appreciation, and free funerals and burials when they died. That was it.

George Green: In one paragraph I read, Dr. Miller states that patients were not denied drugs, rather they were not offered drugs?

Jean Heller: They weren't told what they had so they didn't know what to ask for. The doctors didn't say, "We have the drugs to cure you." They just didn't offer. That was not true that they were denied drugs because they were. The man who checked himself in for treatment was pulled out of there, and denied what he had asked for. I think any reasonable doctor would say, 'If you are a doctor and you have the means to treat someone with a life-threatening illness, and you don't offer the patient... you have denied the patient treatment for the disease.' He is playing with words.

George Green: At this young age of twenty-five-years-old you get the story and you're on the front page of the New York Times. You're suddenly thrust into a spotlight. Tell me about that.

Jean Heller: The story appeared not only on the front page of the New York Times but on the front page of virtually every newspaper in the country. It was the biggest thing that had ever happened to me. Then I went down to Tuskegee for a second time, after the story broke I went to see what impact the story was having on the people there. I ran into one of the men who had been prominent in the story. We sat down on a park bench and he told me, "Before this happened, this was a friendly town. Now people avoid shaking my hand." I just broke down. I realized that the US Public Health Service, which was then the Center for Disease Control, stopped the study the very next day after the story broke. I was sitting with this man and I thought, 'What have I done?' It was horrifying for me because, here he has survived the disease and had been living a perfectly good life until this little white girl from up North came along and told everybody he had been sick and contagious most of his life. Now his friends wanted nothing to do with him. It was devastating. A lawyer who took the case and wanted to sue the federal government, his name was Fred Gray; he was a man from Tuskegee himself. Thank God for federal Judge, Frank Johnson. He gave Gray enough money so that he could administer the eventual settlement. He saw to it that the victims got most of the money. It was such an emotional story. It was still affecting me on the 25th anniversary, when I was working on the St. Petersburg Times. They sent me back to Tuskegee to do a 25th anniversary story. I talked to the last living survivor of the story who has since died. It was a story fraught with feelings of wild success and human emotion, and human tragedy. I was almost a manic depressive. I went from very high highs to very low lows, but came away knowing that I had done exactly the right thing.

George Green: Who were you sharing that emotional time with?

Jean Heller: Mostly my family. I was secretly dating the man who had been the head of the investigative team, Ray Stephens.

George Green: He was a wonder-man?

Jean Heller: He was a wonder-man. People felt deeply about Ray. I did, too, in a different way. He was the one who encouraged me to pursue the story when he saw the letter. I prominently share the spotlight with him, even though I wasn't working for him anymore. He was the guy pushing me from behind.

George Green: How many other times in your career did you get that kind of high?

Jean Heller: May be a dozen.

George Green: What happened in-between the highs?

Jean Heller: You don't have one Tuskegee story after another. I was fortunate. I had maybe a dozen huge stories in my career, but in-between it doesn't mean I wasn't doing good work. My employers must have agreed because they kept giving me raises and promotions. I never really had a down time in my career. I just had normal times. I would consider those very high highs to be abnormal! The only time I lost it was the second time I came in second place for the Pulitzer Prize. Everyone thought I was going to win for national reporting. That was the same year that Meg Ritter, at the Washington Bureau, broke the story that Thomas Eagleton had gotten electric shock treatments for depression, and had just been named the government's running mate. They made the mistake... I considered it a mistake and so did a lot of other people... when they published the story, they took it to McGovern. McGovern said, "Can you give me a day or two to deal with this?" They said, "Yes." In the interim, McGovern got Eagleton to step down. So, when they finally published the story, it was after the fact. They won the Pulitzer Prize for mishandling that story. I finished second on the syphilis story.

George Green: So you came second twice. The first time you were part of a team.

Jean Heller: I kept arguing that two seconds equal first, but couldn't get anyone to go along with it! I might just add that that was a very low low. I felt that they had grossly mishandled it and let McGovern take the story away from them. I thought they should have deducted points for that. I think part of it is that no one took AP seriously enough. I think if the Tuskegee story had been broken by the Washington Post or the New York Times or the Chicago Tribune, it would have won the Pulitzer Prize. AP did it so... what the heck.

George Green: How often do you look back on that second prize?

Jean Heller: A lot less now than I used to. It used to bother me a lot for fifteen to twenty years.

George Green: Finishing second really had an emotional impact on you?

Jean Heller: Yes. Not debilitating, exactly. It's still one of the only great disappointments in my career.

George Green: What happened at the very end?

Jean Heller. I have to go back to 1991. I was in the Washington Bureau at the time, and bought some commercial satellites from a Soviet satellite agency. They showed that the first Bush Administration was dramatically exaggerating the buildup of Iraqi troops in Kuwait. If you remember, the first Gulf War was justified because the Saudi's asked the United States and its allies to come in and protect it from the invasion by the Iraqis after the Iraqis had overrun Kuwait. The Bush administration was saying that in September, 1990, there were a quarter of a million Iraqi troops and tanks on the Kuwaiti border, ready to go into Saudi Arabia. On that basis they began preparations to actually send troops over there and intervene, because the Saudi's asked them to. We hired two intelligence officers; both of them were experts on satellite imagery. We spent a weekend together looking at these huge photographs of the main airport in Kuwait, the desert, the border with Saudi Arabia, and there was no evidence of any significant buildup whatsoever. One of them said, "When you send massive numbers of troops and tanks across the desert, the tanks leave tracks in the sand and can last for centuries. You can even look at satellite photographs of North Africa and still see tank tracks left in World War II. They just don't go away." There were none. There was no significant number of airplanes at the Kuwait City airport. There was no evidence of bunkers for ammunition, no evidence of toilets, no evidence of food distribution apparatus, no medical apparatus, absolutely nothing... just an empty desert. The Bush Administration kept telling us, "No, they're there. Our photographs are better than your photographs." Ray Stephens and I, we subsequently got married, had spent four years in Jackson Hole, Wyoming, which is where Dick Cheney was Congressman. He would always stop by the paper. He, Ray and I would sit around drinking coffee. Pete Cutty was his Press Secretary at the Pentagon. I said, "Pete, if you've got these photographs show them to me and I'll back off." He kept saying, "I can't show them to you they're classified." I said, "I'm not asking to publish them. You prove to me that what I'm telling you is not accurate, and we won't to do the story."

To this day those photographs are still classified. They won't release them. I don't know if and when they ever will be. Both the Defense Department and Colin Powell, that after the war ended, 'There weren't nearly as many Iraqis in Kuwait as we expected.' So that was huge. One of the experts, Peter Zimmerman, was able to go public and he quoted in the story which obviously gave it a great deal more credibility. I did a bunch more stories because they were so closed-mouthed about what was going on during that particular war. It was very difficult for journalists to cover. It was just this flood of stories that I was producing.

I was asked to become a manager at the St. Petersburg Times, to move to Florida. They thought I had energized the Washington Bureau and wanted me to energize some other people in the same way. I was hesitant about it but had Ray at my side. He was ready to retire and thought it would be a good move. So, we came down here and I kept getting promoted and promoted, higher and higher, until I realized that management is not where I wanted to be. Phil Gailey asked me to come over to the editorial board. I spent about two years on the editorial board. I had a lot of fun but it wasn't challenging. I yearned for more of a challenge. I asked if I could be allowed to go back to reporting. They found a good fit for me and welcomed me back to reporting. I broke another big story very quickly. I was on a roll again.

Then you flash ahead to 2003. It was a buildup to the second Gulf War. Around 2001 after September 11, 2001, we had gone to Afghanistan and were preparing to go back into Iraq. Colin Powell and George Bush were making the case that we had evidence of weapons of mass destruction. This woman from the New York Times had information that the evidence was not what it appeared to be. I had the same information. She chose not to write it; someone had convinced her that the information she had been given was not correct. I had the same information and I had the same source, one who had been so valuable for us during the first Gulf War. He told us how to learn for ourselves that 'the aluminum tubes that the administration was describing as part of the center, used for enriching uranium, were in fact such low-grade, they could never possibly have been used for such a delicate job... and they were in fact just rocket launchers.' We later learned this was exactly true. I went to a man, a major editor at the St. Petersburg Times, and said, "I want permission to pursue the story." He said, "I've already made plans. I'm not interested in that story." That would have been another shot at the Pulitzer Prize, not just for me but for the paper. More important, it might have stopped the war.

George Green: It might have changed the whole world.

Jean Heller: I walked out his office thinking to myself, 'F*** him, F*** this paper, F*** this industry.' I have never been as crushed and angry at work, as I was that day. Obviously I am still angry about it. I'm angry at all the life that has been lost as a result of that war. It didn't have to happen. I'm angry at the indifference of a man who was so excited about getting reporters and photographers embedded with the troops, that he didn't want to upset anybody in Washington who might exclude us. This was in 2003. I might have actually walked away from the profession at that point but in July, 2003, Ray took a bad fall. He cracked his head on the tile kitchen-floor and three days later he died. I stayed. A journalist was what I wanted to be and it's what I was. It was my life, so I stayed.

George Green: You are smart enough to know that if you did nothing you could really go into a bad spin.

Jean Heller: Exactly. A lot of my support was at the office.

George Green: How long did you hang onto the paper for, before you finally said, 'I'm done'?

Jean Heller: They told me I was done.

George Green: Tell me about that.

Jean Heller: A good friend, David Ehrman the television producer, was sick of TV and I was disillusioned with journalism. We decided to create a new business for ourselves. Both of us were established writers. I had two novels published, helped people with their manuscripts. He had been the vice president of Disney for acquisitions at one time. He decided what unpublished manuscripts Disney might buy the movie rights for, so he had a lot of skill at evaluating books and manuscripts. I had a lifetime's worth of reading and was a book reviewer. We put those skills to work, helping people who had scripts, manuscripts and books they want done. We decided we would work slowly and see if we could develop it into something that would sustain both of us after we retired. I took two weeks' vacation in order to complete a project for a client; I took two weeks' vacation from the Times. When the first week ended and I got to the second week, I realized I had less vacation in front of me them behind me. I began to get sick at the prospect of going back to the Times; it was actually making me ill. When I got back on a Monday, my boss took me aside and said, "We think you have lost your fire and it's time for you to hang the career up." Even though I was sort of ready to do it, I had hoped to hang on until I had twenty full years with the paper. I was a year and three months away. It was a devastating thing to hear, but I couldn't disagree. Listening to Pete telling me it was time to hang it up, was devastating.

George Green: Was there any celebration? Was there any decency in the way he handled it?

Jean Heller: He's a very decent guy. He was crying, too. He said, "We'll keep you on the payroll until you make nineteen years, and then we'll pay your health bills until you're old enough to qualify for Medicare." There was a package but it was like a buyout. Basically they bought me out. It worked out fine because the business that David and I started has been very successful.

George Green: Tell me about the recovery.

Jean Heller: I would find myself waking up in the morning, thinking, 'I've got to get up and shower and go to work,' then lying in bed and kind of smiling, saying, "No I don't have to do all that. I can put on a pot of coffee and go across the hall to my office, and go to work there." There was elation that was false because there was also a lot of fear. I would think, 'How am I going to pay the bills?' Over eighteen to nineteen months I thought, 'I wish I had done this five years earlier!' We were doing business copywriting, we went back to school and took courses. If somebody needs a website optimized, we are hired to write the text. We do brochures, writing whatever businesses need written. If someone did want an entire team, we can put together videographers, photographers, webhosts, graphics people, printers; whatever you need. We are just not all in the same building.

George Green: What was it like in comparison to being a journalist?

Jean Heller: At first we were taking any kind of business that came. As time progressed, we learned to focus on what it is we really like to do. We found that if it's something that doesn't absolutely fascinate us and motivate us, then we are not going to do the type of job that we insist on; we are not going to produce a job that is up to our standards. If it's not worth doing, it's not worth doing well. After four years of intense misery, every morning I wake up and feel free. I can do today what I want to do today, and choose to do the work that's on my schedule because I love it. I feel fulfilled.

George Green: Now you are happy and it is not money that has brought this emotional state to you, what advice would you give to those people who find themselves in the same situation? What advice would you give them to help them along?

Jean Heller: When people get to be our age, I find so many of them live in the past. They have been looking back for fifty years instead of looking forward. I managed to force myself to look ahead and stop dwelling on the past. You can have situations of real stress but they don't permeate your life; they are not with you every day and every night; they are events that eventually will come to an end. If you're still working, start thinking now about what your alternatives are; set up an alternative life for yourself that will be satisfying for you and generate some income. If you have just lost your job or are not working, you probably have a little bit of separation money that gives you a little latitude. As difficult as it is and as low as you feel, think about not what you've lost but about what there is out there for you to grab onto. Find a niche in society where your skills are needed. Look at what skills you have, what interests you have, how can you turn something that you love to do into something that will keep your pulse current? Think about turning your hobbies into your profession. Don't only to keep busy but keep busy with something that you really enjoy. I am a firm believer that mental stimulation helps keep your brain young.

Jerry Argovitz

Super Agent then, and he could be now

Jerry Argovitz was born Texas in 1938. He grew up in the Texas Panhandle, in a small town known as Borger. Life was different for him as a child, perhaps not as easy as it may have been for others. Being Jewish he faced some discrimination, from children at school, until one day his father reminded him that he had options. He could walk or run away, negotiate the issue at hand, or fight. Jerry took up boxing... and chose to fight!

After high school he chose to study dentistry, mostly because he felt the profession had great incentives and perks. He attended the University of Texas, but soon found himself roped into the football team. This ultimately meant he had less time to study and his grades reflected this fact. He left university and took up an offer for a boxing and baseball scholarship at a junior college in Borger, Franksville Junior College. At the same time he worked with two dentists and achieved the grades he wanted. Having done well, he went back to the University of Texas and was accepted into dental school the following year. Facing further discrimination there he was kindly transferred to the University Of Kansas City, Missouri, with the help of one of his professors. He came out top of the class.

He began practicing dentistry in 1964 in Houston, Texas. During that time he was elected president of the Kevin Achull Ministry in Houston, and became active in the politics of the society. Although he loved his profession as a dentist, he wanted more options (which his father had told him he had), and so chose to study real-estate while continuing his work as a dentist. He succeeded in real-estate and also got into the field of banking. Soon he was proving himself to be a true entrepreneur.

Jerry then went on to join Dr. Norman Vincent Peale, Kevin Roberts and Zig Ziglar in the National Lecturing Tour, giving motivational talks around the country. By this time, Jerry realized he was too busy to provide his wife and three adopted children with what they needed. He and his wife ultimately went separate ways, fortunately happily so.

When he finally chose to retire from dentistry, he set up a financial management clinic. At a cocktail party he was introduced to the world of football. After seeing how unfair the deals were, on the side of the players, he realized he had to help them; provide them with what they were truly worth. He signed seven players, asking them to trust his judgment; that he'd get them what they deserved. Jerry's first major breakthrough was the signing of Bill Simms on a three year, million dollar contract; a first in NFL history. This, of course, had the press and professionals in football in a state of disbelief, as Jerry had never set foot in the football-agent industry before.

Jerry was able to see through the system that dictated the futures of the players. He was exposed, first-hand, to corruption, bribery and false talk. Through this exposure he was able to fight for players and became known worldwide as the 'Super Agent'.

Due to his ethics and viewpoint he began to face a lot of criticism, not surprisingly from those he in turn criticized. It was clear that things in the U.S. weren't looking too promising for him, so he took two players to Canada. Of course he got them signed but, more importantly, this decision to move to Canada would become a life-changing experience for him.

In Canada, David Dixon asked Jerry to help him put the USFL together, which he did. Dixon, being so pleased with Jerry, then offered to sell him the franchise. After making this decision Jerry signed a number of top players and they went on to be the first franchise expansion football team in the history of professional football to win their division. The Houston Gamblers was founded and owned by Jerry. He then went on to introduce new rules to the game, such as 'instant replay', the 'sprint offense' and others.

In his book 'Super Agent', Jerry talks about his plan to reform the corrupt world of college football. This has been his passion, a heart-felt purpose of Jerry's since he first became active in the world of football.

He lives today in Rancho Mirage with his second wife, Lori. Although he wanted to take a step back and perhaps play a little golf, he feels the fight is far from over. Jerry is an entrepreneur, an achiever, a philanthropist and most importantly, a man on a mission.

Interview with Jerry Argovitz

George Green: Tell me a little bit about yourself.

Jerry Argovitz: I was raised in a small town in the Texas Panhandle called Borger. It was rough and rugged. We had a twenty-thousand population, and about six Jewish families. My grandmother from Poland pretty much raised me, because my parents were working. I never realized I was different except the way kids treated me. I wanted to participate in sports and it seemed like I was always the last one chosen. I never realized what anti-Semitism was growing up, but I realized I was different because other kids would bully and say nasty things. I was getting in all these fights. My dad told me one time, "Son, there's other things you can do." I was born in '38, so this is probably '48, '49; he says, "You have options." It was the first time I heard the word 'options.' "I'm proud of you for standing up for your heritage and not letting kids push you around. Sometimes if you get in trouble you have to walk away or run. Sometimes you have to be able to out-negotiate your opponent." I felt like these options weren't too good. The third thing he said, "If you're going to fight, you've got to learn how to fight." I knew I wasn't fast enough to outrun anybody. I knew I wasn't smart enough to out-talk anybody. So, I started fighting. I took up the golden gloves in boxing and it worked out well. Once I got out of high school I wanted to be a dentist; that was a goal I had for myself. Things never seemed to work out too easy for me. Looking back, I was the underdog. But it made me work harder, made me strive harder, made me more passionate for achievement. I think that's what helped me succeed. You have to fail to succeed.

George Green: What made you go to dental school?

Jerry Argovitz: I was from a small town and the dentist had a beautiful daughter. They lived in a beautiful home, they always drove beautiful cars, and I liked working with my hands; building model airplanes. I was a cub scout and a boy scout, and so I thought that would be a good way to make a living. My dad thought I was going to come into the hardware store with him, but I had no interest in that, and I had no interest in staying in Borger, Texas. I went to the University of Texas and joined a fraternity. I was a walk-on football player my freshman year, which wasn't planned. I went out for the team. I made the team and my grades just were mediocre at best. I wasted my freshman year. I had a scholarship to a junior college in Borger, Franksville Junior College. They offered me a boxing and baseball scholarship, so I went back there, got a job working with two dentists, played sports and made good grades. I went back to the University of Texas and did well, and I got accepted to dental school the next year. I found out with the University of Texas dental school; they had a limit of four Jews to a class.

George Green: There was a quota?

Jerry Argovitz: There was a black guy and we became friends. He used to tell me, "Argovitz, thank God for your Jewish ass, otherwise they'd be kicking my black ass." True story! Another incident that happened in dental school; one of my mates, I had more training than all the new students in dental school, I was always getting low grades and he was always making high grades. So, he came to me on our final. He said, "I've watched this discrimination and what's going on with you. I just want to do something. I want you to turn in my model, my bridge, and I'm going to turn in your model. Nobody can tell who really did it. The professors are grading it." So we did that. My bridge came back; he made an A. His bridge, he was a straight A student, his bridge came back and I made a C-. We could never tell anybody about it but the writing was on the wall. At the end of my sophomore year they said they were flunking me. All of a sudden the war was going on. I was married and had a baby. I'm looking at being thrown out of dental school, being drafted, and here I've got a wife and kid. I take my case to the assistant dean at the dental school. He gets me able to repeat my sophomore year at the University of Texas. I was getting harassed so much, one of the instructors came to me one day and said, "I want you to go over and talk to Fred Elliott." Dr. Elliott said, "I think you have all the qualities to be a dentist. You just need to change venues." He got me accepted into the University Of

Kansas City, Missouri. I went there on probation. If anything wasn't passing, I was out, that was the understanding. I graduated top of my class in dental school. I had a lot of honors. Second chances, I think, are important in some people's lives. I had some good second chances and I believe in giving second chances.

George Green: You go to work as a dentist. How long did you do that?

Jerry Argovitz: I went into the practice in Houston, Texas, and practiced dentistry nine years. I also became President of Kevin Achull Ministry in Houston. I was quite active in the politics of the society and the future educational courses I put on. I built up a hell of a practice. I loved the profession but I got involved in other things. I realized several things as a dentist; it has the highest rate of suicides, the highest rate of divorces of all professions. Most dentists at age sixty-five are still practicing dentistry. That's not what I really saw for myself. I wanted to have options, I was leaving out options. So I went back to school. I wanted to learn about real-estate.

George Green: You were still practicing dentistry.

Jerry Argovitz: That is correct. Then I got a lot of knowledge in real-estate. I wanted to find land that was maybe fifteen years out of development. The few bucks I had I invested on my own, and then I began to syndicate packages. That went from land into apartments. It all worked out well. I got into banking. I was always looking forward, always had an open mind. I could do this, this, this, and this, and then you close this deal here...

George Green: At that point of your life were you excited.

Jerry Argovitz: Yeah, definitely. After a while it wasn't just the money, it was a matter of achievement. Then I got on the National Lecturing Tour giving motivational talks with Dr. Norman Vincent Peale, Kevin Roberts and Zig Ziglar, around the country. That was a great high. Life was good. But then I realized, 'I'm married'. She had three children; all my children were adopted. So we got divorced, friendly divorce, but there was a void in my life. There weren't enough hours in the day. I was doing so many things. When I retired from dentistry, I set up a financial management clinic. I had accountants; I had numbers of people who could really understand what these people needed to do. Anyway, I found myself at some point in time with a void because once you've had the success of making money, money wasn't the issue anymore. I just missed the contact with people. As a dentist it was such a close interpersonal relationship with people that trust you, that believe in you; "Open your mouth, close your mouth, spit..." You tell them, they'd do it. I missed that as I got further away from it.

George Green: That was the turning point.

Jerry Argovitz: The turning point in my life... I was at a cocktail party one night. I look and here's this attractive black man, got a nice suit on, six or seven guys around him and they're talking about football. Someone asked me, "What did you think about Earl Campbell's contract?" Earl Campbell's a great football player, signed with the Houston Warblers. I said, "If it's what I read in the paper, my grandmother could have done a better job and she's been dead ten years." This black gentleman approaches me and he says, "You don't know a thing about football contracts. That was the best football contract for a rookie in the National Football League." I said, "You're right. I don't know a thing about football contracts, but you don't know anything about the present value of money either." I asked the guy what he did and he told me. I told him, "It sounds like, to me, the guy you're working for is making all the money and getting all the credit, and you're doing all the work. If you really get serious about this business, call me. Here's who I am." His name was Gene Burrough. Gene was a recruiter. He went after the top players. The majority of his players were African-Americans; they all came from poor families. They had no money. So, he would give them money and he would get them to sign contracts with him. They'd pay the money back when they signed the contract. He was representing Troup International at the time. Two weeks later I get a phone call. He wants to talk to me. He said that he's leaving Troup. I said, "Tell me about how the business works." He said, "I meet these young men, find out what they need, and I give them cash right there, and they sign this." They were signing a note and they promised to pay the money back. Then he said, "The next thing is they sign this. This is an agency agreement between the player and the sports agent, but we don't date this agreement until they graduate." I said, "Isn't this illegal? You're not supposed to have an agent in college. And you're giving them money." He said, "That's just against the NCAA rules. They can't do anything to you. Everybody does it, that's how the business is done." I said, "I'll make you a partner. I'll give you forty-percent of the profit. But here's the thing; I'm not going to give a player any money because I believe in changing rules, not breaking rules." He says, "If I can't have money to get the players, I can't sign any players. How am I going to get some player to come with you, when you've never negotiated a football contract before?" I said, "That's up to me to do. All your job is, is to get the players from where they are after they're eligible, to sign to Houston, Texas." So, no one in sports had ever heard my name before, and all of a sudden I wind up with seven of the top players in the entire draft.

George Green: 'Who is Jerry Argovitz?'

Jerry Argovitz: That's what everybody wanted to know. There were all kinds of rumors going around. I got these players for one reason, because they trusted me. When I met with them, got to know them, I asked them probing questions. I wanted to know about their family, I wanted to know about their brothers and sisters; I wanted to know how they were raised. I was learning as much from them as I was teaching the players. But every one of these kids, I asked them, "I'm your fairy godfather, I'm going to get you the money. What's the first thing you want to do?" Every one of these kids told me, "I want to buy a home for my mother, or my aunt, or my grandmother," - whoever raised them.

George Green: I want to hear about Billy Sims.

Jerry Argovitz: Okay. Billy Sims was drafted by the Detroit Lions. I went to try to meet with Russ Thomas, the General Manager, before the draft to tell him, "I don't think you should draft Billy until we can do a contract, because when you draft him we can't sign him." They were going to give him a three-hundred-thousand dollar signing bonus. That's thirty-thousand dollars a year for ten years. I took out my Sports Illustrated...

George Green: ...With the picture on the front page; million-dollar Larry Bird.

Jerry Argovitz: I laid it on the desk and politely said, "This is what I'm interested in. Larry Bird's the first player drafted in the NBA. He got a million dollar signing bonus. That's what I want for Billy. That's what we'll start with, a million dollar signing bonus." He said, "Basketball and football are two different sports." I looked at him and said, "No kidding." He said, "This is a contract that we're going to sign. There aren't any more contracts. This is the offer. When Billy's ready to play football, play here, the contract will be waiting for him. So, when you decide to get him to sign it, let us know." I looked up at him and said, "You know what, Russ... you drafted him, now let's see if you can sign him. When you decide that you want to start paying him fairly, call me." I got up and walked out. A lot of other teams wanted Billy. But they couldn't deal with the Detroit Lions. I give Russ Thomas credit for making me the agent I became because of the way he acted, the way he looked at my client. He looked down on him; a bullying effect. Fortunately for me I took it personally, the way he dealt. I went back to all my players and said to them that the NFL's a total and complete monopoly. I put their hands in mine, and said, "If they can separate us, if they can divide and conquer us, we're finished. So I'm going to have to withhold your services, which means you won't show up until you get paid right." I said they didn't have to worry about money. If a player needed ten-thousand dollars or twenty-thousand dollars, I went to my bank. This was after they graduated.

George Green: So after they graduate, you could help them out before they sign a contract.

Jerry Argovitz: Sure. I signed seven bank loans for them. Money wasn't an issue; they didn't have to worry about it. So I said, "All you have to do is train, work out, and be in the best shape you can be. Let me handle negotiations."

George Green: And the press was covering the absence of these players.

Jerry Argovitz: Every day. I was very vocal about the NFL and about the monopoly, how unfair it was, how un-American it was, how unconstitutional it was that they could take a twenty-one-year-old person coming out of college football; you can't play... the NFL wouldn't draft you for four years, that was another thing... What I found out when I became a sports agent was that the system was rigged against the players. The NFL and the NCAA were in collusion against the players. They NCAA offered the NFL a three-farm system. Players couldn't work during college, so they had no money. They set the agents up to give money to the players. The whole system was corrupt, everybody was cheating. The players were cheating, the coaches were cheating, the colleges were cheating.

George Green: Now all your players joined hands and said, "We're going to support you, Jerry."

Jerry Argovitz: That's it. 'We're with you all the way. You tell us what to do, we'll do it.' I'm getting calls every day from the press.

George Green: It's a major story in sports. 'Billy Sims holding out, not going to sign. What is he going to do? Not play football?' That's the question.

Jerry Argovitz: We had all those options. Bill Ford, owner of the Ford Motor Company, he was owner of the Detroit Lions, calls me a 'Machiavellian idiot'. I said, "I don't know what that means, but if it's something good, thank you. If it's something bad, same to you, buddy." That was my quote in the newspaper. Some of the press was bought by the team, so they're always going to make you look like an idiot, but a lot of the press was interviewing Billy, interviewing me, and the fans start supporting us. I said, "When was the last time Detroit's won any football games? Probably thirty-years-ago!"

George Green: You're going to tell me; Russ Thomas comes to his senses and calls another meeting...

Jerry Argovitz: Russ Thomas calls another meeting and he says, "Give me a contract." We agreed on a contract. When he sends it, it has an option year; three years, and the option year. We didn't want the option year. Option year means you get another year, at the end of three years you play another year, but all you get is a ten percent raise. We said, "Russ, we don't want the option year. Here's when we'd do an option year. At the end of the third year, if Billy does all the things that we want him to do, if he's all pro, he leads the team, and he's everything we want him to be, then on the fourth year, the option year, let's just fill in the blanks on the next three years based on what he did the first three years." And Russ Thomas looks at me and he says, "Brilliant. Wonderful."

George Green: It would be negotiated at that time predicated upon his performance.

Jerry Argovitz: Predicated on his performance for the first three years. That's how I negotiated the option year. He thought that was a brilliant idea, we all shook hands on it. Billy shook hands with Russ, we were all in the room, so everybody knows what the deal was. We signed the contract and Billy was happy. He got the first million dollar cash signing bonus in the history of football, at that point, for a rookie. Now this was not deferred. We took a million dollar loan, spread that over several years and pledged that to the loan. So, we got a million dollars tax free because it was a loan, he didn't pay taxes on that.

George Green: So this was the first time in football he had gotten a loan over a period of time and avoided paying taxes on a million dollar bonus.

Jerry Argovitz: And his deferred signing bonus; it had enough money in it to defer whatever taxes came down there.

George Green: Now it seems to me the other football teams say, "Woah, what have Thomas and Ford done? What are we in for?"

Jerry Argovitz: They were pis-ed. How could this happen? Who is he? They started doing a lot of investigation. I didn't know about them, they didn't know about me, so it kind of worked out alright. Billy got the best contract. Then we had Curtis Dicky in Baltimore. Curtis was the fourth player drafted in the first round by Baltimore Colts, and Billy was the first player taken in the draft. We go there; they offer us some ridiculous contract. Trying to deal with Dick Symansky; he was just a puppet for the owner, Irsay, and that's what I found with so many of the General Managers. They're just moving their mouths like a puppet, but the owners are pulling the strings. They have a salary system and that's the way it was done. Since I wasn't part of the 'good-old-boy's' society, and I didn't need the money, I didn't have to hurry up and sign my player to get paid. A lot of agents had no money; they had to sign these players quickly to get paid. When I went to Baltimore we were getting nowhere fast. Curtis already missed two preseason games because he was holding out, and this kid was as poor as a church mouse. But he had confidence in me. Finally I said in the paper, "I'm not getting anywhere with Symansky. If the owner really wants to sign this player and is serious about it, I'm sure we can sign a deal in less than a couple hours." That went in the newspaper. Somebody asked me, "How was it dealing with Symansky?" I said, "It was terrible. The man has an IQ of nine. He's hiding behind what they did last year and how they run their operation." I was in the paper against the owner and the system. It was just so foreign to me to think; once somebody drafts you they own your rights. The next day I get a phone call from Bob Irsay (owner of the Baltimore Colts). I just happen to have a transcriber, like a tape recorder. I could talk into it, you can tape it; transcribe it so you know exactly what you're saying. He says, "Argovitz. This is Bob Irsay."

"Yes sir?"

He said, "You said you could get this contract done in an hour, let's get started. How much you getting?"

"Getting for what?"

"How much is the player paying you to negotiate the contract?"

I said, "Mr. Irsay, I don't see if it's any of your business or not, but the player's paying me six-percent of his contract to negotiate it."

"Here's the deal. I'm going to give you six-percent and we're going to get the contract signed. We're going to do it within an hour." I said, "Wait a minute. Let me understand what you just said to me."

He said, "I'm going to pay you six-percent also, and that's between you and me. And that's six and six, makes twelve." I said, "You just offered me a bribe." He said, "Oh, no, no, no. I just wanted to see what you were going to say." I said, "Mr. Irsay, you can forget about that. This conversation's over." Then I hung up the phone. I immediately called Pete Rozelle's office in New York.

George Green: Pete Rozelle was the commissioner of the NFL. He was the number one guy, and what Pete Rozelle says, goes.

Jerry Argovitz: I thought, "How could an owner of a football team offer you a bribe and then you're going to go play on that team with that owner?" I called him and I said, "You have to make my player a free agent. I can't deal with this man. I'm not going to put him in that environment. The man offered me a bribe." He says, "Can you prove that?" I said, "Yeah, I can prove it. Definitely I can prove it." He says, "Don't do anything. Let me make a phone call." So then he has his lawyer call the lawyer for the Baltimore Colts, Bob Irsay's lawyer, and tell him, "You better get this deal done and take care of this guy because he's got something. Obviously he must've recorded the conversation." So that's what happened. That's how Curtis Dickey started playing.

George Green: These ball players; you're making them feel like human beings and giving them back some self-esteem, and they're making money. The word is Argovitz is a super guy, Super Agent; hated by the teams, loved by the fans and the players.

Jerry Argovitz: I get a call one day. By this time in my agent career I was getting black balled. They were out telling all these players, "If Argovitz is going to represent you, we're not even going to draft you." Now they're telling all these young kids that.

George Green: That's collusion.

Jerry Argovitz: It was pretty nasty stuff. But it drove players to me. I took two players to Canada, two first-round draft picks, which had never been done in the history of the sport. Don Shula, Miami Dolphins, first-round draft take over straight went to Canada. Gary Pittsburgh, first-round draft pick, I took to Canada. Both those teams were in collusion and just stonewalled me in negotiations. So that's when I took them to Canada. Now the next year's when they started... now they're really against me. They were fighting it because I was upsetting their apple cart. Nobody had ever really gotten that close to turning everything over and exposing them like I was in the press. We only signed one player that year, Gary Anderson. Gene (partner) and I are saying, "You know what? This doesn't look like there's much of a future. They're really down on us." My deal was, I wasn't going to be part of the system. My deal was I wanted to change the system, I was an advocate for the players and I wasn't going to change to be part of their system. I get a call from David Dixon who has a USF franchise. He asked me to help him put together the franchise...

George Green: U.S. Football League?

Jerry Argovitz: USF Football League. So I became an advisor to him, we became very friendly. I signed a bunch of players to the USFL, top players; he owned the franchise. After I helped him that year to put the USFL together, he offered me to buy his franchise. All of a sudden I just changed hats! That was a very exciting time for me! We won our division title. We were the first franchise expansion football team in the history of professional football, as an expansion team, to win its division. And also I did some other things in football that changed the sport. I had an idea about instant replay. I said, "With TV and the way it is, we can have an instant replay." So, our competition committee passed that rule and then, when our league folded, the NFL adopted that rule. So, I feel good because some of the things I did in pro sports changed the way the game was played. I put in the 'run and shoot' offense...

George Green: That was a major, major event in football; the run and shoot.

Jerry Argovitz: Yeah, it's called the 'sprint offense' today. We had a great team. The USFL was partners with ABC. We were partners with ESPN. ESPN was a new cable company at All Sports channel.

George Green: What about the 'no huddle'?

Jerry Argovitz: Well, we did that 'fast pass play'; we were doing all these things.

George Green: But that's a major thing that's even done today, the 'no huddle'.

Jerry Argovitz: We sped up the game. We called the signals at the line of scrimmage. I had guys playing for me that weighed 138 pounds, five feet - six inches. I gave the chance for little guys to play professional football. When we had the USFL we had TV contracts. We had a lot of positive things going. One of our partners that lives in New York decided that he wanted to have an NFL franchise, not a USFL franchise. So, when he bought the league his whole thing was to create a merger through a lawsuit, through litigation with the NFL. He used me because he had filed me as his sports agent. And he always knew I said the NFL was a total and complete monopoly. He knew the only way we could sue the NFL for being a total and complete monopoly was if we were competing at the same time of year. We were playing in spring, they were in the fall. So, his thought was if we moved from the spring to the fall, now we can't play in the fall because of their monopoly and we can't get a TV contract.

George Green: You opposed that move.

Jerry Argovitz: I absolutely opposed the move. I said, "The best thing we can do is stay where we are, be what we are as a springtime league." I drew up a five-year plan and presented it to the league, on what we had to do about awareness; about acceptability. I said, "If you're going to have a lawsuit you can't have it in New York, and you can't be the face of the lawsuit." That was my buddy, Donald.

George Green: Donald Trump.

Jerry Argovitz: Donald Trump. But Donald was pretty stubborn, very stubborn. He was able to encourage the league, the other owners, and move them to the fall. Very persuasive. We had a major lawsuit. We won the lawsuit and got a dollar, and the league folded.

George Green: You have been one of the earliest and strongest advocates for college football players, and you must be pretty happy at what's going on today. You are the father of that total movement; to try to get equality to the degree that players can live comfortably - not be paid millions, but certainly can be compensated enough so that they can afford to live a normal life while they're playing football.

Jerry Argovitz: Well, they don't have to break the rules because that's the only way you can survive. You can't live without money. You know, an eighteen, nineteen, twenty-year-old man cannot live without money and enjoy college life. So, I thought that again was wrong.

George Green: So the battle goes on. What happened to make you come down here, relax, play golf? You are currently in a different spotlight. It's not as intense as it was. Emotionally, how does that feel?

Jerry Argovitz: Well, I've been out of the spotlight for some time in my life, and I wrote a book.

George Green: 'Super Agent' is the name of the book.

Jerry Argovitz: Super Agent. There's two things that happened. One was writing the book. I give my wife a lot of the credit because she's the one who pushed me to write the book. I wrote the book for several reasons. One was; my Dad always said, "You have great stories, great sport stories. You'll need to tell your stories." Loni (wife) wanted me to write the book for vindication, from the Billy Sims lawsuit. She'd met Billy and she said Billy had told her that, 'Doc did nothing wrong.' So, she wanted me to write the book for that reason. Writing this book took me two and a half years. I talked to all these players. Some of these kids I hadn't talked to in twenty-five, thirty years. What I really found out was; the impact with these young men after talking to them, some of these kids almost started crying. I think they did cry when they heard my voice on the phone. This is just unfinished business to me, this NCAA stuff.

George Green: You're still fighting that battle as best you can through your contacts, but your life is different now. You're involved in charity organizations. Talk about this dimmer spotlight.

Jerry Argovitz: Well, I miss being a part of young athletes' lives. I can see the difference I made and the life lessons I taught them. A couple years ago we started sponsoring. We'd give them the Argovitz Spirit Award. We would award this to one or two or three of the kids in this area who were exceptional athletes, who needed some help. Some of them needed some financial help, but a lot of them just needed some mentoring. So I took some of these kids under our wing. We provide them with a scholarship and I mentor these kids. I put them through a mentoring program three times a week. We've got two kids at USC that we've helped put in school. We've got a kid that's now going to, looks like, Portland State. I'm doing work with five young men.

George Green: Your golf game, it still...

Jerry Argovitz: Sucks.

George Green: But you, as an entrepreneur, as a philanthropist, as a helper of young people, as a Super Agent, as a great dentist; what advice would you give young people that are starting out? What should they be doing to get ahead?

Jerry Argovitz: I try to break things down into what I call 'life's lessons'. One thing is; if you're getting ready to do something and you're not sure, you have to think about it for five seconds, it's absolutely wrong to do. The next thing is; in life there's three things you can do to never, ever get into any trouble, and build character and integrity. These three rules are, one; do the right thing. Two; always do the right thing. Three; repeat rules one and two! You've got to be able to look in the mirror and you've got to be the number one person; important to yourself. If you don't believe in yourself, the vote's unanimous. Temptation is going to always try to get you in trouble. You've got to stay out of trouble. As a young man, you don't get second chances. If you're a minority, they're looking for reasons to get you out of commission. The big difference today in sports; there's so much money involved. And if you do something wrong, in fifteen seconds with instant media the whole world knows. There's two kinds of people. The smart people and the stupid people. Smart people do the right things, make good decisions. Stupid people do the wrong things and make bad decisions. The other thing is, I tell these kids that, 'See my house, see how we live here?' I let them know I wasn't always this way. I used to shine shoes on the streets of Borger, Texas. I had a little shoe shining kit. I threw papers. I'd always figure out a way to make a nickel or dime here or there. Smart people aren't the ones who know all the answers or make straight 'As'. They're people who know what 'they' don't know and they surround themselves with smart people they can trust.

Al Rosen

Listen, you can't learn about life from a book

Albert Leonard Rosen was born on a leap-year in February, 1924, in Spartanburg, South Carolina. His parents divorced soon after he was born which led to his mother, together with her mother, moving Al and the family to Miami. Being an asthmatic as a child it was recommended that he live as far south as possible.

After graduating from Florida Military Academy in St. Petersburg, Al enrolled in the University of Florida where he played for the Florida Gators baseball team. During his second semester he left university to play minor league baseball.

In 1942 he was called to serve in the US Navy, then went straight back to baseball in 1946. While playing for the Pittsfield Electrics, he was given the name 'The Hebrew Hammer'.

Al was indeed dedicated to his religion, refusing to play on High Holy days. On numerous occasions he faced anti-Semitic insults from the general public and even from fellow players. Being an amateur boxer, he had the strength to defend what he believed in. He did not take insults too lightly and although he never fought back physically, he was tough and able to stand his ground in any argument.

In 2010, the documentary 'Jews And Baseball, An American Love Story' (narrated by Dustin Hoffman) was released. The documentary takes a look at the issue of Anti-Semitism in baseball and highlights Al's career as a player, while discussing other Jewish players, too.

In 1947, while playing for the Oklahoma City Indians, he was elected 'Texas League Most Valuable Player'. Then, in 1948, he was chosen as Rookie of the Year.

At the age of twenty-three Al was already a major league player. In 1950 he took over as third baseman for the Indians, leading the American League with thirty-seven home runs; more than any previous American league rookie.

Al played with the Cleveland Indians in the American League for ten years (1947 to 1956) and hit over one-hundred home runs for five years in a row. He was a four-time All-Star, leading twice in home runs and twice in RBIs (Runs Batted In). He was a .285 career hitter with 192 home runs and 717 RBIs in 1044 games.

After retiring in 1956 due to injuries, he went on to become the president/CEO of the Yankees for a year, then president of the Astros for five years. Finally, he became president and general manager of the Giants from 1985 to 1992

Al has been married twice during his life, only marrying a second time to Rita Nee Kallman after his first wife of nineteen years, Teresa Ann Blumberg, passed away. He has three sons, one stepson and one stepdaughter.

Al 'Flip' Rosen will always be remembered as one of baseball's best; dedicated and determined. Today he lives his retired, content life with his family in Palm Springs.

Author's note: *Quote from Cleveland Indians Manager, Al Lopez:*

"He (Al Rosen) came up with two black eyes. His eyes were swollen shut; completely shut. After the game we got on the train (in Cleveland) and went to Philly. When we got there the next morning, Rosen couldn't see at all. So, the trainer took him out to the park in the morning and put ice-packs on his face. Rosen spent the whole afternoon on the training table until finally he could open his eyes. He played that night and got four hits."

Interview with Al Rosen

George Green: Tell me a little bit about your early days.

Al Rosen: It all started when my family moved to Southwest Miami, Florida. I was about four-years-old. I was an asthmatic as a child and in those days they didn't have cures for asthma. The doctors told my Mother that the best place for me to be is out in the sun, as much as possible. So I started hanging around playgrounds, of which there were quite a few where I lived. We settled in Miami at the site of what is now known as La Habana. In those days life was different. It was in the depths of the Depression, and my brother and

I were kind of thrown out of the house to go play ball. We played on the streets, in the sandlots; we went over to the high school where they had a diamond and played from morning to night. And that's the way I grew up. I grew up in America Legion baseball. I played softball in a men's league when I was fourteen and loved it so much that I wanted to make it a career. I finally got an opportunity. I went for spring training at the behest of a former hall-of-fame pitcher, Herb Pennock, who at that time was the director for the Boston Red Sox.

George Green: And you were how old?

Al Rosen: I was seventeen. I went up to Virginia where they had their spring training and I was there for about three days. The manager called me in and said, "Son, go on home. Get a lunch pail because you're never going to be a ball player." I was crushed. But fortunately I ran into a man; in those days we called them Bird Dog Scouts, fellas that scouted around. They knew some of the scouts who were professional scouts employed by baseball teams. This fella said, "A friend of mine called me last night. He lost his third baseman." It was a four and a half hour bus ride from Suffolk, Virginia, down to Thomasville, North Carolina. I went down, met the manager; signed a contract with the Thomasville North Carolina and North Carolina State league. I didn't know at that time they had a working agreement with Cleveland, so in essence I became property of Cleveland. I played that year in Thomasville and had a good year, but then I went into the Navy where I became an officer in a small boat division. After the Navy I came out and found out I was property of the Cleveland Indians... went to a spring training camp with all of their minor leaguers, was assigned to Pittsfield, Massachusetts, in the Canadian-American league... I had a good year. Went from there to Oklahoma City and the Texas league... I got called up by Cleveland for the last couple weeks of the season and made my debut in Yankee Stadium. I struck out. I stayed with Cleveland for a little while, and then I went to spring training with them the next year and was optioned out to Kansas City. From there I got called up again.

George Green: They kind of owned you in those days, didn't they?

Al Rosen: Cleveland owned me. Then I stayed with Cleveland in 1949 for half the season and was shipped out to San Diego. In 1950 I was given a regular job at third base. I led the league in home runs as a rookie, and then I went on to become Most Valuable Player in 1953 unanimously, which was the first time it had ever been done. I was with the Indians. I finished my career when I got hurt. I felt I couldn't play at the same level that I was accustomed to playing and I didn't want to hang on. I didn't want to be 'just another player'. I was used to playing at the highest level, and when I couldn't do that any longer due to injuries, I decided to pack it in.

George Green: You said it was time to turn the lights off in baseball and turn the lights on in something else.

Al Rosen: In the brokerage business. I stayed in the broker business quite some time and later got an opportunity to be the President of the New York Yankees when George Steinbrenner bought the club. We were very good friends. He lived in Cleveland.

George Green: The light just went back on, didn't it?

Al Rosen: It was just huge. But the unfortunate thing is that George and I, while we remained friends through all the years, we couldn't get along business-wise. I resigned from the Yankees. I went to Houston, took over that ball club and stayed there for a number of years. I then had the opportunity to go west to San Francisco with my very good friend, Bob Lurie, who owned the club. I finished out my career with the Giants in the national league.

George Green: How about the comparison of excitement of a manager versus one as a player?

Al Rosen: They're not compatible. Playing is something so special because you only have one chance to play and it's a short-lived career. Unfortunately my time was cut short by injuries. I had always hoped to play until I was in my late thirties, but it didn't work out that way.

George Green: What was the emotional response you had when you were no longer in that spotlight?

Al Rosen: I've been very fortunate because along my life there were a lot of disappointments; a lot of times things were unjust. So, I was able to make the adjustment quite well, I think. I've never had any regrets. My only regret, I think, was the fact that had I played in today's world, the kind of medical attention the players get today would have prolonged my career. When I was playing, there was always somebody to take your job. We lived by that sort of thinking; 'Don't get out of the line-up because somebody can take your place and you may never get back in.' It's different today. Players get out of the line-up, they get tremendous medical attention, and had I gotten that kind of medical attention I probably would have gone on the disabled list, been out for a few months or a few weeks, come back and been well. I went on to other things that I enjoyed, and had a very full 'sporting' life!

George Green: At the height of your career in the fifties; what kind of salary level were you at?

Al Rosen: In 1949 I was making six-thousand-dollars a year playing baseball.

George Green: A major league player, six-thousand-dollars a year?

Al Rosen: And I thought I'd died and gone to heaven! The biggest salary I ever made was 47,500 dollars. Today, players are making huge amounts of money.

George Green: You were the 142nd Jew in baseball. Did you run into much discrimination on your way up the ladder?

Al Rosen: Yes, particularly playing through the South. But you handle yourself...you still carry yourself with dignity and don't fall into the trap of trying to solve the problems of the world. Anti-Semitism, anti-black; at that time there were no black players at all and when you look back on history you think, 'What an injustice it was to all those people who had great ability and never had the opportunity to play.' At least I got the opportunity to play.

George Green: Talk to me about what it's like not being part of that world anymore. Emotionally, are you at peace?

Al Rosen: I think a person is happiest if they accept the circumstances. If there's something you can do about it and don't do it, that's incorrect. But when you get to a point where there's nothing you can do about those things, you accept and you go on and make a life as best you can doing other things. I've enjoyed every moment of my life as a retired person, never had any regrets, never thought about getting back into the game. My time has passed. I had already been at the top. Any place I went from there was either going to be parallel to or less than. I was at the point where I felt I can retire and do things.

George Green: What would you say to youngsters who are trying to make it in the sports world?

Al Rosen: Keep playing. The more you play, the more you learn. You can't learn life on a baseball field, football field or basketball or whatever. You can't learn it out of books. You can't learn it by listening to somebody else telling you what to do. You have to do it yourself. Of course, you refine your game by listening to coaches and managers, and golf pros and tennis pros, but basically you have to have the love and the desire and the overwhelming feeling that you're going to be the best. If you go through life feeling that you've got something to contribute and you're willing to pay the price, which is hard work and determination, you have a chance to succeed. If you sit on the side lines and never give it a whirl, you can only look back and say, 'I wish I had.'

George Green: You can look back and never have to say, "I wish I had," because you can say, "I did."

Al Rosen: Well... it's been a great run!

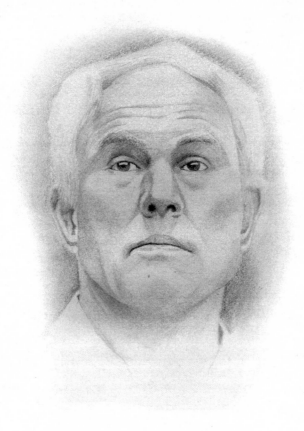

Mitch Kupchack

Lakers then, Lakers now, Lakers forever

Mitchell Kupchack was born in Hicksville, New York, in May, 1954. He started out in the game of basketball when he attended Brentwood high school in Long Island, New York, and played a major role in the successes of the Brentwood division between 1970 and 1972.

After high school he attended college in North Carolina where he became an All-American on the North Carolina Tar Heels Men's basketball team. Mitch played with the gold-medal-winning team in the 1976 summer Olympics in Montreal. In the same year, Mitch was drafted by the Washington Bullets and was added to the NBA All-Rookie team. In 1978 he played with the team that won the NBA championship. In 1981 he signed a contract with the Lakers after Earvin 'Magic' Johnson told the owner that with Mitch on their team, they would win.

Unfortunately, due to a knee injury, Mitch was out of the game between 1983 and 1984. He rejoined the team briefly again in 1985, then retired after that season, in 1986. But just because he stopped playing, this did not mean he would leave the game. Indeed, Mitch went on to learn how to run and manage NBA team operations, and was an apprentice to

Jerry West (also initially a player for the Lakers who then went on to become head coach and general manager of the team). This led to Mitch receiving his MBA from the UCLA Anderson School of Management in 1987.

Mitch then succeeded Jerry West as general manager for the Lakers, but was not considered as having all the powers of an NBA GM until 2000. During his time as GM for the Lakers he has seen many ups and downs, some of which have led to him being criticized for his decisions. However, he has been noted for being 'right' more than 'wrong'.

In 2014 Mitch chose to accept an extension on his contract and, therefore, remains general manager for the Lakers Basketball Team. He has held his position for over twenty-six years now. He lives today in Brentwood with his wife, Claire. Together they have a son and a daughter.

Interview with Mitch Kupchack

George Green: What was it like to be playing on a gold-medal-winning team?

Mitch Kupchack: At North Carolina, the coaches there made sure that they kept your ego in check. Sometimes, the more you achieved the harder they made you work in practice, just so you didn't start feeling too good about yourself. At the conclusion of the season they call you up and they tell you that you made an All-American team. For me it was a sense of accomplishment. It makes you proud. The Olympic experience is a crowning achievement in my athletic career. There is nothing that can quite measure up to an Olympic experience; when they play the national anthem and you get the gold medal.

George Green: Was that moment as good as the Lakers 1985 championship against the Celtics?

Mitch Kupchack: There is an NBA championship every year, but there's only an Olympic gold medal every four years. When you're feeling great, it's hard to say that one feeling was better than the other.

George Green: After you injured your knee you didn't play again until the '83, '84 season. How does an athlete feel when they get that kind of injury?

Mitch Kupchack: I had been injured before so it was nothing new to me. We were on a winning streak and then, one day later, your career is in jeopardy. You're going from the top of the mountain to the bottom of the heap, pretty quick. I had a lot of support by the medical people. I did have a very secure contract which makes a difference. One day I was part of the team and then I came back two years later. I wasn't really part of the team, you move on.

George Green: When you made some of those trades and you are getting criticized from no less than Kobe Bryant, how does a manager handle criticism from some of your key people?

Mitch Kupchack: It doesn't make your job any easier, but I understand where he was coming from. He wants to win; he doesn't want to wallow away the middle portion of his career on mediocrity. The media attention makes it even worse. We're all used to it now in terms of general managers. That's what we do and we get used to it. We get compensated well. It's a great job and there's nothing to be unthankful for.

George Green: You retire after the 1986, '87 season. According to my research, you focused on the program, learning the trade of running NBA team operations. What makes an athlete do the right thing like you did?

Mitch Kupchack: I got hurt at twenty-seven years. I was looking at the end of my career and knew I had to go through rehabilitation for two years. I couldn't see myself going through rehabilitation a couple hours a day, and then having nothing to do the rest of the day. I decided to enroll in the business school at UCLA. The more I got into it, the more I enjoyed it. Once I started I wanted to finish.

George Green: You retire and become assistant general manager under Jerry West, and then general manager of the team when he leaves for the Grizzlies (Memphis). Did you expect that position or were you surprised when Jerry left?

Mitch Kupchack: I was surprised when Jerry left. I wasn't surprised that I found myself following him. There was never an indication that that wouldn't happen. Jerry endorsed me. One day you're working with Jerry West, the next day he is gone. It was just me; it was an awkward feeling. There was a lot of work to do and all of a sudden the weight of the world is on your shoulders.

George Green: After Shaq (Shaquille O'Neal) leaves; people questioning your skills as general manager - how do you feel with that kind of pressure?

Mitch Kupchack: It's all about winning. When you win, everything you do looks good. When you don't win, the stuff you do will take criticism. That's understandable.

George Green: What advice would you give not only athletes but business people or anybody who's had ups and downs - how do you go forward? How do you overcome the lows of a career?

Mitch Kupchack: First you have to prepare yourself for your job. You'll be in certain situations where you have to make decisions and rely upon the people you trust for input, but make the decision that you feel is right. You are going to have to live with that decision for the rest of your life. The last thing you want to do is make a decision because somebody else told you to. You have to be prepared to live and die with what you decide. There is time to reflect and show remorse for going through some tough time, but you have to let it go. That should be your attitude; 'I'm going to deal with the adversity and no matter what happens, I'll recover and forge ahead.'

George Green: When you deal with this adversity, is there anybody in your world that you look to for guidance and support?

Mitch Kupchack: Everybody has people that they look to for those things. I had my family, a coach at the North Carolina team, Stan Kelner. Certainly Jerry became a person I trusted and went to for advice.

George Green: Athletes who find themselves finding nothing else in their world than basketball; what should they be doing with their lives when all they're looking for is that spotlight again?

Mitch Kupchack: There's nothing wrong with being involved in a sport for your whole life.

It's enjoyable and satisfying based on accomplishments. I see nothing wrong with being a manager for fifty to sixty years. I would encourage players, before they retire, to reach out and try to prepare themselves for their retirement. Once they retire or their career is over; if they're not prepared they're out there in the unemployment line, when they could have prepared somehow for life after basketball. If you can stay in the sport, stay in the sport.

Brief Update Interview with Mitch Kupchack, May 2014

George Green: Compare the spotlights, the intensity of being a player and the intensity of being a manager.

Mitch Kupchack: There's nothing that compares to really being a player. You're in your twenties playing a game that you played for fun as a kid. Of course it turned into a real profession, but it was still a game. You got paid well. People looked up to you and made you feel good. You get to compete at the highest level. It's hard to compete with that period in time. When Jerry West came to me and said, "Mitch, I could use some help on the front office," - that was a beacon of fortune and I moved in right away. Working with him was a blessing. It's hard to compare the two. One is a special time in your life when you're young and you're playing a game, and the other time you're so involved. Basically everybody else is going home after a long day of work and you're driving to Staples Center, and people say, "Where are you going?" You say, "I'm going to work. I get to sit and watch a game." It doesn't get any better. Since I retired we won seven championships.

George Green: Have you ever thought of what happens down the road, when you really want to throw the towel in? Is there going to be another spotlight down there?

Mitch Kupchack: No, I really haven't. Every now and then I'll drift and say, "I wonder." But the job is so demanding and invigorating, there's so much to look forward to every day.

George Green: Stimulation and challenge.

Mitch Kupchack: Challenge, I guess. I don't see myself retiring and playing golf and really doing nothing. I like to stay busy and I think I'm young enough to work many more years. So, I don't think that's a vision right now. I think my vision is to kind of re-craft what we have here in the next two or three years, and then take a look and see where we are.

Fred Claire

Think Blue!

Fred Claire was a member of the Los Angeles Dodgers' front office for thirty years, advancing from publicity director of the team to the position of Executive Vice President with responsibility for player personnel decisions and baseball operations.

In a distinguished career with the Dodgers, Claire served the team as a publicity director, vice president of public relations, promotions and marketing; Executive Vice President in charge of day-to-day operations, and Executive Vice President and General Manager in charge of player personnel.

Claire joined the Dodgers in 1969 and he proved to be an award-winning executive at every stage of his career. Claire was directing the team's marketing efforts when the Dodgers first hit the three-million mark in attendance and established a period of record-setting attendance figures.

In April of 1987, Claire was named General Manager of the Dodgers. When the team won the World Series in 1988 he was selected Major League Baseball's 'Executive of the Year' by 'The Sporting News'. Claire became the fifth Dodger executive in the team's history to win the award, following Larry MacPhail (1939), Branch Rickey (1947), Walter O'Malley (1955) and Buzzie Bavasi (1959).

Since his departure from the Dodgers in June of 1998, Claire has maintained an active schedule as an educator and as a consultant to a variety of businesses, in addition to an on-going civic involvement.

Claire currently is a lecturer at Caltech in the first sports business class ever offered by the prestigious university. He has served as an instructor at the University of Southern California, and helped to launch the successful class of 'Sports, Business and the Media' that is offered by the Annenberg School. He also is a founding member of the advisory board of the Long Beach State Sports Management Program.

Claire is a partner in 'AriBall', a leading company in the world of sports analytics. Since his days with the Dodgers, Claire has had an on-going role with MLB.com as a columnist and analyst. A book on Claire's career with the Dodgers, 'Fred Claire: My Thirty Years in Dodger Blue', was released in March of 2004 by Sports Publishing LLC. The book was co-authored by Claire and Steve Springer of the Los Angeles Times, and it was recognized on the Los Angeles Times' Bestsellers list. Claire was a leading member of a group that pursued the purchase of the Dodgers in 2011 and early 2012.

Claire is a member of the board of directors of the Rose Bowl Operating Company. His civic involvement also includes board of director positions for the Special Olympics of Southern California, the Los Angeles Sports Council, and Life Skills FORE Pasadena Youth, Inc.

During the time Claire headed the Dodgers' public relations and marketing efforts, the team received the Diogenes Award for ethics in marketing by the Sales and Marketing Executives of Los Angeles, and the Dodgers were saluted for achievements in marketing by both Major League Baseball and the Advertising Club of Los Angeles.

Claire served Major League baseball in a number of capacities, including a role as a member of the Board of Directors for MLB Properties, as a member of the Broadcast Advisory Group and as a member of the Baseballs Operations Committee. In 1990, Claire received the Award of Honor from the American Baseball Coaches Assn. He has served as a member of the Board of Directors for the RBI program (Reviving Baseball in Inner-cities). Prior to joining the Dodgers, Claire spent twelve years in the newspaper field as a sports editor, columnist and baseball writer for the Long Beach Press-Telegram, the Pomona Progress-Bulletin and the Whittier Daily News. During the time Claire was the sports editor of the Progress-Bulletin, the newspaper was saluted for its sports section by the California Newspaper Publishers Assn.

Claire was graduated from San Jose State University with a Bachelor of Arts degree in Journalism. He holds an Associate of Arts degree from Mt. San Antonio College. Claire started his collegiate career at El Camino College and was selected as the college's first Alumnus of the Year. In March of 2000, Claire was inducted into the California Community College Sports Hall of Fame. He and his wife, Sheryl, live happily today in Pasadena, California.

Interview with Fred Claire

George Green: Give me a little bit of background.

Fred Claire: I was born in a very small town in Ohio, Jamestown, where my father owned the comer drugstore. I guess from my earliest memories; I had a great sense of family, of security and love of sports, particularly baseball and basketball. Then my father decided to make a move to California. I found myself in a much larger community, but continued my interest in sports. I found an interest in journalism and writing. I graduated from Torrance High School and then went to El Camino College and then to Mt. San Antonia College before graduating from San Jose State with a degree in journalism. I had written a number of letters to newspapers in Southern California. I had an interview with a Pomona newspaper. The managing editor said, "We are going to have an opening in two weeks." I said, "Frankly, I cannot wait two weeks." I drove to Fullerton, had an interview with the managing editor of the newspaper. The secretary said he had a three hour business meeting, if I could wait. I said, "I can't wait three hours." I drove to Whittier and was hired by the Whittier Daily News and started the next morning. You have to get after it and make it happen. I worked a year or so at the Whittier paper then I moved to a Pomona newspaper and was sports editor there. I loved that job. Then the paper was sold. I wasn't pleased with some of the things that were happening in our department. About that time, I had a chance to interview for the job with the Long Beach Newspaper, covering the Angels. I accepted a job covering the Angels and then in that off-season had an opportunity to move to the Dodger beat. In 1969 I had the chance to become the team's director of publicity. So, that started my career with the Dodgers.

George Green: I am interested in the emotional highs and lows, and how you enjoyed what you did every day.

Fred Claire: When I started with the Dodgers it was a very small staff. We were the 'image builders' and the contact with media, the fan base, the whole presentation. It was great to work with a tremendous gentleman, Red Patterson. It wasn't so much a job as it was a total passion. Walter O'Malley was replaced as president by his son, Peter O'Malley. I had just started and he saw the need for growth in this area. I was very fortunate to be part of that progress. Those were some great years. I could hardly wait to get to work! Peter gave me a lot of responsibility.

George Green: How much sacrifice was there in your personal life? You were 'this close' to becoming a workaholic.

Fred Claire: I was consumed. I wanted to take the responsibility that was given to me and do the job to the best of my ability. A job in baseball is very demanding from the standpoint of the time required with long days and nights during homestands. At one point I considered accepting an offer from the National Football League in its creative services department, but decided to remain with the Dodgers.

George Green: Were there any lows before you became the GM?

Fred Claire: I loved every minute of my time with the Dodgers, but in looking back I know that I didn't spend the time with my family that I should have. We all make our decisions as related to commitments to our job, and I'm blessed to have three wonderful children; Jeff, Jennifer and Kim.

George Green: Let's talk about that moment when you were going to become the next general manager of the Dodgers.

Fred Claire: Al Campanis had been asked to appear on Nightline. He was asked why there weren't more 'blacks ' in important positions in baseball. Al, trying to defend the game, said some things that were explosive. Within forty-eight hours, Peter made the decision to ask him to resign. Peter called me and said, "You have to take this job of the general management of the Dodgers." I said, "I will take it only under one condition." He asked, "What is that?" I said, "I get full, total, complete responsibility - because I know the importance of the job. If they're going to run me out of town, I want to be sure that they run me out for my decisions and not someone else's." Peter said, "You have the job." When Peter was asked, 'How long does Fred have the job,' he gave the most accurate answer; 'He has it today!' That is the way I did the job. I'm going to do it today. I'm only going to do one day at a time. The record will show that I was the longest serving general manager in Major League Baseball.

George Green: One season later you were the general manager of the World Champion Dodgers. That had to be one of the great moments of your life.

Fred Claire: I really had the feeling that we were going to win. And I was so hoping we would win the World Series because I wanted to take the opportunity to pay tribute to the scouts, the player development people, the people who were the foundation of our organization. That was very important to me because of my respect for scouting, for player development. You win a world championship; you think, perhaps, there will be others but you need to savor the moment.

George Green: After the World Series in 1988, the rest of your time as the Dodgers general manager was perhaps less successful. You made three transactions which turned out poorly and overshadowed the success of your early times. How did you feel about that?

Fred Claire: When you make a move, you have to be thorough. In preparing for a move or a decision, you call upon the resources that you have then you make the decision. You take the responsibility for it. As a rule of management, when something good happens give credit to the people around you. When a decision proves not to be a good decision, the smart thing is to accept the responsibility. It puts you in place to continue to lead people instead of faulting people. When you are a general manager and making player moves, one will always have successes and failures. It's the nature of the business.

George Green: At the time you made the decisions that were supposedly best for the team, then you paid for it later.

Fred Claire: Part of my philosophy is that everything we do will come to the surface. I always respected the viewpoint of the media and of the fans, because I know the fans cared greatly about the Dodgers and I always wanted to give the very best that I have to give.

George Green: Talk about Fox taking over.

Fred Claire: Fox purchased the Dodgers because of the interest in regional cable television, not in the baseball business. An executive of Fox put together a deal to trade Mike Piazza and Todd Zelle...

Author's note: *when Peter O'Malley sold the Dodgers team to Fox in 1998, he was replaced by Bob Graziano as president.*

...Graziano called me the night of the trade and said, "This will be an announcement tonight," meaning the trade that was sending Piazza to the Marlins. I said, "Well then, there will be two announcements because after the trade is announced, I will announce my resignation." The Fox executive who made the trade didn't realize that the trade wasn't even official, because Gary Sheffield of the Marlins had a no-trade contract. I decided not to resign in view of the mess we were in due to the trade being made without a proper structure. When we finally got things in proper order the announcement was made. And when we made the announcement I was very candid. The next night one of the writers came up to me and said, "Fox is very upset with you because you were so candid about how the trade came about. You're not going to be here very long." I said, "Be that as it may, I made the announcement in an honest and straight-forward way, because that was how I was taught to do business as a member of the Dodgers." In June, 1998, I was informed that I was being relieved of my duties as general manager. I was told by Bob Graziano that 'If you want to stay on and help Tommy lasorda as the interim GM, you can.' I said, "You have told me that my contract will be honored, which I appreciate. If I do stay on, would I be compensated for that?" He said, "No." I said, "So, in other words, tomorrow I can go tee up and play golf?" He said, "That's right!" I said, "I think I'll tee it up!" Bob was under the guidance of Fox, he was in a difficult position. So, that was the end of my Dodger days. I said to Sheryl, "I want to go someplace where it's blue and green, and peaceful and quiet." We stayed up at Lake Arrowhead. Sheryl would go down by the pool and I would sit at a typewriter. I put all of my thoughts on paper, and when it was over I put it in a folder. I didn't think about writing a book on my Dodger career at that time, but a few years later I was approached by Steve Springer of the Los Angeles Times about doing a book, and I thought the timing was right. That led to 'Fred Claire: My Thirty Years in Dodger Blue'.

George Green: That night you were fired; I want to know, emotionally, how you felt.

Fred Claire: On that night I was in a bit of a state of shock in that I knew the business world I had been involved in for three decades had suddenly changed. Later on, I felt like a tremendous burden had been removed from me. I never would have given it up. I don't quit. I didn't lose my credibility. I didn't give in. I had only lost a job. I knew I could get another job, so I didn't feel a burden. I was excited as the days went on, about what I wanted to do, about the opportunities that might be there, about having time that I'd never had, to enjoy and explore.

George Green: There were no negative feelings towards the Dodgers.

Fred Claire: No.

George Green: You've done some really interesting things. You're not in the same spotlight. How does Fred Claire reinvent himself and go on to the next eleven or twelve years?

Fred Claire: Many times, when one leaves the spotlight, they absolutely have to find a job that they enjoy and, most importantly, brings them satisfaction. What I really focused on is 'What is it that I want to do?' I wanted to assist young people and give guidance by teaching. One of the first things I did was inquire of USC if there might be an opportunity to teach in the area of the business of sports. I was fortunate in that USC was starting a class titled 'Sports Business and the Media'. Immediately I filled a void. That was interesting for me and very beneficial. There were some opportunities that were coming my way that gave me the opportunity to explore rather than to actively pursue. A friend of mine came to me, he was with a company involved in 'shoulder rehab'; he wanted me to join this company, later to be named Performance Health Technologies. I said, "I don't know physical therapy or the medical." He said, "Yes, but you have the contacts in baseball." So, that started me with a position which kept me active. And then there were some other opportunities.

George Green: Were there any disappointments in contacts?

Fred Claire: No, because the train is moving on. I had the opportunity to start writing about baseball. Part of my job put me in direct touch with other general managers. Many of the people I was close to, I have been able to maintain contact with. With the Dodger train leaving, there was another train coming up; that is if you stay active. You have to make it happen otherwise it's not going to happen. You have to look and be excited about new opportunities.

George Green: My identification was President and General Manager of KABC Radio. I wanted to establish my own identification. How much of that went on with you?

Fred Claire: With the Dodgers there is always that connection, because that was my most visible position. I have never been troubled by that because that is where such a great part of my career was. I don't think one can disassociate oneself from that highly visible position; one can try, but I don't think you really can. That's how the general world thinks of you. If somebody were to say my name, they're going to say, "Oh, Fred Claire, the Dodgers."

George Green: And that's okay with you.

Fred Claire: That's great with me.

George Green: Sometimes we want to be recognized for the new train, and not the old one.

Fred Claire: I don't know that we can really do that when we have spent so many years in one organization. Maybe if you're at an age and stage where you can reinvent yourself, but for me I know the Dodgers are always going to be there. I am content with a different stage, a different career. Recognition, if it has been positive, is rewarding. I've always felt fortunate in that there is a recognition that seemed to be advantageous to me, without being a burden. I enjoyed being removed from the stress, from the greater visibility. I like going out to breakfast with my wife or friends, and just being me. I think you have to let go. My mother would read scriptures. There was one that she had (she has been gone for fifteen years now); 'Sometimes it is only through letting go that I can go open the way for new good to come to me.' Somehow these words stayed in my mind.

George Green: What advice would you give to others to let go and move on, rather than dwell on the past?

Fred Claire: You have to take an active role in shaping your path. It's not going to find you; you have to find it. Part of it is identifying what is important to you, and your passions. We fall short at times. We have to find those things we really enjoy. It is important to maintain a relationship with people who are part of your past, from a friendship standpoint. Beyond that we need to find those things that we're excited about. We need to be productive. We have to fill voids. We may not have high, prominent, positions - but that is more than okay with me. Good health is the most important asset that we have, not a good job. The job isn't who we are. The job is what we do. Don't ever do anything against what you know to be right.

Brief Update Interview with Fred Claire, May 2014

George Green: I have the privilege of talking to a really good friend of mine, Fred Claire; former General Manager of the Dodgers who is living a very active life. What's been keeping your life busy?

Fred Claire: Well, I was very fortunate, as you know, to spend thirty years with the Los Angeles Dodgers. Since Dodger days, and that now encompasses fifteen years, I've stayed very active on a number of fronts. But my main thrust has been doing the things that I really enjoy with the people that I enjoy being with. Many of those have come into civic causes where I get a satisfaction in using my experiences to help. I live in Pasadena and I am a member of the Board of Directors of the Rose Bowl Operating Company. I'm on the board of the Los Angeles Sports Council, and also the First Tee program; the wonderful golf program for youth in Pasadena. I've stayed very busy on the educational front as a lecturer. I had the honor of teaching the first course business class ever at Caltech. That ran from January to this past March, and we will have our second class in 2015. I wanted to let students know about opportunities in the business world of sports, and I have been pleased to see that there is great interest.

George Green: Can you compare the emotional feelings that you had then and now, being out of one spotlight and now being in another?

Fred Claire: When I became the General Manager I enjoyed every bit of that because I enjoyed the challenge. I've always been someone who has enjoyed seeing the results of your efforts judged, accounted for, literally on a daily basis. But it was all consuming, and you know me well to know that I was just totally dedicated around the clock. So, there is more of a 'peace' now in having a schedule where I can spend more time with Sheryl, my wife, and my family, in teaching young students, in assisting in good causes. I recognize at the age of seventy-eight that you have to use your time. You have to treasure your time, and I've tried to do that.

George Green: I don't look back at KABC much. I miss doing editorials, but that's about it. I have a new life and I believe in going forward.

Fred Claire: You have to. Letting go of the past gives you tremendous opportunities to fill your days for the present and for the future. We all have to let go, and I think that that thought is important. It's not that we don't treasure those things that were so much a part of our lives, but to be open to new things and new opportunities, letting go is very important. I like to think that I've handled that well and not tried to cling to something that is no longer there.

George Green: Very well said. What advice would you give to young people wanting to get into the sports business?

Fred Claire: The most valuable asset that we have is our own credibility. If you lose it, it's nearly impossible to get it back. The other part is the attention to detail; returning the calls, knowing more (hopefully more than your competition), paying attention to everything that crossed your desk becomes critically important. It reminds me that I was so fortunate to work with and under the great Walter Francis O'Malley. He was once asked, "What is it, Mr. O'Malley, that makes the Dodgers successful, certainly one of the most successful businesses of all time?" He said, "When the phone rings, we answer the phone." Pretty simple, pretty basic - the attention to detail. He was also asked once, when I was in his company, "Mr. O'Malley, what is it that you want to be remembered for?" Walter said, "I want to be remembered for planting a tree." I think that brings us to the very essence of what you're writing about. What do you want to be remembered for? We're really talking about a legacy, and for Mr. O'Malley that legacy of planting a tree was 'growth'. That tree was Dodger Stadium, his family, international baseball and, indeed, those are the things, at least in my mind, that I remember him for; the growth that he helped to stimulate during his lifetime.

Steve Garvey

When a school's named after you, you've done something right

Steve Patrick Garvey (AKA Mr. Clean) was born in Tampa, Florida, in December, 1948. His father was a driver for Greyhound Bus Services and his mother, a secretary.

When Steve was seven-years-old, his father was assigned to collect the Brooklyn Dodgers baseball team from the airport and transport them to St. Petersburg, where they'd play an exhibition game against the Yankees. On that day, Roy Campanella told young Steve, "You work hard and study hard and maybe someday you'll be a Dodger." Consequently Steve served as batboy during that game which saw the Dodgers' win over the Yankees. From that day on, Steve's ambition was to be a big league player.

From 1956 to 1961 Steve served as batboy in the Tampa Bay area for the Brooklyn Dodgers, the New York Yankees and the Detroit Tigers.

After graduating from Chamberlin high school where he became a phenomenal hitter in the Little League, he went on to Michigan State University where he excelled in football and baseball. Steve recalls how his football coach encouraged him to be a multi-sport athlete.

In 1968, Steve was drafted by the Los Angeles Dodgers and made his Major League debut in September, 1969. In 1974, he won the NL MVP award (National League Most Valuable Player). Then, in 1978, he hit four home runs and added a 'triple for five extra base hits' in the National League Championships Series. Again he earned the award for Most Valuable Player. Overall, with the Dodgers he played over 1727 games over fourteen seasons and was selected for eight All-Star games. Through 1974 to 1978 he won four Gold Glove Awards consecutively, and in 1981 was presented with the Roberto Clemente Award (given to the player who best exemplifies the game of baseball, sportsmanship, community involvement and the individual's contribution to his team).

In 1982 Steve went on to sign with the San Diego Padres. His home run in the deciding game of the 1984 Championship Series ultimately put San Diego in the World Series for the one and only time. Steve went on to break the National League's record for consecutive games played (1027 games in a row), and this led to him being featured on the cover of Sports Illustrated as baseball's 'Iron Man'. This streak ended, however, when he broke his thumb in a collision at home plate against the Atlanta Braves.

Steve retired during the collusion year, 1988, at the age of forty-years-old. Neither the Padres nor the Dodgers wanted to sign on his terms, so Steve decided to go out on his own terms. After nineteen years he no longer heard the sounds of fifty-thousand people cheering for him; the spotlight was off.

Fortunately he had already prepared for that inevitable day when his baseball career would come to an end. On the sidelines, in the mid-1980s, he'd created the Steve Garvey Celebrity Blue Marlin tournament, as well as the Steve Garvey Celebrity Skiing Challenge. In 1989 these were featured on episodes of ESPN and were co-hosted by his present wife, Candace Garvey. He also continued to focus on a project he called 'Pay Sports'; a career counseling service for athletes, with the purpose of helping sports stars make the transition from competition on the field to life in a business world.

In 1988 Steve founded Garvey Communications, involving himself in television production, including infomercials. He also began hosting the television show 'Baseball's Greatest Games' (available today as a DVD series).

Currently Steve serves as a member on the board of the Baseball Assistance Team, a non-profit organization dedicated to helping former Major League, Minor League, and Negro League players through financial and medical hardships. Having a strong understanding of the world of business and public relations, he consequently founded the Garvey Marketing Group.

Steve also went on to succeed Frank Sinatra as the national chairman of the Multiple Sclerosis Society. In addition he assists various other causes and organizations such as the Special Olympics, Juvenile Diabetes, the Blind Children Center, the Sisters Of Carondelet, United Way, Ronald McDonald House, St. Vincent DePaul Center, Pediatrics AIDS, the Starlight Foundation and ALS (Lou Gehrig's disease).

Nowadays, Steve also holds positions on a number of civic committees and corporate boards. Some of these boards include the Catholic University of America, the University of San Diego, and the Scripps Clinic and Research Foundation. His efforts in these areas mentioned above have certainly earned him praise and trust from those who surround him, and he is recognized for his discipline, commitment and dedication to these institutions.

On a more personal note, in 2012 Steve underwent an operation to treat prostate cancer. This urged him to continue to raise awareness for diagnosis and treatment of the disease.

Steve was often called 'Mr. Clean' due to his 'clean and respectable' personal life during his early playing days. Manager Tommy Lasorda once commented, "If he ever came to date my daughter, I'd lock the door and not let him out." However, this name faded over time as Steve found himself facing difficulties, including law suits, after a few of his relationships turned sour. After achieving great success he was confronted with numerous personal challenges, some of which resulted in the diminishment of his good name.

Despite moments of negative publicity and even bankruptcy, Steve was named Michigan State Baseball Distinguished Alumnus of the Year in 2009. In 2010 he was inducted into the Michigan State University Hall of Fame, and was featured in the LA Times as one of the three 'Spartan Athletes' that have helped Los Angeles professional sports teams win seven world championships. Steve Garvey Junior High School, in Lindsay, California, is named in his honor.

Today Steve lives in Palm Desert, California, with his wife, Candace Thomas. Together they have three children. His road was paved with both gold and thorns; his spotlight bright then dim. However, over the years, with his extensive experience in professional sports, business, television, entertainment and humanitarianism, his spotlight certainly still shines today.

Interview with Steve Garvey

George Green: I would like you to talk about Michigan University and being an All American.

Steve Garvey: I was born and raised in Tampa, Florida. My mother was an executive secretary and Father was a bus driver. When my grandfather passed away my grandmother moved in with us. She was handicapped; she was a semi-invalid. She'd contracted a disease called Seringomelia, a rare neurological disease which affected the use of her arms and hands. She was quite inspirational. I always loved sports. In March, 1956, my Dad had a charter order to pick up the Brooklyn Dodgers at the Tampa International Airport, and take them to St. Petersburg to play the Yankees in a spring training exhibition game. The next morning we go pick up the bus and drive to the tarmac of Tampa International Airport, and about ten minutes later the K. O'Malley landed, which was the prop jet of the Dodgers at that time. The first man off that plane was Lee Scott. Then came Walter Alston, Peewee Reese, Gil Hodges, Duke Snyder, Charlie Neil and all the boys of summer! Invariably most of them would pat me on the head. I had a flat top then and was a little chubby. The last guy was Roy Campanella. He patted me on the head and said, "Steve, you work hard and study hard and maybe someday you'll be a Dodger." That day I lugged the bats and helmets. I became the batboy and played catch with Gil Hodges. It was a thrill! The Dodgers won that day. We took them back to the airport and I had a couple of broken bats, an autographed team ball and a couple of other balls. They got back on the plane and took off. When we got home, I went into the bedroom and tried to go to sleep. I kept smelling something but I couldn't figure out what it was. My Dad came in and said, "It's pine tar." I never forgot that smell the rest of my life. That night I dreamed about being a baseball player and being a Dodger.

George Green: And? What happened then?

Steve Garvey: Then I started playing little league the next year, but continued to be a batboy because the Dodgers would request Dad each time they came over. So, until about the age of thirteen I would be a batboy for the Dodgers. It really was an honor for Dad, because they thought enough of him to request him each time, which is quite a statement. Once in a while he would have the Tigers or the Yankees and I would be their batboy, too. It was a chance to collect items like baseballs and bats. What I would do with a broken bat is, each night after dinner, I would go out and swing the broken bat, the heavy bat. I think that's what really developed a lot of my strength in my wrist and forearm and my swing. God blessed me with a little better eye-hand coordination than most of the kids, and by the time I was nine or ten I was pretty-well dominating our league. In high school I played football, basketball and baseball. Basketball practice started by the time football season was over and I was an All-State quarterback, so most of my focus was on football and baseball. I played defensive half-back at Michigan State. In high school I received a lot of honors and had a good scholastic career; had about twenty-five college offers to play football or baseball. I wanted to play both. I was tired of the heat in Florida. I signed the letter of intent with Michigan State and never regretted it. I played two years of baseball and football there. I was first team All-American baseball in my sophomore year, and starred in nine games my sophomore year in football. Entering school in 1966, signing with the Dodgers in 1968, meant that I would have two more springs before I graduated. We put that in the contract, the Dodgers agreed to it, and it took me an extra trimester at Michigan State, which was really for student teaching. So, I graduated in 1971.

George Green: What were you going to teach?

Steve Garvey: I was going to be a Physical Education Coach. I didn't realize that they had so little money! I think an Education degree gives you a good foundation; child psychology, public speaking, presentation, communication skills. People say, "Did you miss not teaching?" I say, "In some ways, but I've done so many other things like lecturing, putting on clinics, putting on camps and so forth, that it gave me a chance to teach and communicate."

George Green: In 1968 you go to Ogden?

Steve Garvey: They gave me a choice. I could have gone to Daytona Beach or Ogden, Utah. I said, "Gosh, I'm tired of Florida, the heat and the humidity. Ogden, Utah, is that up in the Mountains?" They said, "Yeah, it's about four-thousand feet." I said, "What time do I leave?"

George Green: You batted .368 in 1968 your first year and .373 in Albuquerque in 1969...

Steve Garvey: I go to the hotel the first day and there is this 'cherub' of a guy talking to about four or five guys my age. He turns around and says, "My name is Tom Lasorda and your life is changed forever." He was the manager. Bobby Valentine, Bill Buckner and Tom Psoric were also in that draft. It was probably the greatest draft in Dodger history. Next summer we played and won the league on the last day of the season. It was a great experience.

George Green: Were you the straight man of the group?

Steve Garvey: Yes, very much so.

George Green: You were probably true to character; buttoned down. You had a lifetime plan when you were nineteen years old, didn't you?

Steve Garvey: Oh, yes. I was a pretty conservative kid. I pretty much always had a game plan. Being an only child I had a lot of responsibility. One of the biggest was taking care of my grandmother, who was handicapped. I think that taught me a lot in growing up about sacrifice, about taking care of another human being, about compassion, about understanding.

George Green: Your Dad was a bus driver. I suspect that there was not a big monetary environment. I think you got more discipline?

Steve Garvey: Oh, sure. Definitely so, because you watch how hard he worked and how hard my mother worked. He worked every day and sometimes he was gone for a day or two; may have only been off one day a week.

George Green: When did you realize that education was as important in your development as athletic ability is?

Steve Garvey: I think education is very important. From the beginning I did have difficulty reading. What changed that was, after I became a batboy; the interest I developed in baseball; I started wanting to learn more about it. I started reading magazines and papers. I went from being the worst reader in class in the second grade, to being the best by the fourth grade simply because I was stimulated by a subject and the subject was sports. When I lecture now I talk to parents about 'the greatest gift we can give our children is education; both social and scholastic'. The ability to read far overshadows any of the skills simply because; if we can't read we are truly at a disadvantage. We are truly handicapped. That's why I credit the Dodgers and baseball and my love of sports for making me a better reader.

George Green: You played eleven years with the Dodgers.

Steve Garvey: Yeah, September 1969 was my first month there. It was the end of the season, and then 1970 to 1982.

George Green: When did you realize that you were really an upper echelon player?

Steve Garvey: During the '74 season when I finally made the transition. I had a shoulder separation at Michigan State playing football my freshman year, which curtailed my throwing. I had a good strong arm but after the shoulder separation it was never the same again. So, I had some problems throwing. When I signed I always could field well, but... scatter-armed, so to speak.

George Green: That's the first year you got two-hundred hits.

Steve Garvey: In '74, yeah. But I needed to win the position to be able to get out there and do it every day. So, in '73 Ron Cey and Ken MacMillan had finally joined the team. They were third basemen and I was a man without a position. I went to the outfield and played a couple of games in left field and didn't have a real strong arm. I ended up being the twenty-fourth guy on the team. I thought, 'I will work hard; a good work ethic.'

George Green: You were converted from an outfielder to a first baseman?

Steve Garvey: Really third base. I didn't play enough outfield to be considered an outfielder. Dixie was the batting coach. But Monte Baskel was the fielding coach and Monte helped me make the transition. When I was a man without a position I became the first pinch-hitter, so to speak. If you needed a pinch-hitter in the third or fourth inning, I was the guy who went up there. And, I got a few hits. So, all of a sudden in the sixth or seventh inning they needed a pinch-hitter. They would call on me and I would get a few hits. All of a sudden I was leading the pinch-hitting and was the guy you brought in at the bottom of the ninth or the top of the ninth, when you needed a run and the game was on the line. All of a sudden I was nine for twenty with ten RBI's and leading the league. But it was July 23rd, a double header against Cincinnati; Freddy Norman beat us. Freddy used to just drive Walter Alston crazy. I got a pinch hit in the eighth inning. In between games he asked me if I wanted to play first base. I started first base and then got two hits. We beat them, split the double header. We took off for Cincinnati and the next day I started that game and played seven straight games at first, got two hits a game, and won the position in the last half of that season. It helped solidify my position as a first baseman. Then, 1974 was my pivotal point or turning point year. I went out, got two hundred hits, leading the league in home runs and RBI's through the All-Star game.

George Green: Batted .312?

Steve Garvey: Yep, had all those MVP statistics; MVP of the All-Star game and was the only write-in candidate ever to start a game. I had over one-million write-in votes. I go to the playoffs and was MVP of the playoffs.

George Green: You were the first player in National League history to have over four-million votes.

Steve Garvey: People actually write my name in, which is a tremendous achievement! It has never been done since, and may never be. It was my break-through year.

George Green: While you are remembering all these wonderful dates, I'll give you one; August 28, 1977.

Steve Garvey: That was probably my five for five for five day; St. Louis. About ten minutes before the game, Steve Brener, the publicist for the Dodgers, comes over and says, "There is a lovely girl, about twelve, who was in a gymnastics accident. She is a quadriplegic. Would you come over and talk to her?" I looked over and saw this beautiful long blond-haired girl and I went over. Her name was Annie Ruth. I said, "Hi, Annie, how are you?" She goes, "Hi." She had difficulty speaking because of the respirator. I told her that I heard she was a big Dodger fan. She said that she was. She said, "Can you get a hit for me today?" I said, "Oh, sure, Annie, that's easy. My first hit today will be for you." It was also Nun's Day at Dodger Stadium. I thought, 'If I don't get a hit today, with this pretty girl as an inspiration, then I'm really in a slump.' So, first time up against Bob Force I hit a double down the first field line. I get to second base, look at her, tip my hat, and she had a big smile. I said, "God, thank you." Next time up, I hit a double and then hit a home run, and then hit a grand slam.

George Green: You had two homers and one grand slam? Five runs, five RBI's and fourteen total bases. What a day!

Steve Garvey: Yeah, on the cover of the Herald Examiner the next day, front page with my hand up and got two standing ovations. Over the years I have taken her to charity events and dinners. She has come to my events. I have seen her and talked to her. People say that I have really helped this girl. I say, she has been a tremendous inspiration for me. Here's a girl who went to USG, graduated with a degree there, started painting and got into the greeting card business; uses a brush with her teeth. I have seen her through the years, and just thinking about her now - I'll probably call her in the next couple of days because I really miss not talking to her. She is a true inspiration. It's a great example of what happens with chemistry.

George Green: 1977 was probably the best year of your career, wasn't it? Fourth straight Gold Gloves, thirty-three home runs, 192 hits. In Lindsay; a Junior high school was named after you.

Steve Garvey: Probably. That was '77. Next February (Interview in 2009) will be the twentieth anniversary of the naming of the school which I go up and visit twice a year.

George Green: Tell me about that.

Steve Garvey: A fellow from Orange County, a principal, went up and took the job at Abraham Lincoln Junior high school in Lindsay and found that there were some morale problems and problems between the cultures of the kids there and the ethnic backgrounds. He decided, 'let's do something different'. He thought a name change would help. I became a finalist with Elvis Presley and Elton John. He called me and asked me if I would mind, if I won, if they could put my name on the school. I asked him if I could think about this because there are not too many living people with names on a school. It is quite a responsibility and I wanted to talk it over with my family. I did and the next day I called to say, 'If I become the person they want, then let's give it a try and let's see if it works.' It became Steve Garvey Junior High and they became the Dodgers. They changed their colors to blue and white. They named the library after Tom Lasorda; The Lasorda Library. I told them that they should have made the cafeteria named after Tom Lasorda, which is what they eventually did. I go up each year and there are a lot of kids who come up to me now who are not kids anymore. They have families and they are in their thirties. They remember the first day I came, and the assembly, and the cheerleaders, and the band, and the gifts, and the commitment I made them.

George Green: How many baseball players have junior high schools named after them?

Steve Garvey: None that I know of. Usually politicians, presidents. If you look past the National and International visibility of who I was as an athlete; I did go to Michigan State, I did get a degree. The charitable work that I did... all those things that I did do round out the person, and I think they knew that if I made the commitment I would stick by it and see it through the duration. Over the twenty years a lot of things have happened to me, challenges, and times when I have had to go in and talk to the kids about things that have happened to me, that are not easy to talk about, but are life lessons. I have always said that I'm just a human being. I am fallible, I make mistakes, but I try hard and try to learn from my experiences.

George Green: In `77 and '78 you became the only Dodger to have four twenty-hit seasons, and forty-six hits out of a one-hundred at bats in September. Any final reflections on those wonderful years of the 70's with the Dodgers?

Steve Garvey: I just think that the 1977 team was the best team I ever played on. When I look back at the post-season play, obviously we were frustrated in the 70's against the

Yankees in Oakland in '74. We had our opportunities but didn't capitalize on them. I think that the quality of the players that I played with, their ability level and the team work was something I will always admire and list as a virtue in my career. The infield being together; Lopes, Cey, Russell and myself, for nine-and-a-half years was five-and-a-half years longer than any other infield, and I will bet that this will not be broken for a long time, simply because of the change in the opportunities and options players have now of mobility. It is very difficult for a team to keep a player for three or four years, much less nine-and-a-half years.

George Green: 1982 was your last year with the Dodgers, before you went with the Padres.

Steve Garvey: Well, the problem with the Dodgers is that they came up with what we wanted in terms of length of contract. We wanted five years, they would only go three. Language of the contract; they wouldn't do the language we wanted. It wasn't real difficult. The difference in monies was over 2.5 million dollars which was a lot at that time. All I wanted was parity relative to what their team were going to be making. Their philosophy was that it was always better to get rid of a player a year too soon than a year late. But in this case it was five years too soon. If you look at what happened then; although the Dodgers won in 1983 and 1985, I think one of the reasons they didn't get to the World Series was the senior experienced leadership that a Cey, Lopes, Baker or myself could have provided wasn't there. It was a matter of judgment. As I look back now, if I knew then what I know now, I probably would have taken the contract simply for the sake of the fans.

George Green: So, you leave the Dodgers.

Steve Garvey: I never thought I would.

George Green: Neither did any of us, as fans. We thought you were as much a fixture as the Statue of Liberty.

Steve Garvey: If the Dodgers would have gone for the years and the wording of the contract, the dollars and cents would have been superfluous. But I just got no feeling that they wanted to compromise. The five years I spent in San Diego were successful because I helped them win for the first time; go to the World Series.

George Green: If you had to describe the euphoria or feeling, what is it like to be an athlete with all this adoration coming at you from every single angle?

Steve Garvey: It's inherent to those professions where the individual stimulates other human beings and raises their level of excitement and anticipation, and does something extra special. The feeling of accomplishment and achievement by what you do, is measured by the response from your audience, which in this case is the fans. For the politician, it's the audience; for the actor, it's the audience. When I hit a home run in the bottom of the ninth against the Cubs in game four of the playoffs, sixty-thousand would cheer for fifteen minutes. It's difficult to top that!

George Green: Was that one of the great moments?

Steve Garvey: Yes, oh sure. People still come up and say where they were when I hit the home run that night. But, that moment with sixty-thousand on the stands and fifty-million people watching on television, that's still is not as great as the one cry from the birth of my daughter. That is still the greatest accomplishment of my life... my children.

George Green: How serious was your attempt at politics?

Steve Garvey: I never made an attempt, really.

George Green: Didn't they say you were going to run for Senator at one time?

Steve Garvey: Dick Young's wife thought I would make a good politician. I told him that I do my reading and I read the New York Times Op Ed column, and I do my share of voting. I told him that maybe someday if I think I can make a difference... Well, next day in the New York Daily News; 'Garvey thinks about politics.' It's been one of the first three questions anybody asks.

George Green: When was the last baseball game you played?

Steve Garvey: The last game was a pinch hit in a pitching appearance in 1987, in San Diego.

George Green: After the `87 season that was it, right?

Steve Garvey: Retired in January of '88 during collusion.

George Green: When you say collusion, what do you mean?

Steve Garvey: The owners were found to collude in `86, `87 and `88. They paid one-million dollars into a fund distributed by the association over the last few years. They asked, 'Did I want to go out by trying out in Spring Training for some team, and giving them the subjectivity of just cutting me at a whim after the great career I had, or would I go out on my terms?' I decided it was time to leave.

George Green: You finally decided that you were done. What goes through your mind?

Steve Garvey: I started a sports marketing company in 1983 in San Diego, Garvey Marketing Group. I had been involved in that for five years. I started a career-counseling company for athletes called 'Pay Sports' in 1982.

George Green: Please explain some of those things because that was unique in the business. No athlete had ever done that.

Steve Garvey: Nor had anyone else ever created a career-counseling company that was focused at and for athletes, in helping them make the transition from sports to business. The term we used was, 'After the cheering stops'. It is a very high profile business which we started as a not-for-profit, simply to provide a service for athletes. It was a seven-step process from initial contact to placement. We used industrial psychologists, we use testing, we have a group of counselors on staff. Through the years Pay Sports provided a valuable service and wrote the book, essentially, on career counseling for athletes. Probably the most high-profile program that was established was one with the NBA in which eighty-percent of the basketball players were involved in the program for a period of three to four years.

George Green: It is your opinion that most athletes are not prepared for the transition after the cheering stops?

Steve Garvey: I think less than ten-percent are prepared. The managers and agents essentially are gone once the player stops playing. It is a rare agent or manager who helps the player prepare before he retires for that transition; helps him develop another skill. Unless you have done some theatrical work for which you have a manager or agent, and that's very rare, most of the players haven't developed that secondary skill. Ten-percent to twelve-percent have a college degree. Maybe forty-five-percent to fifty-percent have gone to college but are nowhere near a degree, and have played for so long that what they learned probably is outdated, especially in high technology now. Our testing focuses on where the aptitude lies for each individual, what they want to do, where they want to live, how we could provide extended education to help them develop a skill. It is not based on dollars and cents. It is not continued lifestyle, because it is very difficult for any of these players to leave professional sports and be making several hundred, thousand dollars and step into a position where they will be making the same. Usually the CEO, President is making that kind of money, maybe, if he is lucky. Not somebody who has just come from another profession and is stepping in. He hasn't had the on-the-job experience or education for it. The athlete would come to us. The first question would be; 'What would you like to do? What would you like to make?' They would say, 'A public relations job for maybe one-hundred-thousand or one-hundred-and-fifty-thousand dollars. ' Within an hour they would be reduced down to high anxiety, so to speak, about what reality really is. We probably tested eight-hundred, nine-hundred athletes over the years and placed two-hundred. I'd like to think we saved some lives, some marriages.

George Green: What happened to the five-hundred you didn't or couldn't help?

Steve Garvey: They probably failed to complete the steps needed to be in position for placement.

George Green: What does the athlete who doesn't find a public relations job do? A sales job, representative job? What happens to the bulk of athletes that don't have the benefit of getting a Steve Garvey to talk about their career?

Steve Garvey: Basically, they go into sales. They take the visibility of their name and they use it to sell products and services. There are some that do have business skills, professional skills. Some are entrepreneurial. Some are in their own businesses. We used to take athletes who wanted to start their own businesses and get them involved in franchises, and have the franchises teach them and educate them on running that business.

George Green: Any success stories you can think of?

Steve Garvey: There are a lot of them, but I think the most important thing is there are companies like Anheiser-Busch , Pepsi Cola, Merrill Lynch and two or three more that work with us on intern programs on the off-season, that understood the value of the athlete who is used to hard work and dedication. They communicate pretty well and if given the right education preparation, can be a viable associate.

George Green: As a professional consultant to athletes now, do you ever have any emotional setbacks because you aren't in that bright spotlight anymore?

Steve Garvey: Most athletes do. Fortunately, in my case, I was the guy they cheered for. I was the guy that ended the game. I was the guy that was the MVP. I was the guy that played in the ten All-Star games and we won all ten. I was the guy who was the 'Iron Man' up until Cal Ripkin.

George Green: How many consecutive seasons?

Steve Garvey: Seven and a half, 1207 games.

George Green: If you had to give advice to somebody who came out of a spotlight, cheering crowds; whether it is an athlete or a businessperson who is at the top of their game - what do you tell them to prevent them from comparing those wonderful moments of heavy spotlight to an ordinary life?

Steve Garvey: There is nothing that can compare with that. Unless you go into the political arena where people are cheering for you, or another high-profile arena where there is an audience. You are not going to be in that situation again. So, what you do is, you take that wonderful part of your life and the accomplishments, and take those memories with you as a fond time and don't try to duplicate them. If you try to duplicate them, you will fail. You cannot do it. Close that chapter, open a new one in which now you have an opportunity to create another arena that is much smaller and has less visibility; that doesn't have as much adulation and audience to it. Create your own star there. Everything is relative. All spheres in business are greater or smaller.

George Green: What do you tell guys who are downsized? Do you tell them to find a smaller star or light?

Steve Garvey: Not necessarily a smaller star, because every profession relative to that profession has a big light to it. What you want to do is you want to be the MVP of your next job or position. Magnitude. What you want to take with you are the same things that made you successful in the fishbowl, so to speak. That is hard work, dedication, humility, commitment, passion...

George Green: Everyone has their own spotlight on them, don't they?

Steve Garvey: Oh, sure. My Dad had one. He was responsible for forty-two people on a bus every day.

George Green: When he thought about himself and what he was doing, did he feel he was accomplishing something, and did he have a strong self-image?

Steve Garvey: I think if you take pride in what you do and you do it well, that's very important; no matter what it is. If you take that equation for success and apply it, and remain humble and keep reaching and keep inspiring people, or you get to a position where you are not only responsible for a specific job, you are responsible to lead people; I think that is what you did, and that's what I do, and it's very important. We all want things. It all depends upon what philosophy you grow up with. I wasn't born and baptized Catholic right away. My parents waited until I was twelve or thirteen. Once I became baptized and became involved in the Catholic Church, I started to grow spiritually as well as physically and mentally.

George Green: Religion has been a very important thing in your life.

Steve Garvey: Yes, it has been a very strong foundation.

George Green: This faith and belief is the thing that helps you overcome all kinds of problems.

Steve Garvey: Yes, I can take all of those problems and let them go, knowing that I do have faith. With that faith, God will help me. It is not always my time. Very rarely is it my time. It's His time. I cannot control another person, all I can do is control myself and my actions, thoughts and words. It's not easy. But that's why you can strike out in the bottom of the ninth and feel bad about it, then you can go to the clubhouse and think about it for a while, take a shower and go home and know that you did your best.

Tommy Lasorda

You can't dodge the spotlight!

Thomas Charles Lasorda was born in September, 1927, in Norristown, Pennsylvania. Tommy's first involvement with baseball was through the Philadelphia Phillies in 1945 as an undrafted free agent (a player not under contract with any specific team). In the same year he began his professional career with the Concord Weavers.

In 1946 Tommy left to join the army for a year. He then returned to baseball in 1948 with the Schenectady Blue Jays of the Canadian-American League. In May, 1948, he struck-out twenty-five Amsterdam Rugmakers (New York) in a fifteen inning game, setting a record (at the time). Soon he gained the attention of the Dodgers Major League baseball team who drafted him from the Phillies chain.

In August, 1954, Tommy made his major league debut for the Brooklyn Dodgers. He scouted for the Dodgers for a few years then managed the Ogden Dodgers. In 1969 he became the Dodgers AAA Pacific Coast League manager. Tommy went on to become the manager of the Los Angeles Dodgers in September, 1976.

Tommy led the Dodgers for twenty seasons (1977 to 1996). Under his management the team won 1599 games, eight National League West titles, four National League pennants and two World Series championships. He also managed four all-star games. Tommy's involvement with the Dodgers, also as a pitcher, lasted fifty years.

After retiring in 1996, he continued to remain actively involved with the Dodgers in various senior positions, including vice-president and interim general manager. In 1997 he was added to the Baseball Hall Of Fame in New York.

Tommy will always be known as a great leader and one of baseball's great personalities. He has been quoted for stating, "I want to die a Dodger." Tommy and his wife, Jo, presently live in Fullerton, California.

Interview with Tommy Lasorda

George Green: You've been out of that intense spotlight even though you've been very visible doing a lot of things. How are you handling this transition?

Tommy Lasorda: I'm handling it fine. I gave up the managing because of my health. When I had a heart problem I decided to step down as manager of the Dodgers. Nobody made me step down. I just decided that I could not do the job like I'm capable of doing, because of my fear of my health problem.

George Green: It is a different situation that you're involved in now. How are you handling that difference?

Tommy Lasorda: I miss managing, there's no question about it. I miss it terribly. But I gave up something that I loved very dearly for something I love even more dearly, and that's my family and my life. If I had just completely severed my relationship with baseball, I think it would have been really drastic. But being that I'm vice-president for the Dodgers, I'm still doing a lot of things that I enjoy doing. It made the transition a lot easier.

George Green: If somebody called you tomorrow morning and wanted you to manage a team, would you do it?

Tommy Lasorda: No, I wouldn't do it. I gave up the best job in baseball. Why would I want to manage for somebody else? My uniform's been retired. So, I think I've reached the top of the mountain and I think that's about the end of it. I have not been forgotten by the people that I've retired with. They've all remembered me; they've all treated me great. They all know that I have the ability to help them and that's what I've been doing.

George Green: Everything is going exactly as you want it to go.

Tommy Lasorda: I think it is. I feel like I'm happy with what I'm doing. I'm visiting the minor leagues. I'm working with young players. I'm teaching. That's what I enjoy doing. I do a lot of speaking which I enjoy doing. I never dreamed that I would ever be vice-president of the Dodgers.

George Green: How do you cope with the fact that the two spotlights are not the same?

Tommy Lasorda: I don't care about spotlights; that doesn't make that much difference to me now. It's never easy when you make a transition; never easy for anybody. It wasn't easy for me either. You've got to be doing something that you enjoy. It naturally was tough for me to leave managing, I did it for twenty years on a major league level. I did it for eight years in the minor league. I did it for six years in winter baseball. When you make the change, it's not an easy change. But you have to face reality. After all, I was in a position where I was concerned with my health, so I stepped down. I'm still with the Dodgers and I'm spending more time with my family and I enjoy it.

George Green: I think the key line of advice is that you've got to face reality to whatever situation that you're in.

Tommy Lasorda: I think that if you're going to be unhappy after you make a transition, then that's a sad situation.

George Green: I just want to know what advice you would give to other people going into a transition.

Tommy Lasorda: Don't look back. Look ahead. You can't change what has happened. Try to enjoy yourself, try to make another area where you could be happy, and that's what my advice would be.

Brief Update Interview with Tommy Lasorda, May 2014

George Green: How often are you going to the ball games now? Are you at every one of them?

Tommy Lasorda: Oh, yeah. If I'm not there then I'm out of town visiting our minor league teams.

George Green: I presume that baseball will continue to be the most important thing in your life until you die?

Tommy Lasorda: Absolutely. I want to die a Dodger. I'm eighty-six now, I've been with the Dodgers sixty-five years.

George Green: I presume that's a record in baseball?

Tommy Lasorda: I don't know if it's a record but it's a goddamn good shot at it!

George Green: And I'm hoping Jo is well and by your side?

Tommy Lasorda: Jo is well, still living and we're both very happy.

George Green: I presume you're still doing charity work.

Tommy Lasorda: Absolutely. I speak all over the country.

George Green: Baseball has been your life for sixty-five years. It's going to be continued. You're one of the most well-known people on this planet, and I had so many good times watching you speak. You're one of the great people that I've met and I wish you good health.

Tommy Lasorda: Same back to you, George!

Donn Moomaw

The football field, the father and forgiveness

Donn Moomaw was born in October, 1931, in Santa Ana, California. As a child he remembers one very special Christmas when he (eight-years-old) and his brother (ten-years-old) received the best gifts ever. His father had acquired second-hand football uniforms, including shoes and helmets, from the junior college then hung them next to the tree on Christmas morning. This ultimately sparked the love for football, in the hearts of the Moomaw boys.

Donn attended Santa Ana high school and then UCLA where he joined the football team as center and linebacker. He exceled in football and went on to become an All-American. He recalls that throughout this time, he never felt as good as the fans perceived him to be, and instead of thriving on his ego he continued to play believing that performing at his best was merely what was expected of him.

When his football career ended he turned to a deeper life, a spiritual life and thus became a Presbyterian minister. He served as pastor for the Bel Air Presbyterian Church in Los

Angeles from 1964 to 1993; the church attended by Ronald and Nancy Reagan, among others. Their trust in him grew strong which led to him performing the invocations and benedictions at both Reagan's presidential inauguration in 1981 and his second inauguration in 1985.

The attempt on Ronald Reagan's life was a shock to the country. During the time Ronald was in hospital, Nancy called upon Donn to visit him and pray for him in the hospital.

Donn then remembers the day when a mistake, call it human error, led to the collapse of the life he knew. Involved in a sexual scandal, Donn was cast out of the church and left to fend for himself after years of service to a spiritual family he deeply loved.

He recalls how his own family, his wife and five children, were there for him but those he'd known from the church were gone with the wind.

Crisis defines a man, and this is what happened to Donn. He found solace in the concern from others he never knew, even those who had been persecuted for crimes that landed them in prison for years. He learned, over those years, more about life, faith and spirituality than the average man would ever find the time to learn. Due to this, his faith and understanding of the spiritual became stronger, and he became wiser. To speak and live from experience makes one's word that much more viable.

No longer allowed to return to the church he'd served for twenty-eight years, he later was able to start preaching again as a guest at the St. Andrews Presbyterian church. In 1997 he was welcomed to the pulpit of the eight-hundred member Village Community Presbyterian Church in Rancho Santé Fe.

Unlike some performers, athletes, entertainers or business men, Donn didn't find it that easy to 'jump back' and strive to climb another mountain. It took him several years to find the forgiveness he deeply longed for. But fortunately, he did find it!

Today he and his wife, Carol, still live in Bel Air and are at peace, thankful for the wonderful friends they have now and the wonderful lives they have been blessed with. Donn is respected again today and will continue to be respected for his wisdom, his spiritual teachings and his devoted faith.

Interview with Donn Moomaw

George Green: I'd like to hear a little bit about your highlights; the career of Donn Moomaw.

Donn Moomaw: When I was eight and my brother was ten, my father being a junior college professor; we obviously didn't have lavish Christmases. One Christmas we heard him down in the kitchen. My brother and I knew something special was up. Christmas morning we came sliding down the stairs to see who was to be the first to go into the living room; see what was in front of the Christmas tree. Our chins dropped to our chests when we saw in front of the Christmas tree; football uniforms. My father had prevailed upon the coach to give some reject uniforms to him and he had polished the shoes, painted the helmets, repaired the jerseys and so on. We had those suckers on before anyone else was up in the neighborhood, and we were out in the back vacant lot. In a real sense that was the beginning of my love for football. As a junior-high boy, I remember one day playing a game against another school and I scored a touchdown. My mother came late to the game and she drove her car up to the edge of the playing field. Five of the girls in my class ran over and told my mother. Man, I could see them animated about how 'Donn had scored the touchdown'. And I think that was the beginning of a very heady feeling of euphoria outside myself. Most of my life, I judge myself on the basis of what I've done, not on the basis of who I am. Through high-school I was All-American in Santa Ana, and then All-American at UCLA, in all my three varsity years. I never had a very high self-esteem, all the way through.

George Green: All the way through high school you weren't feeling good, even when you were an All-American?

Donn Moomaw: Even when I was student body president. No. It was something fundamentally messed up within my system that would not let me experience myself as others were experiencing me.

George Green: So when the people were cheering, you still didn't believe the publicity?

Donn Moomaw: I believed the publicity and all the rest, and that got me high. It didn't change the fundamental nature, though, of my esteem.

George Green: What happens when the cheering stops?

Donn Moomaw: What happens to us when we don't have anything behind our name? All we do then is reflect back on what we used to do. Crisis usually readjusts everything that we're doing. You have family crisis, you have financial crisis, but how to live without the audience? I had an audience all my life.

George Green: What was it like being the pastor to President Reagan, were you not involved in inauguration?

Donn Moomaw: I had a charmed life and a wonderful opportunity to serve the inauguration of president Reagan. Mr. Reagan and Mrs. Reagan had been members of the church.

George Green: Before he became governor?

Donn Moomaw: He became governor while he was there and then he was elected president. I went through all the crisis that he went through. As his pastor, as his friend, he had a strong capital punishment conviction; pro capital punishment. And yet, I knew even with that conviction, if you have a chance to save a man's life, it's a gut-wrenching thing. So I went over that day with him, and the many pellets were dropped. I asked him to kneel and pray. And we knelt and we prayed through that time to the first execution. A minute after we got off our knees, the warden of the state prison called in and told him, "It's over." He then asked me to pray at the inauguration. It comes down to this: your ultimate accountability is not to your political party. It's not even to your immediate family. Your ultimate accountability is to God. At the end of the day, can you reflect upon it when there is no more shouting, no more televisions in your face, no more reporters hustling around, no more of your aides pulling at your coat? How do you feel about your day? And we talked about moral responsibility...

George Green: Could you believe that you were probably the most popular, well-known minister of all time for that moment?

Donn Moomaw: Fortunately, the things leading up to it, being in front of crowds, being honored, being the campus hero and those kind of things, I think prepares one to put this in perspective. It was very heady and very affirming, very validating,

George Green: Did you ever feel it was going to go on forever?

Donn Moomaw: No. I knew too much about highs and lows. But I knew there'd be other times. I always wondered, 'why me?' That's probably the question I will ask God someday; "Why me? Why did I get all those wonderful perks, and how could you trust me with that kind of stuff..." because I know myself. But it was good to be by his side in those very difficult moments. When Ronald was shot, I was in Bermuda at an insurance convention.

Author's note: *from Wikipedia; The attempted assassination of United States President Ronald Reagan occurred on March 30, 1981, sixty-nine days into his presidency. While leaving a speaking engagement at the Washington Hilton Hotel in Washington, D.C., President Reagan and three others were shot and wounded by John Hinckley, Jr. One of them died decades later of related injuries.*

At about 10:30, I was on the plane going to Washington. I'd already talked to Nancy. Nancy had some White House people meet Carol and me at the airport, rushed us to be with her at the White House, and we had a remarkable meeting with Frank Sinatra and Barbara, Billy Graham and his associate T.W. Wilson, Lou Evans and Colleen Evans who were in a sense his East Coast ministers at National Presbyterian Church... and Charles Wick and his wife. Amazing conversation, to hear this real eclectic group sharing. Billy Graham led in prayer. Then she asked Carol and me if we would go to the hospital with her that night. We went that night and down the hallway. Every five feet were Secret Servicemen standing sentinel, just like pillars. They were ready for anything. Then we went into his room. He had pipes going everywhere. He had just been operated on that morning yet he was very alert, wanted to talk about the church. We had a very deeply personal time, talking about his faith, talking about his hope. He had an incredible feeling that he was being spared for a reason. He didn't see it as a failure or even as hardly a bump in the road. But his crisis made him a better person. He handled it well. The crisis doesn't make or break an individual, it reveals an individual. With all that kind of adulation and everything that I had experienced over my life, it was very humiliating, a sincere crisis, when I faced up to some compulsive needs, and compulsive habits, in my life that I needed some correction in. It was brought to my attention by some loving people, almost like an intervention. I looked at myself. At first you deny, you rationalize, you intellectualize, you spiritualize, you evade and you blame. After all of those you crawl out from behind the rationalizations. Then you say, "What a stupid idiot." But you don't do that while you're still in the denial; you're not a stupid idiot, everyone else is wrong. I was leading a congregation to build a sanctuary and there was a lot of disappointment, a lot of rejection; the letters. It's hard on a person who's letting the audience set the agenda, letting the audience tell you who you are. You're a good boy one day and you feel cruddy the next day.

George Green: You had overcome a lot of crisis, then you became a professional person to help other people.

Donn Moomaw: To meet other people.

George Green: You're preaching to others. You're telling other people how to think, how to have their faith, how to believe in themselves, how to believe in God and how to live a better life. You're doing all this stuff, how are you dealing with some of your personal ups and downs?

Donn Moomaw: First of all, I have a strong faith in prayer. I have a strong belief in the forgiveness of God. So, if it's a personal thing that got me into crisis, I knew how to handle that with my faith. There was great peace that would come often too fast to recover. There's something about recovering too fast.

George Green: You don't go through the grieving process.

Donn Moomaw: Well, the grieving process and the learning process. Are you going to treat God like a sugar-daddy, or a benevolent grandfather who says, "Boys will be boys." I could begin again, use those experiences. When you begin to bring God into your need for fulfillment, boy you can manipulate God into craziness! So, most of my life, I think my faith helped me through crisis, and I have indomitable spirit that tomorrow's going to be better. I had a doctor once tell me, 'if I can't recover in one good night's rest, then I'd better really get some serious help.' All through my life I've had small groups of men around me who we call 'covenant groups'; guys that would share themselves and let me share myself with them. I was pretty transparent in those groups. I have a wife that's a beautiful support, and the children; amazingly supportive of Daddy, their unconditional love of their Dad.

George Green: Going through transitions you were a master and a professional at overcoming crisis.

Donn Moomaw: That's right.

George Green: You certainly didn't get over what happened five years ago in one day.

Donn Moomaw: No, I sure didn't. I don't think I got over the things before. I think I had enough anesthesia around to help me through them. But this has caused me to take a look at the core of my being. I have done what we all do. I had my spiritual advisors but I also had some very solid medical help; psychiatrists, psychologists. Public humiliation is a tremendous bell-ringer. Even though the things that were written were false, for some of us we need a very serious bell-ringing before we'll get to the point, and begin to not be so controlling, and begin to understand something about surrender; not be defensive, not be denying, not be rationalizing. All those neat escapes that we've used, we use them because they work... for a while. My own way of getting around them was temporary. I began to see some hypocrisy and phoniness in my own life.

George Green: For the first time, you said, "I'm not able to do this as quickly as I thought."

Donn Moomaw: I knew it was not going to be a simple 'surgery' to become who I really am; who God created me to be, not who I let society create me to be. I knew there were dangers in crowds. I knew there was danger in giving power away to other people to establish my worth. It's very heady business being a minister in a church. No one gets as high as a pastor because you're dealing with spiritual things, and there's nothing more serious in life than spiritual things. One-hundred and fifty people come out of the church and tell, "Bang on, boy, you really did it today." And you come home and your kids say, "Daddy, this week you really disappointed me..." and you want to say, "Do you know who I am? Do you know what these people said about me this morning?" So it's a fragile world, the world of spiritual leadership. A bunch of healers took me under their wings and would not be sucked in with any of my background or my charisma, or anything else. They cut through the fat and called it what it was. I was there for three weeks to begin with; seven hours a day. Took me about a week to begin to go, "Aha." And it was 'surgery' without anesthesia. But if the surgery's right, it'll make you a healthier body.

George Green: What were those emotional moments like?

Donn Moomaw: The saddest day of my life was when I was in my third week at Scottsdale. My therapist encouraged me to think very seriously about resigning. I wasn't asked by anyone to resign. I resigned. I think there were people that agreed that it was the right thing to do. There was some pressure, but it wasn't definitive. If I wanted to fight it, I could have fought it. But I knew there was enough truth in it; the need for affirmation, the need for approval, the need for validation seemed to be insatiable.

George Green: That disappointing day of your life, I would think that you got lower emotionally.

Donn Moomaw: I'd never been lower.

George Green: Talk to me about the way up.

Donn Moomaw: Well, there weren't many people that knew how to minister or how to be there for me. I never got the support from these close friends. Where were the phone calls that I thought I'd get from some of these people after I left? They weren't there. It forced me then to look in other places for my help, rather than from people. But not all the angels are in the Presbyterian Church, or in the church, period! There were a lot of people that came out of the woodwork, that ministered to me and to Carol. I mean absolute strangers. A guy out in Scottsdale, Arizona, who's now in prison for eight years for child molestation. I was so repulsed by him when I first heard his story. Then I heard about his background. I heard how many times he'd been abused. He reached out and touched me at the deepest level of where I was because he was deeper yet. He was a greater dodo than I ever was, and he was not necessarily an orthodox believer, but he wrapped his arms around me in the name of Jesus, and I came alive. Those that were not there were clumsy. It was a clumsy situation.

George Green: They were embarrassed, didn't know how to help. You got the cold shoulder from the entire congregation.

Donn Moomaw: But I got terrific affirmation from those who I knew had been wounded themselves in some circumstance. I couldn't read the scripture or I didn't read the scripture. But then I began picking up the scripture again and read it through different eyes. I was censured for four years. I could not do any ministerial work for four years.

George Green: How did you get by? How did you live financially?

Donn Moomaw: How did I get four kids through private school? I don't know. Some way it happened. The last four years I did some work outside that was non-ministerial. I worked for American Golf, for instance, who owns two-hundred and fifty golf courses. I worked for David Price, a very good friend who was in our church. So, one year I had good salary. It was never a huge crunch. I don't have a whole lot of savings. I got a three months' severance after twenty-eight years. My probation's over, though. January 1st it was over. Then on January 10th, I accepted an interim call to the Rancho Santa Fe Presbyterian Church to be their interim pastor. Now I'm doing everything ministerial. My four years is up.

George Green: The relationship between the church down the street, with the city here in Bel Air, can you go back there?

Donn Moomaw: No. The day I said goodbye to my congregation there were 1700 people in the congregational meeting. I said, "This is my last Sunday with you." I said, "Sometimes you sit around the family table and some of the children say they have to leave. And you all grieve. But then there's a time when the father has to leave and he doesn't have enough time to tell the family all the reasons for it, but he has to leave. And I'm asking you to believe that I've prayed this through, and thought this through, and I have to leave." And then I broke down and cried like a baby. I had never done that before.

George Green: That's real.

Donn Moomaw: It was real. And everyone was crying because we have a family relationship. But when I had the custodians bring in all my office stuff over; they said I'm not to go on the campus.

George Green: That's cruel and unusual punishment. What about the concept of forgiveness?

Donn Moomaw: Regardless of what happened, I felt terrific peace with God. In the early days it bothered me terribly that I wasn't finding a whole lot of peace with the family of God. Now it doesn't make that much difference. I had depended on them for my worth; I wasn't going to be dependent on them for my affirmation of forgiveness. Most individuals have their own stories, and they would come out of the woodwork. Today, I'm having more profound ministry because I'm a pastor and I'm pure. Knowing my story, I'm able to minister now in those areas like never before. As you accomplish you're rising up, and other people are rising you up.

George Green: If you had to open your eyes two years from now, where do you want to be?

Donn Moomaw: I'm having such a wonderful time in Rancho Santa Fe as an interim pastor. I want to be, in two years, right where I am now both in my service opportunities as a pastor, and also in my inner feeling of peace, because I'm living in obedience. I'll probably have another interim; go to a church where there's people that really need a pastor but are not going to enthrone you and wait for the next person.

George Green: It's ninety percent spiritual. Headiness is not as important in your life anymore.

Donn Moomaw: Not at all.

George Green: You're learning how to live in the different spotlight; it probably has as much depth.

Donn Moomaw: Far more depth, and far more inclusiveness.

Brief Update Interview with Donn Moomaw, May 2014

George Green: You and Carol have found peace in the world and you're still living in the same place.

Donn Moomaw: Well, I'm having a wonderful retirement life and Carol and I are having a good time. We're not pressured to produce anything and to do anything. I have time to read and time to meet people when they want to meet with me. I'm enjoying, very much, these latter years. Sometimes I wish I could fill the days with more meaningful endeavors, but that's okay, too, because I've had those days.

George Green: I know there was a lot of fill-in church work you were doing when we chatted last, and you were just at the tail-end of being forgiven. I thought that at this point of your life right now, you and Carol really are people of peace and tranquility, and you have found what you wanted to find; peace of mind.

Donn Moomaw: No question about that. We have had twenty years since all that happened. We've had twenty years of wonderful growth, peace and a new sense of commitment, and we're doing fine. It just seems like the way it's supposed to be. We had great days at Bel Air Church, twenty-eight years of wonderful ministry and we have great memories. A few regrets, of course, but no bitter feelings at all. I just thank God for the opportunity to serve there in such a dynamic area in the church. I'm a winner for it.

John Severino

I did it my way!

John Severino (nicknamed Sev) grew up in Hamden, Connecticut, with his Italian father and American mother. During school he worked at odd jobs, including snow shoveling, to earn his pennies. As he got older and stronger he went to work for his father, a bricklayer, as a laborer.

He played football in high school and, even though he considered himself an average player, he was offered a football scholarship by the University of Connecticut. He accepted and went on to major in economics. Once he'd completed his studies he moved to Boston with his wife whom he'd married in graduate school. There he took on a job as an insurance salesman and was comfortable, until a friend suggested he interview for a position at a TV station in Maine, Portland.

Through the interview he was offered a position as football coach for a team owned by the owner of the station, the Atlantic Coast football team. John accepted the job and in his spare time began selling television time. After a year there he moved on to WBZ Radio, also in Boston, where he sold radio time.

Preferring television, he drove to New York and interviewed for a position at WABC TV.

After a year as salesman there, they promoted him to Chicago national sales. He did extremely well, selling time for all ABC stations, and was then promoted again; this time to New York national sales. From there he was asked to become sales manager at WLS TV in Chicago. He then moved to Detroit for some time, after which he was asked to be General Manager, Vice-President General Manager at WLS TV Chicago. As you may have gathered by now, John did a great deal of traveling throughout his career! He thanks his wife for always being able to adjust, and remaining supportive despite their having two children to raise!

With only three years' experience in television, John was now heading a forty-million-dollar company. After four years there they moved him along to Los Angeles. Through hiring a few well-known senior names, John was able to put KABC TV news operations on the map. After seven years with them, he was asked to move up to be President of ABC. Capital Cities then bought the ABC Company and numerous changes were made. John worked for a few years under Capital Cities, but left the moment he was offered a position as President and CEO of Prime Ticket Network, after twenty-three years with ABC. He took Prime Ticket and made it into the largest regional sports network in the country.

At the age of sixty-five he decided it was time to retire, but things didn't work out that way. He was head-hunted by a European company called Central European Media. He joined them and, through his expertise, was able to convert a once-floundering company into one of the best in Europe, running the stations in the same way he'd run those in the United States. He owned shares in the company, too, which helped him to remain motivated. At the age of sixty-eight he decided that he'd done as much as he could, and again wanted to retire. After a few months of taking it easy, CBS approached him and asked him to be President of CBS. He accepted the position, but didn't last too long due to the fact he was older now and a little tired. After two years there he retired, this time for good.

John explains how retiring (for good) was one of the best choices he's ever made. He lives now in Los Angeles with his wife, great friends, financial comfort and all the time in the world to do whatever he likes. John looks back on his career in television and regrets nothing; he loved what he did and was expertly good at it. His son David Severino currently works as a manager in radio. He is considered a 'chip off the old man's block'; very successful in his own right!

John Severino is a legend in the television business. Accomplishments like running ABC and CBS, and owning his own TV stations in Europe, are some that very few others can claim. He is truly one of the great names in television, and is strongly remembered by everyone who worked with him. Although he ruled with a tight fist, he was also extremely generous and kind to the many thousands of loyal employees under his management.

Interview with John Severino

George Green: We call him Sev because that's his nickname. Just give me a quick summary of you.

John Severino: I grew up in Hamden, Connecticut. I'm a first generation Italian. My Dad was born in Italy. My Mom was born in this country. He didn't have a job where he had a lot of fun. A lower middle-class family, we went through life well. I worked every summer. I sold newspapers when I was a youngster. I shoveled snow in the winter for fifty cents or twenty-five cents. I shoveled sidewalks. I went to high school then, as I got older, I went to work with my Dad as a laborer. He was a bricklayer and I was carrying bricks up and down the ladders, mixing mortar and working on all kinds of construction, running jackhammers, breaking concrete. I knew that was not what I wanted to go into the rest of my life, because it was hard work and it was tough. I played football in high school; I wasn't a great star, I was a lineman, I was a guard. My senior year, someone from the University of Connecticut contacted me and asked if I'd be interested in attending the University of Connecticut on a football scholarship. No one in my family had ever gone to college before. My Dad thought that might be a good idea! He couldn't afford to pay the tuition and the room and board, but with the scholarship we could do it. So I went to the University of Connecticut. When I started there, the football office suggested that I major in physical education. I said, "You know, if I'm going to go to UConn, I think I need more than physical education." I decided to major in economics which was a wise thing to do, although I didn't realize it was wise at the time. After graduation I thought maybe I'd like to coach football. Then I found out how much money you could make doing that, and I said, "No, I don't think that's something I want to do." So my wife and I, we had just gotten married when we were in graduate school, we drove to Boston and I interviewed with a number of companies. I figured one of the ways I could find out if I was going to be a good salesman or not was to try selling insurance. I went to work for the Liberty Mutual Insurance Company, trying to sell small businesses insurance, workman's compensation, fire insurance, business insurance. Talk about getting thick-skinned pretty quickly! I'd walk into a liquor store and I'd say, "Hi, my name's John Severino and I'm with the Liberty Mutual Insurance Company. I'm here to save you some money on your fire insurance." And the guy would look at me and say, "Get out of here, will you kid?"

So you got thick-skinned very quickly. I did that for a year and thought that was an okay job, nothing spectacular. Then someone suggested that up in Portland, Maine, there was a TV station; the fellow that owned the station also owned a semi-professional football team. I went up and I had an interview with this person. He did in fact own the Atlantic Coast Football League. He didn't have any positions open in TV but he did have a position open as coach of the football team. I started coaching his football team and during the off season I sold television time. I did that for a year. I thought, 'I like this TV business. This is fun, but I've got to get more than Portland, Maine, because this is not the center of the television industry.' So, one day I got in the car and went to different TV stations in Boston, trying to get a job. None of them were interested. One of the sales managers at one of the TV stations thought there was a job open in his radio station which was downstairs, same building. I went down there, interviewed with the people and got the job at WBZ Radio in Boston. So, I had one year in TV, now I was selling radio in Boston. I did that for a year then I thought, 'I want more than this.' I got in the car one day and drove to New York. I went around and interviewed with all the TV stations there, and one station was interested in hiring me. That was WABC TV. I was just a kid, twenty-five, twenty-six-years-old. I took a job there as a local salesman and called on advertising agencies, selling television time. I did that for a year and then they decided to promote me to Chicago National Sales.

No one from WABC had ever gone to National Sales before, and all the other sales people tried to convince me that I would be ruining my career rather than advancing it. But I didn't listen to them. I was there a year, did very well selling national television for all the ABC stations, then I got promoted back to New York National Sales. We moved back to New York and I sold National Sales in New York again for the five ABC stations, for a year. Then they came to me and asked me if I wanted to be the sales manager at WLS TV Chicago.

I thought, 'Sales manager's better than local sales.' So, we moved back to Chicago and I was a sales manager in Chicago for a year. They asked me if I'd like to be the General Sales Manager in Detroit. So, we went there. I was there a year and then they said to me, "Are you interested in being the General Manager, Vice-President General Manager at WLS TV Chicago?" I said, "Yes." So we moved back to Chicago. Now here I am with a brand new bride and we have two small children.

Thus far we've lived in New York for a year, Chicago for a year, New York for a year, Chicago for a year, Detroit for a year, and now back to Chicago. Thank God my wife was able to contend with all these many moves! I'm a thirty-three-year-old kid at that time, and my total experience in television was one year at WABC, one year at WLS, and one year at WXYZ. I had three years' experience in television and I was running a forty-million-dollar operation. I was a kid! The Chief Engineer would come to me and say, "We're going to move our antennas to the Sear's Tower, what do you think?" I'd say, "I don't even know what an antenna is." So, I had to learn what the news department did and how that operated, and I learned how the programming department, advertising and promotion departments worked. I knew sales pretty well, but that's about all I knew. I managed that station in Chicago for four years and I loved Chicago. People will put Chicago down because of the bad weather. Well, if you're in the TV business, that bad weather is a blessing because the people are inside watching TV! We became the number one station in Chicago. I learned from the ground up. They came to me in 1974, after four years of managing Chicago, and said, "We'd like you to move and run the station in Los Angeles." I came out here and figured it can't go wrong, it can't go anywhere but up. We had a very weak news operation at KABC TV. One of the things that worked for us very well in Chicago was hiring one of the older senior anchor people away from the competitor station in Chicago. There was a fellow whose name was Jerry Dunphy who was anchoring the news over at CBS.

Author's note: See Jerry Dunphy's interview.

I met with Jerry Dunphy. He was under contract so he couldn't get out. Then one day he called me up and said, "You know, they're unhappy with me here and they want to team me up with somebody else, and I don't like that." I said, "If you could get a release from your contract then I could offer you something at ABC." He said, "Let me see what I could do." His boss was a guy by the name of Russ Barry. The next day I was playing tennis in a tournament, and Russ Barry was at the tournament playing. He called me aside and said, "I may be releasing Jerry Dunphy from his contract. Do you have any interest in hiring him?" I said, "Absolutely not. He's old, he's over the hill. I'm looking for young people." He said, "That's what I thought." So, he gave Jerry Dunphy a release and I talked to Jerry that night and said, "You get over here with that release right now." So he showed it to me and we showed it to our attorneys, and they said, "You're fine, you could offer him anything you want." So, to make a long story short, I hired Jerry Dunphy. As soon as it was announced, Russ Barry called me. He said, "I hear that you hired Jerry Dunphy." I said, "Yes, I did." He said, "I thought you said you weren't interested." I said, "I lied!" That was the end of it. We teamed Jerry Dunphy with the first woman to ever anchor a Monday through Friday newscast. Her name was Christine Lund. People said, "You can't put a woman on there." I said, "I think it'll work." They finally agreed.

Then I had to sell the people in New York on the fact that, along with Jerry Dunphy, I had to buy his baby-powder-blue Rolls Royce from CBS! I met with my boss at ABC; he was on board one-hundred-percent to hire Dunphy. I said, "By the way, there's a car that comes with this. We've got to buy the car." He said, "Nope, no cars. I won't give anybody a car." I said, "I've got to have the car otherwise the deal isn't going to work." We went back and forth for a while and finally he said, "Okay, I'll make an exception." As I was walking out of his office he said to me, "I bet it's probably a Cadillac!" So we had Jerry Dunphy and we hired everybody that had any kind of name at all in Los Angeles. At KABC Radio, we were able to cross promote each other. When those people were on KABC TV they could end their story by saying, "...and I'll be on KABC Radio tomorrow," and vice-versa; when they finished their story on KABC Radio they'd say, "...I'll see you on KABC TV tonight, Channel 7." That promotion, I thought, worked terrifically!

George Green: You had the most amazing crew, Sev, because you ran a wonderful television station. We went right along with the tide and our KABC Radio station became number one. From there you went over to ABC television as President of the whole company.

John Severino: Right! They came to me in '81 after seven years and said, "We'd like you to come to New York and be President of ABC television." I said, "You know, President of ABC television is a long way to come from being the son of a bricklayer in Hamden, Connecticut! So I think I'll take a shot at that job." So, I went on to New York and worked at ABC as President of the network for five years. We became the most successful, most viewed television network. We were the number one profit network and the only thing that went a little bit haywire was that this other little company called Capital Cities came in and bought us out.

George Green: That's when Dennis Swanson rehired you to go back to channel 7.

John Severino: Leonard Goldenson actually worked me back into channel 7. Then I came back to Los Angeles to be President of KABC the second time. That was under Cap City. I did that for four years and again we were very successful. Then one day I got a call from a head-hunter. They hired me to be President and CEO of Prime Ticket Network. They gave me a piece of it, which is what enticed me into going.

George Green: You were fifty-five-years-old at that time and you were with ABC for twenty-three years before joining Prime Ticket?

John Severino: That's correct. I went over and I looked at what we had at Prime Ticket. What we had was not very much. We had some of the Laker games and some of the LA Kings games, and that was it. The rest of the time we had a ticker-tape presentation. The ticker-tape would just read across the screen with sports news and that was it. We didn't have any advertising sales. The only income we had, which wasn't enough to cover expenses, was from the subscriber base and we were getting eight or ten cents a month per subscriber. That didn't go very far. So I said, "The only way we're going to make this work is if we make this like another Los Angeles TV station. We're going to promote it like a TV station, we're going to sell it like a TV station, and we're going to program it like a TV station." The first thing I had to do was get some people over there who I could rely on; experts in various fields. I went back to my roots at KABC and since none of those people were under contract at KABC, I hired them all to come over to Prime Ticket. There were twenty-one of them. That didn't make me one of the favorite guys at Cap City. I got a call one day from the President of Cap City and he said, "What are you doing?" I said, "I'm trying to start a new business." He said, "Well, you're taking all our people." I said, "Well, they're not under contract." He said, "We don't give contracts." I said, "We do." He didn't like that, but that's part of the rough and tumble of business. You don't give a contract; you're going to lose your people. So those people came over with me. They took a risk, a big risk.

George Green: So, what happened?

John Severino: We took Prime Ticket and made it into the largest regional sports network in the country. We had all the Laker games, all the Kings games, and I made deals with USC football and UCLA football and USC and UCLA basketball. Then I got on all the programs for the Pac 10, and then we started a bunch of other programs. We started pro-beach volleyball and swimming; every kind of sport you could think of that hadn't been exposed on TV before. Then, trying to make it look like a TV station, we decided to put on a newscast every night at 11pm. It was just sports news but we sold it like it was a regular TV news operation. We called it Prime Ticket Sports and then we promoted it with kind of a funny campaign; we got a lot of controversy about it! The name of the program was Press Box, and we would say on billboards, 'Don't go to bed until you score,' or, 'Score every night at eleven.' We had those on billboards all over the city! Not only did the billboards work, but the radio stations kept talking about this kind of promotion; 'Is this a good thing to do? Is this alright? Are they going too far with this kind of promotion?' So the radio stations in town were helping us to promote ourselves! We sold it just like a TV station. When I first got there, the revenues were four-million-dollars and we took it up to seventy-million-dollars in four years; we sold it out to Fox Sports. Then I decided, 'Enough.' I was sixty-five-years-old and I figured that it was time to retire. I retired for a few months and I got a call one day from another head-hunter. He talked to me about this company that they were starting called Central European Media. A guy named Ronald Lauder, whose mother was Estee Lauder from the cosmetics company, was the money behind it. Their game plan was to try to obtain licenses to TV stations in Europe and convert those to commercial stations similar to those in the U.S. They hired me to be President of Central European Media Enterprises and I had to relocate to London. I rented an apartment in London. By this time my kids were in college, so that was good! We took that TV station, first of all in Berlin and then the one in Prague, and started to program those like stations here in the United States.

George Green: This time you owned part of those stations.

John Severino: Yeah, exactly. The first thing we did was to have an IPO to raise even more money to get even more stations. What we did was a 'Dog and Pony Show', an initial public offering for Central European Media. The stock price came out at forty dollars a share and we were off and running, because now we had a huge amount of financing. We raised over one-hundred-million-dollars with the IPO, and we put that into the market. I did that for three years. We lived in London, I loved living in London; my wife loved it there. The kids would come over and visit. One week, on Monday, I would fly to Berlin and work in Berlin for a week. The next week I'd fly to Prague and work in Prague for a week. In Prague, the TV station, NOVA TV, was the most successful launch of a TV station in Europe. When we took over that station it was a government station so it had no ratings, zero share of audience. One year later we had a seventy share of audience. The station that was owned by the government; their programming was to put on the Superintendent of the sewers, to talk about how they were going to improve the sewer system. We took 'Baywatch' and we dubbed it into Czech, and we put 'Baywatch' on! You can just imagine where the people were watching! Anyway, that was a lot of fun.

George Green: So now you're seventy-years-old. When are you going to throw the towel in?

John Severino: That's when I said that was it! At that time I was fifty-seven, fifty-eight-years-old and I said, "That's enough." So we came back here. Fortunately we had kept our house here in Encino. Seven or eight months later I got a call from some people at CBS and they said, "How'd you like to be President of the CBS television stations?" I said, "Well, I don't know. Let's talk about it." They offered me a job as President and General Manager of KCBS television here in Los Angeles and I said, "Okay, I'll give that a shot." To be honest with you, at that time I didn't have the fire in my belly anymore. I took the job and as soon as I started, within a few months I knew I wasn't going to be able to replicate the same kind of enthusiasm and energy. I was tired, I had done it all. I had conquered all the mountains that were before me. I just didn't put my soul and my heart into it.

George Green: And your body was not doing what you had thought you could do.

John Severino: Exactly! So I said, "Okay, that's enough." And they said, "Hey, that's enough," because they saw it, too. We agreed to separate. That's a nice way of saying I got fired, but I was ready for it. I was tired and I wasn't doing myself or them any favors.

George Green: How long were you there?

John Severino: I was there two years.

George Green: Somebody says, "It's time for you to retire." You agreed, and then your retirement starts. Now you've got your freedom, you've got time to do what you want to do…

John Severino: My wife was worried; 'How is he going to accept retirement? He's had so many of these highly visible jobs.' Let me tell you this, it took me about fifteen minutes to get into the retirement swing! I don't think I ever looked back. Did I miss it? I missed some of it. I missed some of the people. Did I miss the action? I missed some of the action. But I honestly loved being retired. It didn't take a whole lot for me to say, "Having the ability to do exactly what I want to do whenever I want to do it, is worth tons of money. It's worth a heck of a lot more money than anybody could pay me!" I've never looked back, I've enjoyed retirement. My wife was amazed that I could so quickly adapt to being retired. It was fun, I had a great run. If I had it to do all over again, ninety-nine percent I'd do it exactly the same way. That's the story.

George Green: What advice would you give to young people who are starting out today; they want to climb some mountains… it's a little tougher today. What advice would you give to them?

John Severino: I have two sons and I tell both of them the same thing. The most important thing is not the money. The money's just a way to keep score. You only come this way once. The most important thing is whether you like and love what you do. If you're doing what you like and what you love, it's worth tons of money. I don't care if you're teaching school; if that's what you love, that's plenty of money. If you're in the peanut-butter business and that's what you love, it's worth it. Find out what you love first. Do what you love.

Ken Minyard

Everything's gonna' be okay! Egbok!

Ken Minyard was born in Oklahoma, in 1939. During high school he worked at his local radio station, KTMC. He then moved to California and went to San Francisco State College where he involved himself with the radio and television department; creative arts. From there he cut his studies short and got a position in Santa Rosa at KSRO. After four years there, he went to Stockton and worked at KGOY. Then, in 1967, he moved to Minneapolis and worked with WAOL as program director.

The highlight of his career in radio, at the age of thirty-four-years-old, began in 1973 when he teamed up with Bob Arthur at KABC Radio. Together they created a show called 'The Ken and Bob Company'. Every morning the duo would inspire and motivate listeners to awaken to the new day by reassuring them — EGBOK! — 'Everything's Gonna' Be Okay!' This term was in fact used in the 1980s by hostages in the Middle East who felt the term helped to boost their spirits.

Ken was known as the more talkative of the two, commenting on news events in a quick and quirky manner. Bob was quite the opposite, providing simple one-liners in an often authoritive tone.

'The Ken and Bob Company' topped the charts and ran for seventeen years. The duo never dropped lower than third place in radio during their tenure. They were known for never reading from a script, choosing to rather comment on the headlines as they pleased with optimism and professionalism.

Ken and Bob were awarded their own star on The Hollywood Walk Of Fame in 1986.

In 1990 Bob 'retired' and chose to spend the rest of his years developing a project that would provide homes for Alzheimer's patients in Long Beach. However, in 1991, Bob came forward and wrote a letter to The Times telling them that he had not 'retired' from KABC; he had been fired due to his age. The radio station denied this.

At this time Ken had joined forces with Roger Barkley. This new duo became known as 'The Ken and Barkley Company'. Bob passed on in 1997 at his home in Albuquerque.

Ken continued to work with Barkley for six years at KABC. The show was then replaced which led to Ken moving over to KRLA – AM where he hosted a program with this son, Rick, in the afternoons. Then, in November, 2001, Ken returned to KABC where he paired up with Dan Avey for a morning show.

Ken finally pulled out of radio in 2005, due to his no longer being happy in the industry after several changes were made. He spent thirty-five years with KABC Radio. Fortunately he had prepared himself financially for that day, and had more than enough to support his family. He states that his last year on the air was not a happy one, and goes on to suggest that perhaps the key to good retirement is having less fun just before you retire - then perhaps it won't be so sorely missed?

Ken also feels that show-business people seldom acknowledge the fact that they are retiring. In some cases the person retiring feels diminished somehow; that their spotlight has been put out for good and they no longer serve a purpose. Ken accepts and understands that for many, they come to an age where their services are no longer in demand. Whether or not you can still do a good job is not the point. The point is 'it's over', and coming to terms with this is the key to a peaceful exit from the show-business industry.

Interview with Ken Minyard

George Green: Tell me where you started and go on from there.

Ken Minyard: I was born and raised in Oklahoma. My Dad bought a business in California, so I moved out at seventeen. From my freshman year on through high school, I had gotten involved in the local radio station. I did everything from news to being a disc-jockey to describing the local parade. I don't know if anyone listened but that was great training! I went to college at San Francisco State and was involved in the creative arts department there. I got a job in Santa Rosa at KSRO. I cut my college education short. I went to Stockton, KGOY; I stayed for five years. In 1967 I started a talk show at WAOL, Minneapolis. I was looking to get out of Minneapolis; it was too cold for me! I sent a tape to KABC and was hired at the age of twenty-nine. They could never find a spot for me, I'm sure I almost got fired a couple of times! I did a regular talk show and a lifestyle talk show. People were trying to figure out what to do with me. Bob Arthur was doing the morning show. They plugged me in there and it clicked. That was the rest of my career, basically.

George Green: The radio station's call letters were named after you, as I understand?

Ken Minyard: If you take 'Ken and Bob Company'; that spells out KABC. We were number one for about twenty years after that.

George Green: Talk about the spotlight that you were under.

Ken Minyard: It never felt intimidating. It felt like a family. We didn't sit down with a master plan and cause this to happen! Every morning we really looked forward to getting in there and having fun. I was always very competitive and focused; I still believe that if you're having fun other people are going to enjoy it, too. We didn't just act silly, we paid attention to what was in the news; the old name applied, 'News Talk'. We expanded the meaning of news, not just the serious stuff.

George Green: I think it's well-known that you were the highest-paid performer in Los Angeles.

Ken Minyard: I don't remember but it was seven figures. You always feel the need to perform and justify the lifestyle, but we built a brand; 'Ken and Bob' became a very strong brand in the market.

George Green: Travels were taking the show around the world.

Ken Minyard: That was unbelievable! We were doing it with bailing wire. We didn't have satellites, technology that we have today; we didn't even have fax machine technology. I remember how we thought, 'Wow, you can actually get the news when we are in Berlin or wherever we were.' We went everywhere.

George Green: Now the spotlight is intense. Then what happened?

Ken Minyard: Well, you left!

George Green: I got fired. Things started to change around the station.

Ken Minyard: It certainly did. It coincided with the decision in 1996 to allow the accumulation of stations; consolidation and syndication. That changed the world. It became then you had to make twenty-percent more profit each year, and that meant cost-cutting, and they started buying syndicated programs. The fun went out of broadcasting. The whole atmosphere changed. Certainly, in a personal way, because you left. The way you left was meant to send a signal. It sent the wrong kind of signal; the signal that 'There's a new sheriff in town and we're not going to take any of your c—p.' A very unpleasant time. They didn't want to pay the kind of money that they had to pay, so I was crossed out. I was ready to go. I didn't want to be there anymore. After my thirty years in the business, I thought it deserved a little bit more respect. The way it happened wasn't satisfactory.

George Green: They treated you badly.

Ken Minyard: Yeah. It was not necessary. They could have handled it better and I would have felt better about it. I found out what retirement was like and I wasn't crazy about it. Before that, though, I did have one wonderful opportunity to spend a year and a half working with my son, Rick, and that was a great experience - in that sense that I was able to work with Rick, but not a great experience in terms of the people I had to work for.

George Green: At that time they are trying to change you. You're unhappy going to work and then you're thrown out. Emotionally, how were you feeling?

Ken Minyard: Angry. I had never had an experience like that before. I had never been fired. They said, "We're not firing you. We're terminating your contract." I was angry for what they put me through prior to that. They were really trying to force me to leave early so they could save money.

George Green: Why do companies want people to quit on their own?

Ken Minyard: They would have saved a lot of money if I had thrown in the towel a few months early. I think that was what their goal was; to make it so unpleasant for me that I would walk out. I said, "I can survive anything for six months." I revealed to somebody in the media that my contract was up at the end of the year. They called me in and said, "Do you want to leave now?" I said, "No, I'll be happy to work until the end of November, unless you don't want me to." They said, "Okay, end it this week." They were obligated to pay me but I still had two weeks left on my vacation. It went to arbitration and it was determined that I was owed another six weeks' vacation. It cost them an extra couple-hundred-thousand dollars.

George Green: Anyway, you get a syndication gig that I helped you with...

Ken Minyard: Exactly. You were instrumental with it! After that ended, I guess I felt that I was probably retired at that point. Then September 11th came. I really wanted to be able to talk about it. I needed to put an exclamation point on my career. By November 2001, I was back doing mornings at KABC. The circumstances were different but they didn't have the money to support the show. We couldn't do the same kind of thing that we did before. It wasn't as gratifying for me. I left on good terms. So the key, maybe, to a good retirement is having less fun before you retire!

George Green: You were looking for a new life outside of broadcasting with your wife and family. Tell me about that.

Ken Minyard: I had a great run and was in a position to retire comfortably. We go to movies, travel, go to theater; all of those things. When I retired I said, "When I find something that I really enjoy then I will do it." So far I haven't found anything. I don't feel the real need to do that.

George Green: You are enjoying your life as is...

Ken Minyard: Exactly, I feel bad for people that can't. The hardest thing to admit; you have had your time and the market has dried up; you're no longer relevant. People say, "But you could do a good job." It doesn't make any difference whether you could do a good job. The point is it's over, your through. It is great to come to the conclusion that you've done... that you can say, "I understand, it doesn't bother me."

George Green: And you spend how much time looking back?

Ken Minyard: Not much. I look back on it fondly. It's a whole different life now than I had then. I choose to remember the good times.

George Green: So the things that surround you, that make you happy are your wife, your family, your health.

Ken Minyard: Don't forget my puppy!

George Green: Are you angry anymore?

Ken Minyard: I'm angry that the business we cared a great deal about no longer exists. It bothers me that through pure greed there are a select, relatively small, number of people who, I think, ruined the business. They are just a cash-cow for putting on syndicated stuff and infomercials.

George Green: That business is not what it used to be when I was in it having fun.

Ken Minyard: I agree. But I have a feeling that eventually things will turn back to the radio of serving the local community again.

George Green: Is there anything else that you would like to suggest; advice to anybody else who has been cast out somewhat?

Ken Minyard: Only that one needs to accept what is and move on rather than just dwelling on the past. Be realistic about your situation rather than just trying to cling to something that no longer exists.

Marty Katz

Hated the violin but loves making movies

Marty Katz has worked as a producer and an executive in the motion picture and television industry for over forty years. He was born in a displaced persons camp after World War II, in 1947. Five years later his family moved to America. As a child he showed excellent talent playing the violin, and was even granted a scholarship at the Academy of Music. However, this was not a career Marty wanted to pursue.

His parents then auditioned him for television shows. He finally got to work, but this was unpaid. Being verbal about his opinions regarding certain aspects of these shows, and how they could be better put together, he was finally asked to become assistant producer on a show with Joe Landis.

Marty then went on to serve in the U.S. Army Signal Corps as a 1st Lieutenant Combat Pictorial Unit Commander at the South East Asia Pictorial Center in Long Binh, Vietnam. It was here he made his very first motion picture, albeit with combat footage he shot. In 1969, having been awarded the Bronze Star and various other medals, he returned from Vietnam and began working at Peterson Publishing, then moved across to Roger

Corman's 'New World Pictures' as production manager/associate producer. In 1971 he became Director of Film Production for ABC Circle Films. During the five years he spent with ABC, twenty-five of the fifty TV movies he supervised won Emmy awards.

Katz then joined Quinn Martin Productions as Executive Vice President and supervised six on-air television series from 1976 to 1978, and then moved on to Paramount Pictures, where he was a Producer and Consultant.

In 1985 Marty became Senior Vice President of Motion Picture and Television Production at Walt Disney Studios, overseeing all production and post-production for Touchstone, Hollywood Pictures, Walt Disney TV, Theme Park Productions and feature animations. His expertise put numerous films in the spotlight such as 'Dead Poets Society', 'Honey I Shrunk The Kids', 'The Little Mermaid', 'Good Morning Vietnam', 'Pretty Woman', 'Who Framed Roger Rabbit?', 'The Color of

Money', 'Dick Tracy' and many more. In 1988, Marty was promoted to Executive Vice President of Motion Picture and Television Production.

In 1992 he formed Marty Katz Production based at Disney. Then, in 1996, Marty Katz Productions became an entirely independent company. Since then Marty has worked on films such as 'Titanic', 'Reindeer Games', 'Lord of the Rings', and 'Gangs of New York', among others. Marty Katz Productions still operates today out of Malibu, California.

Interview with Marty Katz

George Green: Why don't you give me a short background of the starting points of your life?

Marty Katz: I was born in a displaced persons camp after World War II, in 1947. My sister, Esther, was born two years later. Five years later, we came to America and lived in Philadelphia. I lived there until I was thirteen, at which point we came to California because I was a concert violinist and they wanted me to audition for Jascha Heifetz. My Holocaust survivor parents sold whatever they had. They bought me a handmade Hoffman violin. On the day I was supposed to audition for Heifetz, I told my mother, "I don't want to do this. This is not my career."

George Green: I didn't know you were a violinist.

Marty Katz: I was a violinist, and my fingertips are still hard from the four or five hours a day I played.

George Green: How old were you?

Marty Katz: I was taking lessons from the time I was five. I'm afraid I broke my parents' heart because I took their ten-thousand-dollar Hoffman, which was their life savings, and said, "I'm not going to be a professional violinist." Then I threw the violin, and their dreams, on the floor and broke it; "That's not my future." I never picked up the violin again until I was on a movie set in Vancouver, twenty years later. I shocked my wife and myself. That was the only time I ever picked up a violin again. My parents wanted me to become an actor, but I wasn't quite sure if I had it. I was thirteen/fourteen-years-old. We tried a couple of shows. I finally went to work for Dick Clark. I was not getting paid, but I was working on the 'American Bandstand' as a production assistant. One day he said to me, "There is a new show, '9th Street West', a teen pop-musical variety show starting. You should go work for them. Maybe they could pay you!" So I went on the show with my sister, and for some reason I went home and wrote a ten page document about what I thought these people were doing wrong. I mailed it to them and thought nothing of it.

I was in Hollywood High School, and I got called into the principal's office. There were these two men who seemed vaguely familiar, and the principal asked me, "Did you write this?" I said, "Yeah." He said, "They want to talk to you." These two gentlemen were from the show, and they said to me they'd like to hire me. I was about sixteen-years-old, going to UCLA in the afternoon after mornings at Hollywood High School, as a part of the MGM (Mentally Gifted Minors) program. The producer said, "We want to hire you on the show as a Production Assistant." I worked for Producer Joe Landis. One year later, Joe went to ABC TV Network and produced the Daytime soap-opera 'Never Too Young.' He wanted to take me with him, but I read their scripts and said, "Kids don't talk this way." Joe said, "What would you change?" So I rewrote the script. He said, "Can you read the scripts and story-edit for us?" I said, "Sure, if you give me a job as one of the characters." So, I was on that series for about nine months. I graduated High School with three years of UCLA college credit, but I never registered for the draft. When I was eighteen I was visited, at my house, by two men with badges who said, "Are you a resident alien?" I said, "Yes." They said, "You're eighteen and you're a resident alien. You have to register for the draft." I said, "I thought that only applied to citizens." They said, "You have a choice. You can go back to Germany ..." I said, "I am not German." They said, "You have to go back to Germany or you have to register for the draft within two weeks."

I got to all my friends in the business and asked them to write letters for me, because I was going to go in the service. I wanted to go to the U.S. Army Motion Picture School in Long Island and work in television in the Armed Forces network. During that same period, I applied for and received an expedited United States citizenship. As soon as I registered I was drafted. Unfortunately, I'm a compulsive test-taker. I took this required U.S. Army test, and they said that I had 'leadership potential'. I was offered an option to go to the Officer Candidate School after basic training. I said, "No. That would mean another year. Besides, I have orders to go to the Army Pictorial Center in Long Island." They said, "No, you're not going there," and they took my orders and ripped them up. "You're going to be an infantry soldier in Vietnam, or you could go to Officer Candidate School (OCS), but it has to be in combat arms." I said, "Which branch deals with photography?" They said, "The Signal Corps," which is a combat arm. So I got into Signal Corps Officer School. I found out that if you graduate in the top ten percent, you can pick your assignment. I became number two in the class out of five hundred and fifty people; a Distinguished Military Graduate. I did what it took. One of our final tests was 'Escape and Evasion'. Ultimately, you were released into the woods at night and caught by the senior classmen. They were allowed to teach you what it was like if you got captured by the enemy. One week earlier, prior to the Escape and Evasion maneuvers, a classmate of mine and I discovered the Prisoner of War Camp location. My associate and I secretly took plastic explosives from a weapons class we attended, and placed a charge in the Prisoner of War Camp perimeter wall, prior to the Escape and Evasion maneuvers.

The night of the maneuvers, two upperclassmen caught me and they took my rifle and strapped it behind my arms. I whacked both of them in the knees with the rifle, so they took me to the camp and tortured me. They had me in a waterwheel, slowly going around, and then they put me in a pit with (dead) snakes. I looked at Leonard, my associate, and gave him the cue. We blew a hole in the camp perimeter and all the Officer Candidate School prisoners escaped! The next day, everyone knew who did it. The General in charge of the school ordered me into his office and said to me, "Moral Courage; Ten. Judgment; Zero... Congratulations, you can pick your assignment." He put a phone call into the Pentagon and got me into the Motion Picture School, but I had to first take a tour of duty in Germany to develop leadership skills. So I went to Germany, and then six months later went to the U.S. Army Motion Picture School in Ft. Monmouth, New Jersey. Afterwards, instead of sending me to the Army Pictorial Center in Long Island, New York, they sent me to Vietnam as a First Lieutenant, Unit Pictorial Commander, with the Southeast Asia Pictorial Center. I photographed everything from the DMZ to the Mekong Delta and, secretly, in Laos and Cambodia.

George Green: So that was the start of your motion picture career?

Marty Katz: When I left the army in April, 1969, I had three days left before discharge. So I figured I would wear my uniform, and I visited a couple of people in the industry. They saw me and I went to work for Peterson Publishing who had a film division. And that was my first opportunity. I did a filmed-on-location musical-variety television series called 'Something Else'. They were the first music videos. The show won the Monte Carlo International Television Festival. I was the production manager.

George Green: So this is 1969?

Marty Katz: 1969. Then I got a phone call and went back to work with Roger Corman. I did a few low-budget movies for him, as production manager and assistant director. It was a great training ground. Then I got a call from Barry Diller at ABC, head of ABC Entertainment. He had this passion to create 'The Movie of The Week'; to have his own in-house division called ABC Circle Films. Barry offered me a position, but I had a long beard. He said, "I'll hire you but you have to shave your beard." I said, "No." I went home thinking 'what an idiot you are.' I shaved the beard. The phone rings again and it's Barry. He says, "You don't have to shave your beard!" I got the job, shaved the beard, and I ran ABC Circle Films from 1969 to '75 or '76. We won twenty-six Emmys, including Best Picture three years in a row, and all of the top creative Emmys.

George Green: Up to this point it's been straight up for you. Were there down moments?

Marty Katz: Not at this point because I was on an upward path. I was learning a lot because I was now really running a company for the first time, and this led to me being a valuable asset for ABC. When I wanted to leave to go to Quinn Martin, Barry said, "I don't want you to go. You should stick with me." I said, "Okay!" I rejected Quinn Martin's first offer. Quinn Martin came back offering me three times more, and other perks. I went back to Barry and said, "I really do have to take this job." He said, "If you have to go, then go." I found out that Quinn wanted to get back at Barry for interfering on the Final Cut of the 'Streets of San Francisco'. That show had been getting complaints about it being too violent, and the network wanted it toned down even though Quinn had 'Final Cut'. The way he got even was to hire me away with an unbelievably rich offer. At that point in his career, Quinn didn't want to work too hard and delegated most of his 'Final Cut' rights to me. I was running the QM Production Company with six on-air network series, and delivering Quinn's 'Final Cut' of each episode to the networks. I did that for a couple of years, at which point I found out through my lawyer that Barry Diller and Michael Eisner at

Paramount were interested in making me a producer.

George Green: Barry came back to you and said, "I want you to come over with me at Paramount."

Marty Katz: Yes. So I went to work there, but I wasn't getting a chance to produce as much as I wanted to. Then there was a movie called 'Heart Like A Wheel'. Jonathan Kaplan was directing. I had worked with Jonathan at Quinn Martin, so Jonathan said, "Would you come along and produce it?" So I went out and produced 'Heart Like A Wheel'. In '82 I also did 'Lost in America'. It's still on the top one-hundred AFI Comedies list of all time. I was the sole producer. Michael Eisner went over to Disney in '85. I got a call from Michael saying, "You got to come over and join me at Disney." I said, "I really don't want to be an executive again." He said, "This is an unbelievable opportunity." I would be coming in as a Senior Vice President and, in a few months, I would become Executive Vice President Motion Picture and Television Production Worldwide, an unprecedented position at any studio, ever. Later, at Disney, I was also asked to develop a technology organization, a committee that would bring together, within the studio and Disney companies, all the latest technology. At that point I had a license to stick my nose into everybody's business. Then our country, our economy, started to tank. 'Austerity One' meant we had to cut a lot of overhead. We already had Disney and Touchstone. We created Hollywood Pictures. It doubled our output. Now we were told, "You're still going to do the same number of movies, but you have to cut all these executives out, and get rid of minor positions." I understood it, and we all basically took on another thirty-percent of our work.

George Green: You took a cut?

Marty Katz: No. I had to do the firing. It was the first time I'd had to downsize. The second time, there had been many employees who had been there for years and years. Their salaries outweighed their performance. It just wasn't worth it. I had to restructure the entire studio. Then came 'Austerity Two and Three'. I understand cutting, but I didn't want to have people working seven days a week in order to keep the same output. So I elected to resign as Executive Vice President and exercised my producer option in my contract.

George Green: You'd be at Disney producing, independent producer, but not the Executive Vice President of Disney.

Marty Katz: Not the Executive Vice President Motion Pictures and Television Production Worldwide. So, this is the beginning of change in my life. Now all of a sudden I'm a producer on the Disney Lot.

George Green: For the first time you're starting to feel, 'I don't have total control.'

Marty Katz: It was interesting to see that people reacted to me differently. Many have moved on to run studios around town. Some of them were afraid to hire me because they didn't feel that they could manage me.

George Green: Here's a first time that you're dealing with rejection by some people who should be appreciative of the work you've done for them.

Marty Katz: Absolutely. I'm the one who got them into the food chain.

George Green: Emotionally, how are you feeling that the light is no longer on you?

Marty Katz: I can get up every morning. I know how good I am. I continue to improve myself. When I don't get a position because I may not have presented myself as well as I should have, that's one thing. I'm honest with myself. I really do a good audit on myself. When I realize it wasn't me; at the end of the day, it doesn't affect my self-worth. It doesn't affect my image of myself. It's disappointing but it doesn't say to me 'you're irrelevant'. Irrelevancy is the big fear. I don't feel like that. I feel I'm in the game.

George Green: That's the key line here; accepting what is and not dwelling on the past.

Marty Katz: Except to the extent it can help you. Don't dwell in terms of negativity. That doesn't help.

George Green: You don't look back at those days and get into a depressed state?

Marty Katz: Never, because each one of those life events took me to another place. And each one of them gave me lessons, opportunities to move forward. I've been asked to become an executive again. I never wanted to do that again. I always wanted to take this new path and I'm still on this path. Does it happen as fast as I'd like it? No. But I'd rather it happen when it's going to happen, than just sit around and worry. I'm always looking to network and work with other people. I have an office, an organization; people working for me. We're reading scripts every day. If it's right, then we take the script to the studios. So, in addition to presenting new projects I've found, I'm still looking to other producers who are looking for people to help them make their movies.

George Green: The door is still open to you.

Marty Katz: I have to open it, though. Part of being vibrant is knowing what's happening. I am sixty-two-years-old. The average age of these executives is probably in the thirties.

George Green: Old age can be threatening.

Marty Katz: It can be threatening and, also, 'old age' can be 'old school'. I'm not old school. I'm considered to be an expert in cutting-edge technology. I've done movies like 'Titanic'. That's the most successful movie I've ever worked on.

George Green: What lessons could you pass on to other people?

Marty Katz: It's really important to develop relationships. People you are meeting on the way up may be people you are meeting on the way down. It's important to not forget the relationship-side of it. You have to sometimes stop and think about the people as individuals not as departments. If you didn't help people and were self-centered, what kind of response are you going to get when you go to them? So the first thing is dealing with people. The next is to be honest with yourself; what are your skills, strengths, weaknesses. Number three; be current, don't rely on what you used to do and what you used to know. And you need to have the courage of your own convictions. You need to be positive and conserve your resources.

George Green: You believe that physical health is as important as mental health.

Marty Katz: My ninety-six-year-old father-in-law, a former SEC attorney; he's writing his seventh or eighth novel for his own edification. He's still driving, when we let him! His hearing is a bit gone. He'll debate politics. He can speak languages. He's an amazing character, but you can see the frailty. You don't get that way unless, over the years, you take care of yourself. You have to take care of yourself. As proof - I play hours of racquetball, squash and tennis on a weekly basis.

Michael Dukakis

Be prepared to give back

Michael Dukakis was born to Greek immigrant parents in November, 1933, in Brookline, Massachusetts. After attending Brookline high school he went on to graduate from Swarthmore College, in 1955. From 1955 to 1957 he served in the U.S. Army and was stationed in Korea. After his service he attended Harvard Law School where he graduated with a degree in law.

With a sincere interest in public issues and affairs, Michael turned to politics. His views and ideals consequently led to him being elected governor of Massachusetts in 1974. He then went on to become the longest serving governor in Massachusetts's history, serving as the sixty-fifth and sixty-seventh governor of Massachusetts from 1975 to 1979, and 1983 to 1991 respectively. Michael also hosted President Ford and Queen Elizabeth II when they visited Boston for the US. bicentennial.

After fourteen years as governor, in 1988, he sought the democratic presidential nomination and triumphed. Unfortunately, in the final election, he lost to George H.W.

Bush. Michael blames himself for this loss, however, claiming that during the elections he was concentrating more on Massachusetts when he should have been campaigning nationally. The last two years of his governorship were flooded with criticism regarding his policies.

After leaving office in 1991, he and his wife, Katherine (Kitty) went to Hawaii where he taught courses in political leadership, and led a series of public forums on the reconstruction of the nation's healthcare system.

In 1998 Michael served as vice chairman on the Amtrak Board after having been nominated for a five-year term by President Bill Clinton. In 2009, at the age of seventy-five, he was mentioned as being one of the two leading candidates likely to succeed Ted Kennedy in the senate, after Kennedy's passing. However, Paul G. Kirk, the favorite of the Kennedy family, was called to fill the seat.

Since then Michael has been a distinguished professor of political science at Northeastern University and a visiting professor at the School of Public Affairs at UCLA. He also partnered together with the late former U.S. Senator, Paul Simon, to write a book called 'How To Get Into Politics And Why'. The book was created to encourage young folks to think seriously about politics and a career in public service.

In January 2014 it was proposed that South Station, the largest railroad station and intercity bus terminal in Greater Boston, and New England's second-largest transportation center, be named after Michael. Although he opposed this proposal, he stated that he would not object to having the North-South Rail Link (a proposed pair of railway tunnels that would connect the North and South stations in downtown Boston, not yet built) named after him.

Michael experienced some dramatic highs as well as lows, and remembers the difficulties he faced during these transitions, both professionally and in his family life. However, he has come out on top emotionally, and today lives happily with his wife, Katherine (Kitty), part-time in Southern California and in Massachusetts. Together they have three children; two daughters and a son. Fortunately, taking his own advice long in advance, he was able to create a life that he could enjoy both in and out of the spotlight.

Interview with Michael Dukakis

George Green: Bring me up to date on Michael Dukakis, on the career and how you got there.

Michael Dukakis: After I graduated from Swarthmore I went in the army for a couple of years. I spent most of that time in Korea. I came back and went to Harvard Law School. I had been somewhat involved in the politics of my town before leaving for the military, so I got deeply involved when I got back. I ran on a seat in a representative town meeting, which is grass-roots politics at its best. Then I began to chair the Democratic organization in my town, a suburb just west of Boston, about fifty-five-thousand people. I graduated from law school and went to work as a lawyer in Boston. A vacancy in the state legislature opened up from 1962. I ran for it and won. I was in the legislature for eight years. In 1970, Kevin White won the nomination for governor. We ran, we lost. I Went back into law, did some TV work, moderating the public television for three years. I then ran for governor in '74 and got elected. I was defeated for re-election in '78. So I had to go through that transition. It was really painful, I got beaten. But it wasn't the first time that I'd had a transition. I taught at the Kennedy School for three years and ran for governor again. I won in '82. I was re-elected in '86 for a full term and then ran for the presidency in '88. So, in a sense, unlike perhaps some other people who've been continuously in public life for an ex-tended period of time, I had these breaks; first between my legislative stint and the governorship, and then between my first and second terms as governor. I pretty much decided when I left public office that I wanted to teach political science. I spent a lot of time on the campuses where I taught, encouraging young people to go into public service. And that's what I've been doing ever since. I teach nine months of the year at Northeastern, three months at UCLA. I'm very much involved in the Public Policy programs in both schools. I spend a lot of time speaking on college campuses around the country, and I pick and choose those issues that I want to become publicly involved in. Some of them are local. Some of them are state. Some of them are national.

George Green: What do you speak about?

Michael Dukakis: My thrust basically is that public service is not only important, it's very fulfilling and satisfying. It's not easy, but if you want to make a difference, and you have an interest in public life, that's where you ought to go, and you ought to take it seriously and use your college years to prepare yourself for what I hope can be a career in public service. And I discuss some of the do's and don'ts, and why's and wherefores', and things that young people can do to begin to enter public life in whatever capacity they think makes sense, that fits them.

George Green: You have gone through the various transitions in life; you went in and out of all those spotlights. Could you compare the intensity?

Michael Dukakis: The first one was the toughest, even tougher than the presidency. I got defeated by somebody for whom I didn't have a lot of respect. Suddenly I'm out in the cold. That was a very tough transition. Fortunately I was able to begin teaching at the Kennedy School, thanks to a very wise and sympathetic dean. I went in there to do a job, and soon became a full-time member of the faculty and had to put together their management program for state and local managers, and really worked hard at it. I think part of what's important about transitions is that you're doing something that you think is worthwhile and useful, and working hard at it. It took a while to get over the loss, it wasn't fun. It was unexpected. I wouldn't call it depression but it certainly... it wasn't a fun time. I was out there trying to figure out, "Okay, what do I do now?" At that time I did not think that it was likely that I would return to public office. I had a young family to support, and I decided I wasn't going to go back to law practice. So, it meant not only adjusting to civilian life but it also meant working hard to develop skills at a brand new profession for me. I never taught before. As I began to develop more confidence in my ability to teach in the classroom, I think I was able to make that transition. As a result of that experience, however, I think subsequent transitions were somewhat easier. I should tell you one other thing; we don't have a governor's mansion in our state. We're one of only three or four states that don't. So you live in your own house, you live in your own neighborhood. I used to take the streetcar to work which wasn't an act, that's the way I was. That's the way I've always been. So, keeping your lifestyle reasonably normal is not a bad idea. There is something to be said for keeping your lifestyle normal, moderate, not getting carried away with the perks of the office. There wasn't a big change. If you continue to live a relatively normal lifestyle in the environment in which you've been used to living; that helps all the way around. There's a lot to be said for making sure that you don't get carried away but you maintain pretty much the same lifestyle you always have.

George Green: Would you say that it took about a year for total re-entry?

Michael Dukakis: No, about six months.

George Green: What is it like when your whole family has got secret servant agents protecting you, and you're suddenly catapulted into a different kind of a spotlight? What was that spotlight like?

Michael Dukakis: I thoroughly enjoyed it. Now, I was the last of the candidates, republican or democrat, to say 'yes' to secret service protection. I never had that kind of security in my life. No bodyguards, no nothing. But as soon as I said 'yes' to secret service, I'm not sure people will understand this; one of the things that happens to you is that you are totally unable to have the kind of easy, informal contact with people. I mean, that's over. From that point on, you're effectively walled off from the public. I was never comfortable in that environment and I was increasingly unhappy. I'm afraid it showed in the campaign. I had the reputation for being a hard campaigner around here, out all the time. There is lots of person-to-person stuff and so forth. That's impossible. You can't do it. Once you say yes to security, you're living in a kind of capsule and you just can't have the kind of contact with the folks that you want to represent. That, for me, was not something I adjusted to well at all.

George Green: The lights never go out with entertainers, there's always another thing around the corner. Sooner or later the curtain's going to go down, but they're going to get a call from their agent and then it'll go up again. Is it the same in politics?

Michael Dukakis: I don't think that's what happens in politics. I mean, when you serve three terms, twelve years, as governor of a state, you know that you're not going to do that again. It isn't because you don't want to, it's just; twelve years is plenty and when you decide you're not going to run again, I mean, that's it. Now that does not mean, however, that you cannot continue to be actively involved in public life in a different way.

George Green: It's a different mountain to climb.

Michael Dukakis: I'm not even sure it's a mountain, but you've been where you've been, you certainly have an ability to command some public attention to continue to be involved, to have an impact perhaps beyond what the average citizen has. And so, you kind of selectively decide, "Okay, I want to get involved in this, or that, or something else." It could be national, it could be international, it could be local. So, unless you become a hermit, you're going to continue this life, but in a different way. The phone around here rings about twenty-five or fifty times a day, and a lot of it has to do with people who are involved, one way or the other, in public life, public causes, public issues and in politics. So you continue to participate actively in that sense.

George Green: Tell me about the re-entry, the first six months after the presidential campaign was over.

Michael Dukakis: I went right back to the governorship. Unfortunately, as I returned, the economy in the northeast was beginning to go south on us. So I got back, and all of a sudden I've got financial problems on my hands. I didn't have any time to sit around. I had a very busy and a not so pleasant two years trying to deal with the consequences of what was a sudden, unexpected and pretty serious recession.

George Green: For Kitty (Michael's wife), when the light went out after that campaign, her light went out.

Michael Dukakis: Yeah, it did, because she had been a very strong and a very effective person all during the campaign.

George Green: She went to alcohol at that point. Were you aware at that time?

Michael Dukakis: Well, I wasn't aware of it immediately. But if you know anything about addiction and alcoholism, folks who are addicts and alcoholics have a great way of covering it up, at least for some period of time. But within a matter of weeks, I knew that something was wrong.

George Green: So then you had a personal problem on re-entry, and you also had a personal problem at home.

Michael Dukakis: Right.

George Green: What character traits do you think someone has to have to persevere in public life?

Michael Dukakis: You certainly have to believe deeply in what you're doing. You've got to be an optimist, not a cock-eyed optimist, but certainly an optimist. If you're a pessimist don't go into public life. You really have to believe strongly that good people working together can make a difference, and that as part of that you can make a difference. You've got to be very tenacious. You've got to anticipate there are going to be some disappointments. You certainly have to be able to absorb a certain amount of criticism. The higher you rise in politics, the more criticism you're going to get, the more visible it's going to be. I think you have to want some very strong support. For me certainly, family was very important. I think you've got to be fairly disciplined with your time. It was very important, in a personal sense for me, to have that time with my family to be, at least for some period of time, away from the political stuff and so forth. I'm not sure that's a normal characteristic of most politicians but it was for me, and it was very important.

George Green: What kind of advice and lessons can you offer to people who are going through transitions in their life?

Michael Dukakis: I've mentioned some of these already. Watch your lifestyle, keep it reasonably moderate. Don't begin living at a level that's going to be impossible to maintain once you've left whatever it is you're doing. That's very important. Keep it as normal and as natural as you possibly can, both in an economic sense and more importantly in a kind of broader, lifestyle sense. Secondly, if possible, have some sense of what you're going to do when you leave that life, in a way that's going to engage your energy and talents and intelligence, and be thinking about that even while you're working very hard at the profession or the occupation that you're involved in. And thirdly, make at least some of that time that you're spending, after you leave whatever it is that you've been doing that's put you in the spotlight; make sure that involves you actively in the broader community.

George Green: Do you ever reflect on those late 70's and 80's and miss the action? How do you deal with that?

Michael Dukakis: I'm not sure I miss it. I mean, occasionally when I pick up the paper, I get more than a little annoyed not just as a citizen, but because I was in a position once where I could do something about that. And so that could be frustrating; where you see things happening that shouldn't be happening, and you were once in a position where either that didn't happen or you were in a position to make sure that didn't happen... or correct them. I certainly think from time to time, 'Well, if I were there I might have done it this way,' or, 'Why are we doing these things when they could be done better?' But not in the sense of 'wouldn't I like to be in the White House, in the Oval Office, surrounded by all the trappings and that kind of stuff. But I will say this; I have a very busy life these days. I've got a full teaching schedule. Kitty and I have a chance to roll around a little bit. California's a very, very special place, both for its natural beauty as well as what's happening out there. It's a hell of a lot of fun to be out there teaching, and I could spend full-time just working on important public issues as a citizen, or former governor, or presidential candidate. I still have the problem of managing my time in a way that makes sense and leaves some time for personal things. It's a busy and engaging life.

Gray Davis

Serving your state, the people and your country

Joseph Graham 'Gray' Davis was born in December, 1942, in the Bronx, New York City. In 1954 he moved with his family to California and was raised a roman catholic. Aside from attending public, private and catholic schools, Gray graduated from North Hollywood University Military Academy, the Harvard School for Boys (now part of Harvard Westlake School). His academic accomplishments ultimately led to him being accepted at Stanford University where he earned a Bachelor of Arts in History. He graduated in 1964 with distinction. He then moved on to Columbia Law School where he won the Moot Court Award and graduated in 1967.

Gray also served in the U.S. Army during the Vietnam War until 1969. He returned home as a captain with a bronze star medal for meritorious service. Those who knew him claimed that he came back from the war a 'changed man', more interested in politics than before. He believed that the burden of war should be felt equally, and decided to try to change America. Today he is still a member of the 'American Legion' and the 'Veterans of Foreign Wars'.

In 1970, Gray volunteered for the campaign for John V. Tunny for the United States senate. He also started a statewide neighborhood crime-watch program while serving as chairman of the California Council on Criminal Justice.

One of his first experiences in politics included helping Tom Bradley to win the elections as Los Angeles' first black mayor in 1973. Bradley's victory ultimately inspired Gray to pursue a career in politics. He then ran for state treasurer in 1974, but lost to the more popular Jesse Unruh.

After this, Gray returned to California and served as executive secretary and chief of staff to governor Edmund G. 'Jerry' Brown Jr. from 1975 to 1981. However, in 1976 he was suspended from the state bar of California for failing to pay his yearly state bar dues on time. Fortunately, after paying each of the dues that followed, he was automatically reinstated. When Jerry Brown went on to run for president in 1980, Gray ran California.

During this time, in 1978, he also met his future wife, Sharon Ryer, whom he ultimately married in 1983. Gray claims that his wife is a cornerstone in his life, constantly supportive, upbeat and caring.

From 1983 to 1987, Gray was elected to the office of assemblyman from the 43rd district, and represented parts of the Los Angeles County including West Los Angeles and Beverley Hills.

After this he went on to serve as state controller for eight years until 1995. During his time he saved taxpayers more than half a billion dollars by taking a stand against Medi-Cal fraud, exposing the misuse of public funds. He was the first controller to withhold paychecks for all state-elected officials, including himself, until the governor and legislature passed an overdue budget.

Gray then ran for the United States senate in 1992. However, his campaign was not successful and was considered one of the most negative in state history. Gray continued to use similar negative campaign ads even during the race for lieutenant governor, but vowed not to let major decisions, in future campaigns, be decided by his campaign staff. After this, many democrats believed his political career was over. But Gray made a wise decision; to create a new campaign team.

Due to this, he experienced a landslide victory in 1994, receiving more votes than any of the other democratic candidates in America. He chose to use his ads as a way to depict republican Cathie Wright as being too conservative for California. He served as lieutenant governor until 1999 and, during this time, focused his efforts on the economy of California, trying to encourage new industries to expand in the state. He also aimed his efforts towards keeping education affordable for middle-class families. He went on to serve as president for the State Senate, Chair of the Commission for Economic Development, Chair of the State Lands Commission, Regent of the University of California, and Trustee of the California State University.

In 1998, Gray won the election for governor with a 57.9% vote. During his campaign he emphasized the need to improve California's public schools which voters supported wholeheartedly. In 1999 he signed laws banning assault weapons 'by characteristics rather than brand name' as well as those that limited handgun purchases, and those that enforced the requirement of trigger locks with all sales of new firearms. He also included a ban on .50 caliber firearms and, in 2001, signed a bill requiring all gun buyers to pass a specific test.

Also during this year, Gray signed senate bill 19 which establishes nutritional standards for food at elementary schools, and bans the sale of carbonated beverages in elementary and middle schools.

Gray also sought to improve relations with Mexico. Under his leadership, Mexico became California's leading export market for the first time in history, which led California's trade with Mexico to surpass Mexico's trade with Latin America, Europe and Asia combined.

During his time as governor, Gray also passed many bills regarding the environment, business and transportation, all of which had significant impact and proved to be highly beneficial.

Sadly, during May of 2001, California hit an energy crises, one that Gray explains clearly in his interview below. Of course, the public turned to him for answers, but wouldn't listen to those he had to give. By April 2003, his disapproval rating was at 65%. With this declining popularity came further criticism in other fields. Ultimately he was blamed for mishandling the electricity crisis, and before long a number of signatures were collected to enforce a recall election.

Gray left office in 2003. He claims that he'd lost touch with the voters despite trying to correct the matter through numerous meetings. On the night of the recall he admitted defeat and thanked California for having elected him in numerous statewide elections. He was pleased with the improvements he'd made in the fields he'd pursued while serving.

In 2004, after his spotlight in politics had dimmed, he joined the law firm of Loeb & Loeb. He also went on to do several media interviews about his legacy, and appeared in the documentary, 'Enron '. The Smartest Guy in the Room', which deals with the electricity crisis and how it really happened. Then, in 2007, Gray was appointed to the board of directors of the animation company, DiC Entertainment, as a non-executive.

Today Gray lives happily with his wife Sharon, and still speaks as a guest lecturer at UCLA's School of Public Policy. He looks back at his life in politics and remembers the effort he put towards changing California for the better. This was only ever his intention. Although his spotlight went out, perhaps simply due to folks not wanting to listen to the truth, he believes he did his best and certainly achieved what he set out to. Without a doubt, many will agree. When asked 'Would you do it all again?', although his answer is 'Yes', on the other hand Gray admits that living a life with light shoulders, free from political burden and worry, is just as wonderful.

Interview with Gray Davis

George Green: You have had some wonderful experiences. I want to know how you felt about the highs and lows.

Gray Davis: My mother raised me to always think the best about people, to be grateful, to get off the canvas if life knocks you down; when you start this journey don't expect to win, understand that there will be highs and lows. Part of life is dealing with whatever fate you encounter. As a young man I helped Tom Bradley get elected as the mayor of Los Angeles. I had quit the practice of law to do that. Then I thought, 'Well there's nothing to this politics.

I'll just run myself!' It looked like everyone else was running for another statewide office, and the treasurer was the only one where an incumbent could make a pretty good stand for election. I didn't think I would have much opposition in the primary. On the last day to file for office, Jesse Unruh filed after having already preliminarily filed to run for his old assembly seat. He was the Democratic nominee for governor against Reagan in 1970. This is 1974. He's trying to reclaim his old seat, so he decides to run for Treasurer. I didn't realize it at the time, but the election was over the moment he filed. I believe when God closes a door, he opens one. I was asked in the general election to help Jerry Brown get elected governor. He was the Democratic nominee. I was in a better position as chief of staff to Governor Brown, I certainly learned more about how government functions.

George Green: Tell me about the excitement as you ran for state controller.

Gray Davis: Jesse Unruh was the treasurer. The treasurer and controller are on some fifty boards together. They had a close relationship. The last week before you can file your papers to run for reelection of the assembly, Jesse calls me and says, "Ken Corey is not going to run. This is not widely known. If you haven't already filed for reelection, let's talk." So, we talked. My wife said, "Go for it." I had the opportunity to run for that job and was able to win the primary election. Then I went on and beat State Senator Bill Campbell. John Garamendi ran a commercial; a picture of a black limousine, the license plate is a picture of me. It says, "People of Beverley Hills count on Gray Davis to make things happen in Sacramento..." or words to that effect. The commercial had a good feel to it. $150,000 came in from people I had never met in Beverly Hills, saying, 'keep up the good work.'

George Green: You ran for lieutenant governor in 1994.

Gray Davis: One of the reasons I ran for lieutenant governor was because I felt that I needed a change. I spent eight years as a controller; that was for four terms. I could have run again. All my advisors thought I should, but I needed to do something different.

George Green: Tell me about the excitement when all of a sudden it's a landslide victory.

Gray Davis: It's very heady. There is no experience like it in life. It's very exciting! I learned early on, not to get too high or low. I always try and curb my enthusiasm. I've learned in life that it's not over until you stop breathing. Good things may still happen.

George Green: You were always trying to encourage businesses to stay in California. That was very important to you.

Gray Davis: Business is the way people get to earn a living from a family, develop a sense of self-esteem and purpose, and without businesses expanding there are no new jobs. Without new jobs there is no revenue, there is no money to support the programs that people want to pass in Sacramento. No business, no jobs, no revenue. So, whether you're a Democrat or Republican, you ought to find a way to be supportive of business. When I was governor, I was fighting for the renewal of the manufacturer's tax credit. That included Hollywood and Silicon Valley. The Democrats didn't seem to have any interest. So I went to the Republicans, and they didn't have any interest. I couldn't believe that. The leader told me, "We used to be focused on this but now we're not. We just want to be on the right side of two issues; birth control and gun control." That's got to change. This is a great state; whether you're Republican or Democrat you need to allow business to prosper and do well. There needs to be a regulatory framework and businesses need to do the right thing by giving your children and their children the opportunity to get the job, to grow, to develop, to become an entrepreneur; whatever they want to do, give them their chance. Without job growth the chance doesn't exist.

George Green: You were then enjoying the highlight of being lieutenant governor and you probably had your eye on being the governor. What are some of the emotional feelings that a politician has when he's running for one of the highest offices in this country?

Gray Davis: It's a great honor to run for governor of any state. I've been in the state since the mid-1950s. I love it! It provides more opportunity than any place I know. When I ran, however, I was a distinct underdog. I didn't start off with the big cheering section on my side. You just have to believe in yourself and believe you can make a contribution. Nobody does this just to see their name up in lights. You do it because you want to change something. I want to change education, make it more accountable, provide more scholarships.

George Green: That was one of your key platforms; education.

Gray Davis: Education and accountability. We spent a lot of money training teachers. We increased their pay. We expected more from them because we wanted to give every child the chance to reach their dream. I used to say, "I believe in the era of higher expectations. We want our kids to reach further. Even if they can't reach their goal, they'll do better because their aspirations reach their sights." I believe within the academic setting, if you don't challenge kids and expect a lot from them, they won't rise to those ambitions. If you believe a child can succeed, the child will take their cues from you.

George Green: When you won the governorship you must have really been on high.

Gray Davis: Obviously the governor is the apex of my political ambition. I felt terrific, but that lasts for about three days. Then you have to get down to work and do something to justify all the trust people place in you. We were pretty clear in the campaign about what we wanted to do. Our focus was schools.

George Green: You accomplished a lot for the state of California, especially in the area of education. Looking back, do you think you got the proper recognition and credit for the good things that you have done? Do people understand what you did accomplish, instead of looking at the negative?

Gray Davis: It's probably human nature to dwell on the negative. I didn't go into this profession looking for constant applause. If I knew I was doing something positive to help the next generation of students or jobseekers, or protecting the environment, then that was satisfaction. Anything beyond that, any newspaper articles or external recognition was great. But I didn't expect it, I didn't crave it.

George Green: That's a major point; self-satisfaction. If you're happy with what you did then it doesn't make any difference whether somebody else is not. There are always going to be people that don't like what you do. If you feel in your heart that you've done a good job, that was good for you.

Gray Davis: Yes, that is exactly how I think you should approach life. You should do what you think is the right thing. We did a lot of things in terms of the environment, created more parks than anyone else. We bought the cornfields and yards that are going to be the first state park in LA. That is being developed now. I signed the first bill in America which prevented greenhouse gases. That was actually a measure, thanks in part to the advocacy by Jerry Brown and Arnold Schwarzenegger. Obama used that when he announced the fuel mileage standards for America, patterned after the California law in writing. Arnold didn't author the bill, but kind of picked up the fact after I left office and kept fighting for a waiver from the EPA. We had a fight in 2002. Detroit said they would take us on. We won every court battle. The EPA turned us down after having given us fifty-one straight waivers. Obama finally issued the waiver and said we are adopting these standards by 2016.

George Green: You worked really hard for a good relationship with Mexico. Were you concerned about illegal immigration in those days?

Gray Davis: I always used to say, "I want people to come here legally. I want them to not jump in the front of the line and discourage other people who are waiting their turn." However they got here, we should treat every human being with respect. I think that's very much a part of the Christian ethic, and that's how you should behave.

George Green: By 2001, your popularity as the governor declined.

Gray Davis: Because of the energy crisis.

George Green: How does a politician deal with that judgment?

Gray Davis: Everyone likes high approval ratings and no one likes low approval ratings. Governor Wilson told me once, during the transition, 'the governor has to be the adult in the room.' No one in politics likes to say 'no'. You rarely hear the word 'no'. You hear, 'I'll think about it. Let me consider...' but not the word 'no'. It's fine to be popular and get elected governor, but at the end of the day you have to do what's right whether it's popular or not. One regret I have is, I could never explain to people how the Enron's of the world were taking advantage of a system created prior to my governorship. I paid the price. No one got a bill from Enron. The way the law that Wilson signed two years before I became governor was written; 'Utilities had to sell half of their plants'. Enron, Edison; they were only about six companies operating in the state. They would sell the power back to this other company. The expectation was that that would be the cheapest power. Electricity you cannot store, so you have to sell it on the day you have it, otherwise it disappears. You can't put it someplace if you don't use it. So, the argument was that that would be the cheapest. It turned out to be the most expensive because of all kinds of manipulation. I'll give you one example; on the audio and videotapes that came out four years after the fact, you could see that Enron was ordering plants to go down, and creating shortages which were leading the blackouts. But one thing they discovered during the energy crisis was; Enron would confuse the people running our electricity grid, into thinking they had put too many electrons on the grid. Too many electrons; you think of too many cars on the freeway and all of a sudden you're at a standstill, and nobody moves. So, they were giving Enron 'decongestion fees' to take these electrons off the grid... which they had never put there in the first place. But they were able to, like in a video game, confuse the people operating the grid. So, they would get all of this money from the state for allegedly taking electrons off the grid... that they never put there in the first place. That was the kind of stuff that we were up against. But because no one ever got a bill from Enron, they didn't understand.

George Green: In 2003 there's a situation; the deficit that budgets the unemployment situation, and then driver's licenses for illegals came up at that point.

Gray Davis: Yes it did.

George Green: Is that one of the things that you would have gotten done?

Gray Davis: No. I felt that was the right thing to do. Many of the police and law enforcement supported that. When someone issues a warrant to you, it is based on your driver's license number. If you don't have a driver's license, it's hard to issue a warrant. Plus, we could keep track of who was on the road. Plus, they had to get insurance. At the end of the day people didn't like it. I believe in standing up for what I think is right. It's not as if we can harvest the crops ourselves. There have been many times, people who were here illegally were asked to go into the fields. They would quit by twelve or three in the afternoon. They can't work a full day. We depend on people being there to harvest our crops and get food to our table, and most of those people are here illegally. Farmers will tell you that eighty to ninety-percent of the workplace is not here legally. Years ago there used to be a program. There used to be a way that you could legally come in. That doesn't exist anymore. People are putting food on our table and we are saying that they can't drive to work. They have to be at the farms at 5 o'clock in the morning. How is that going to happen?

Also, the nannies and gardeners come out here. I don't think you should take the benefit of their labor and then say, "Well you have to take public transportation to get to work." So that is where I was coming from. When you first ask, "How can you let people drive a car who are here illegally?" I wouldn't support that either; they're not just here illegally, they're harvesting food that gets on our table. They're helping watch our children and raise them, as nannies; they're gardening, they're doing odd jobs. They are a force in our economy and in most cases they are paying taxes and Social Security benefits that they never get to receive. So, that was my rationale when you say, "Are you in favor of people being here illegally?" No, I wouldn't be, but it's not that simple. I think there are eight or nine states that permit illegals to get a driver's license. Then there was a bill passed in 2004 or 2005, to go along with homeland security, which made it more difficult than any other state to do that. You had to make a finding that it didn't increase security risks.

George Green: You ran into some tough opposition.

Gray Davis: It was tough to be in the middle and Arnold sort of finds himself in the same place. But that's what governors have to do. No one said the job is easy. It is easier in good times. It is not fun in bad times. People say, "Why are you cutting my program? My child needs special tutoring. My child depends on this after school program." So, it's a great pain. You don't want to hear people suffering because of actions you cannot continue, because the money isn't there. As I told people, and they didn't want to hear it, everyone has a stake in a strong economy. Strong economy provides jobs and provides revenue. Without that, we can't do all the things governors want to do.

George Green: The time of the recall, and then afterwards, was a traumatic thing in your life.

Gray Davis: Very much so.

George Green: You were the guy in the middle. I don't think you deserved it. How did you feel when you lost that election and you're out of the spotlight?

Gray Davis: We had just won reelection in 2002, and they started circulating petitions to recall me before the end of the year. My first reaction was that all the issues they were raising were raised in the last race. This was like the second bite of the apple. My next instinct is everyone, even Governor Reagan, had a couple of weak recalls against. Generally these things don't amount to much, so I'm not going to dwell on it. For a long time it looked like it wouldn't qualify. Then Darryl Eisend put in three-million dollars. That was what put it over the top. That all happened pretty fast. Then it qualified. The election was in October. Arnold took advantage of the opportunity to run, but I don't blame him for the recall. To the best of my knowledge he wasn't active in the recall per se, or in the efforts to qualify the recall. I guess, just because you're working hard and doing what you think is the best job, doesn't mean the people are going to allow you to do it forever. The same people who had the right to put you there have the same right to take you out. Every election was like being on a high wire act without a net. If I lost, I didn't have another job. If I ran for controller I had to give up the assembly job. I ran for lieutenant governor and had to give up the controller job. I ran for governor and had to give up the lieutenant governor job. I used to know that you can't count on this thing working out. In the end we lost. There are some things that could have gone differently in that campaign, but they didn't. I told my wife the day after election, "There are people that want us to move on. This chapter in our life is over. We're going to start something new." I didn't know what it was but I wasn't going to dwell on it. I just knew we fought. We did the best we could with just moving on.

George Green: How important was your wife in the recovery process?

Gray Davis: She was just important, period! Everyone who has met her will tell you that she is just full of joy, very positive. The family was very religious. They were Episcopalians and read the Bible every night. She converted to Catholicism but is very spiritual. She has an upbeat approach to life. She was a big part of every success I had and also a big part of dealing with any failure. Today if you ask her, she likes to joke that if she had known life could be so good after the recall she would have voted for it!

George Green: The intense spotlight goes out. Then what happened?

Gray Davis: You have to make a new life for yourself happily. We had a lot of good friends that helped us. We got a lot of good advice on how to spend your initial time out of office. I had never lost an election that caused me to be out of office. I told my wife we're moving on. We're not having any regrets.

George Green: How long did it take her to enjoy the good life?

Gray Davis: Probably about a year, a year and a half.

George Green: Family and religion was extremely important in your recovery.

Gray Davis: It's been important to us all the time.

George Green: You're still very much involved in the community, aren't you?

Gray Davis: Yes. I'm the senior fellow at the UCLA school of Public Policy. All of the ex-governors are on the Southern California leadership conference which meets once a quarter. I'm constantly being asked to help on this political campaign, or that political campaign, or being asked to speak about and give comments on the activities in Sacramento.

George Green: Life is good.

Gray Davis: Life is good! I still have my say. I was on CNBC last night, but I'm not in the crosshairs anymore. You do the things that you want to do as opposed to things you have to do. I'm grateful for every moment I had in politics, including the six and a half years when I worked for Jerry Brown. The good times, the bad then in between... but I'm also grateful now to be beyond that.

George Green: Do you miss the spotlight?

Gray Davis: No. I don't miss it. Being governor of a state like California is challenging and requires you to be responsible for a whole bunch of things. If the lights don't go on, if the buses don't run, the water doesn't get from Northern California down to Southern California, if there's an earthquake, a fire; the governor has to declare a state of emergency and needs to show up and express empathy with its victims. You're constantly being called upon to make a decision, to make an appointment, to get a bill passed to deal with the challenges that people experience. Every day it is both thrilling and very challenging. So, to not have the weight of all that is very liberating. Would I do it over again? Yes, but now it's time for younger folks to do it.

George Green: What suggestions would you give to other people moving ahead to another spotlight?

Gray Davis: It's a mistake for people to think life is all about them. Life is about serving other human beings. When you leave one position which offered you an opportunity to serve, you can often find another position to be of service. Being of service is fulfilling and allows you to continue to have a positive impact on the people that you encounter. The stage may be smaller, the setting may be more intimate, but you're impacting people for the better. Find a place where you can be of service to another human being. It doesn't matter whether you're coaching your daughter on how to play soccer, or whether you're mentoring a young person working with the County Art Museum. Whatever it is, be of service to other human beings. I find that more fulfilling than anything else in my life. Some say, "I don't have this big spotlight." Well, who cares? You can be of service to people no matter where you are in life, and throughout your entire life.

Brief Update Interview with Gray Davis, May 2014

George Green: The last time we chatted we covered all the bases of your elections, the ones you won, and the ones you lost. You were in a very bright spotlight when you were running for office and you won some elections. You lost some, but you always seemed to love serving the people no matter what office you held. I suspect that you're still having your highs and your lows and I wanted to compare them. Now you're in another spotlight, what are the comparisons?

Gray Davis: Well, I think the best way to put it in a nutshell is; now I give a speech and if people don't like it, it's not my problem. I did the best I could. I told them what I thought. If they like it, great, if they don't, they don't. When I was in office I'd get all worried, 'Oh they don't like it, they're not going to vote for me.' There's a certain freedom and liberation that comes with being a private citizen. I still very much enjoy the opportunity to mentor young people, to play the role of a senior statesman and provide advice, guidance, and encouragement. I can't underscore how important it is to encourage young people, help them believe in themselves, and believe they have a great future in the 21st century.

Getting people to believe they'll have a great future already moves the ball at least halfway down the court. If they believe they'll have a great future, I'm sure they will. That will benefit their country, their family, all the people they care about.

George Green: The last time I asked you the question about what advice would you give to people, you said, "I'm going to answer in the way that I think will be most helpful. It's a mistake for people to think life is all about them. Life is about serving other human beings. When you leave one position which offered you an opportunity to serve, you can find another position to be of service. Being of service is fulfilling and allows you to continue to have a positive impact on the people you encounter. The stage may be smaller, the setting may be more intimate, but you're still impacting people for the better." I love that.

Gray Davis: And I don't think I could improve on that. I certainly believe that as much today as I did when we last spoke. I have a chance now, as a distinguished fellow at UCLA, to interact with students a couple times a year. I have an opportunity as a Co-Chair of the Southern California Leadership Council, which includes Governor Wilson and Governor Deukmejian, to try and be a thought-leader in Southern California and fight for middle-class jobs, for better quality of life. So, yes the stage is smaller, but I still bring as much passion every day that God gives me. You do have an impact on the people you encounter every day of your life.

George Green: You get a great deal of pleasure doing what you're doing?

Gray Davis: Yes, and you get time for some feedback. When you're in office, you're always running to the next meeting, the next speech, legislation you have to sign, and you don't have time just to hang out occasionally with people. I remember being out of office and going to the 80th birthday party of Eli Broad. A woman came up to me and she said, "You may not remember this, but ten years ago you wrote a letter to my boy who had just graduated from middle school. You congratulated him on graduating with honors. He was asked the next year to identify the most important thing that has happened in his life, and he wrote a paper on it. It was called 'The Letter'. He indicated how he was so encouraged and so inspired that the Governor of California would write him a letter, complimenting him on being a good student and encouraging him to learn and to be good to other people." So, just a letter from an elected official or even a former elected official can encourage and uplift people, which is a great gift. It's a form of service because you're just giving encouragement and inspiration to those who follow, and the reward is just knowing that you may have helped them become more successful than they otherwise would have been.

George Green: I think that's a great way to end this!

Michael Reagan

Being the son of a former president 'aint a bowl of cherries

Michael Edward Reagan was born in March, 1945, in Los Angeles, California. His biological mother, Irene Flaugher, was unwed when she gave birth, and consequently gave Michael up for adoption immediately after he was born. As an infant he was adopted by Ronald Reagan and Jane Wyman. Ronald Reagan was a superstar in Hollywood, as was Jane, before he became Governor of California in 1967 and again in 1971. He then went on to become President of the United States from 1981 to 1989.

Michael grew up as a part of the Reagan family in Beverly Hills, California. Ronald and Jane divorced when Michael was three-years-old. For any child, divorce is one of the unhappiest memories to hold. At the age of six-years-old he was sent to boarding school, due to his parents living the life celebrities do, and would only return home for four days every month. At the age of eight-years-old Michael became victim to a molestation incident which affected him deeply and detrimentally as he grew older. Although he graduated, in 1964, from the Judson School, just outside of Scottsdale, Arizona, his childhood left him scarred.

The start to Michael's career in radio was slow; he did not enter the industry immediately after graduating. After school he became a clothing-salesmen then moved on to become the director of a catering company. He, in fact, tried to work at numerous jobs, despite his fear of the world due to the circumstances from his childhood. He worked hard, trying to keep his integrity, but was always seen as the 'son of the Reagans'; not in need of anything. He then found a passion for powerboat racing and consequently became known for his skills as a powerboat racer. He, in fact, set a few world records in this field.

Michael then went on to put his efforts towards raising funds for charities like the United States Olympic team, the Cystic Fibrosis and Juvenile Diabetes Foundations, and the Statue of Liberty Restoration Fund. For efforts like these, through sports, he was finally recognized and received a Victor Award.

His first major role in radio started at KABC in Southern California, after which he moved across to KSDO in San Diego, California. By 1992 he had joined the Premiere Radio Networks with his very own show. His show was later picked up by the Radio America Network. This was where Michael ultimately discovered his own, true identity. It was also at this point that his parents finally accepted his past and a new father-son relationship blossomed after so many years of discontent.

Michael has been married twice. After divorcing his first wife, Pamela Putman, he married Colleen Sterns and together they had a daughter and a son.

After his career in radio, which lasted longer than twenty-five years, Michael took to writing. One of his books, 'Tough Love', is about dealing with being adopted, while others such as 'Twice Adopted' and 'On The Outside Looking In' deal with similar or more personal issues related to his molestation incident.

After Ronald Reagan, his father, passed-on Michael founded an organization known as the Reagan Legacy Foundation, a charitable organization based on causes that Ronald Reagan believed in. Michael also works alongside Arrow Family Ministries where he talks with abused and less-fortunate children in hope of bringing light to their confusion and inner-turmoil. He speaks from personal experience.

He will always be remembered as a young man who faced more pain and difficulty than most in his younger years, but through sheer determination to be recognized as worthy, managed to find his feet on solid ground.

Interview with Michael Reagan

George Green: Give me a brief paragraph, letting us in to who you are.

Michael Reagan: I was born German and three days later I was Irish! My birth mother found herself pregnant by a man who joined the military. Her name was Irene. She found that Jane Wyman and Ronald Reagan were looking to adopt a child. She put me into Jane's arms; I was three days old. It was a big deal that the Reagans were getting a son.

George Green: You had a mother who was very busy and a superstar in Hollywood.

Michael Reagan: My mother and father divorced when I was three years of age. Dad remarried in 1951 to Nancy. Mom was trying to raise Maureen and I as a single mother.

The Hope kids, the Crawford kids, the Reagan kids; all of us ended up in boarding school. I had nobody to talk to because everybody thought I was so lucky, because I was Ronald Reagan and Jane Wyman's son. I was always trying to act out, that people would recognize me; mainly my parents. I just saw them on TV or in motion pictures. I was able to get through it but there was a lot of damage done. You're playing the game out there trying to be liked by everybody.

George Green: You had sadness about not being with your parents, and then you end up with Dad taking you to the Ranch.

Michael Reagan: I really looked forward to the ranch. The ranch was consoling.

George Green: What is the timeframe for the sexual molestation incident?

Michael Reagan: Third-grade. My Mom brought me back to be a day student. She set up an afternoon with the day-camp counselor who would basically babysit us. The counselor had a bunch of kids and he would take us over there and we do trampoline and football and baseball. I was eight-years-old. He took pictures of me in the Santa Monica Mountains.

George Green: Nude pictures?

Michael Reagan: Yes. A couple of days later he took me back to his apartment, telling Mom he was giving me dinner. He had me develop the picture and said, "Wouldn't your mother like to have a copy of this." My life ended that day. I didn't want to have friends. I knew that if they found out, they wouldn't want to be my friend anyway. Everybody has a secret. You see a lot of children who have been through this become alcoholics.

George Green: You described the incident to your father and Nancy. For the first time there was this understanding coming from them.

Michael Reagan: I was scared to death to be in the limelight even though I put myself there sometimes. I was scared because if I became too successful; I worried those pictures would show up in the National Inquirer, or one of these things, and would hurt my father, hurt me, hurt my marriage. I didn't want to have relationships, so you have a father who doesn't understand why he's son always gets to here and quits, always gets to here and leaves.

George Green: Through boarding school your mother and father leave you. That's when you realize that you needed attention so badly.

Michael Reagan: I was in school with all the actors' kids. It wasn't abandonment; you could look at it like abandonment. My mother saw it as, 'There's no father there at the house, twenty-four hours a day. He needs to be learning.' Fourteen-million children go to bed in America every night without a father in the home. Then you wonder why we went to drugs and everything else. Thank God I got through it and I'm able to go out and help other people.

George Green: You had to go through 'Arizona'. You seem to go into another tailspin.

Michael Reagan: I was fired in Arizona because my last name was Reagan. They told me I didn't need the money because my parents were Ronald Reagan and Jane Wyman. The same thing today; people automatically think because you're the son or daughter of somebody famous, you don't have to do anything.

George Green: How did you feel becoming a 1967 Outdoor Champion Of The World? Now you're in a different spotlight, you're racing boats.

Michael Reagan: I was Inboard Rookie Of The Year in 1966, racing powerboats. People would loan me money and give me money. I worked into the system. The bank thought my parents would pay back the loans. I was going into debt, but having a great time. It was great fun.

George Green: That was a turnaround in your life because you are being recognized for what you did. Not only did you drive the boat, but you talked about the boat falling apart and you still won. After winning you still never heard from your Dad and Nancy. You went from a high again to a low.

Michael Reagan: The only time I heard from my Dad was when I disintegrated that boat and ended up on the front page of the LA Times the next day. My Dad called me and said, "Have you ever thought about selling boats, instead of racing boats. I think it's safer." in the 1970s I got into selling boats.

George Green: 1972 - no job, no car, no money, in debt, marriage failed...

Michael Reagan: I started to internalize things. There must've been something wrong with me that my birth mother would give me up. There must have been something wrong with me that Jane put me in boarding school; that all these things are happening in my life. I blamed mothers. It's easier than blaming yourself. 1973 would begin the turnaround. I was living with a friend. He set me up on a blind-date with Colleen Stearns. We will celebrate our thirty-fourth wedding anniversary, November of this year. We have been together ever since. She wouldn't let my anger, frustration, self-destructiveness deter her from what she saw.

George Green: The fact that you were in debt over fourteen-million didn't scare her at all?

Michael Reagan: She got on the phone and called everybody I owed money to, and we ended up paying off every bill that I owed. She took over and began the process of really changing my life.

George Green: Your Dad became the President of the United States. How intense of a spotlight was that?

Michael Reagan: It's interesting because nobody would hire me. The only thing I could do... I worked my tail off in 1980 for my Dad.

George Green: You campaigned in how many states?

Michael Reagan: Sixty-six airplane rides in nineteen states.

George Green: You started getting recognition for your own accomplishments. You continued to race boats, setting a record raising half a million dollars...

Michael Reagan: Colleen and I sat down and said, "What can we do?" I said, "I'm going to go out, race boats and raise money for children." The first one was in Mississippi in 1982.

George Green: You were always known as Michael Reagan, the adopted son of Ronald Reagan. You are searching for your own identity.

Michael Reagan: I think that's inherent in people who grow up in famous homes; you're always looking for an identity. People who are famous today have children getting themselves in trouble. What parents and adults don't understand; it's a way for the children to find their own identity. I talk to a lot of kids who have been adopted, and the number one thing they tell me is, if they could change anything in their lives, is their parents referring to them as they adoptive children.

George Green: After you tell your Dad everything that you had to tell him, you go on with your life, and very successfully.

Michael Reagan: It's really funny. I talk to people today and they say, "How did you make it through?" I said, "I could probably go out to become a mass murderer and people would say; look at his life - not guilty!" luckily enough, certain things happened at certain times. In 1992 I was making deals with God. I found myself in tears, saying, "Maybe the reason I haven't attained as much as I need to attain is because my Dad never told me he loved me." His generation didn't do that. I found myself blaming him for never saying he loved me. God spoke and said, "Next time you see your Dad, give him a hug and tell him that you love him." When he came to San Diego I was doing my radio show. He came to the studio. I went over to him and fulfilled my obligation to God and said, "Dad, I love you." My Dad says, "Well, I love you, too." From that point on, when I would see my Dad I'd hug him and say 'I love you'. When the Alzheimer's kicked in, he could not say my name. He would hug me not being able to talk to me.

George Green: Tell me about your media career; your life today.

Michael Reagan: You put me on the radio July 12, 1983. I did that for a while. I was guest host for Michael Jackson. He was the first guy in talk radio. In 1989, I got a call from a station down in San Diego, asking if I would come and sit in for them. I did three weeks for Roger Hitchcock and they offered me a three-year contract. They changed ownership, started to faze me out of talk radio. They thought I'd be a good newsreader in the morning. Jack tried to train me to read the morning news, and I was terrible. They put me where I would be doing a six to nine at night talk show, then they moved me and I was doing twelve to three, or whatever it was. I did that up until 1992, when some guy became available. They gave me forty-eight hours to pack up and leave. I started my own national show on September 7, 1992. But I could only get it going with people that I had met down in San Diego. I would drive from Los Angeles to San Diego every day to do a show from six to nine at night. It was a two-hundred-and-sixty-two mile drive every day, round-trip. There was no money coming in. I stayed doing my talk radio show until 2009 then I chose to get out. I stayed syndicated from 1993 to 2009. I had over two-hundred stations.

George Green: Did you finally feel that you had found your own identification?

Michael Reagan: Yes. I had my own identification as a radio talk show host.

George Green: Today, are you okay?

Michael Reagan: Yes. I started the Reagan Group. I have my own political action committee. But what's really exciting is I have the Reagan Legacy foundation. If I can help the next generation really understand my father from both sides of the pond, then I think I've done my job. But right now, I'm just busy raising my own family and take care of my family.

Brief Update Interview with Michael Reagan, May 2014

George Green: Bring me up to date on what you did from that point on until 2014.

Michael Reagan: I finished doing the Reagan Room in Berlin. In this last year we were instrumental in finally having an imprint about three foot by four foot put in the ground in front of the Brandenburg Gate, to commemorate my Dad's speech there in June of 1987. It took three years working with the red, red government of Berlin, but they finally succumbed and allowed us to do that. We were also instrumental this year in helping in Poland to put a bronze statue of my father, and Pope John Paul, at a park in Gdansk, Poland, and we're getting prepared to open up the Reagan at Normandy Exhibit. We're excited about that.

George Green: What is the Legacy Foundation?

Michael Reagan: Well, the Reagan Legacy Foundation I started back in 2002, 2003, to supply scholarships to young men and women who, in fact, serve aboard the USS Reagan, my Dad's namesake, that is home-ported at this point in San Diego, California. I do a lot of work with the ship. I have a scholarship program for people or who want to give dollars to our foundation, for those scholarships to the sailors who serve on the USS Reagan. I'm down there on a regular basis. I work with Operation Gratitude in making sure the troops don't think they're forgotten when they are deployed overseas and around the world. When I'm not doing those things, I'm speaking throughout the United States of America. I speak at many events throughout the country. A lot of them political because my last name is Reagan. We are attached to Arrow Family Ministries, where I work with kids who have been sexually abused, kids who have been part of child pornography. I work with foster care kids and abused kids. At this point Arrow houses fourteen young girls who they've been able to take out of human sex-trafficking, which is a horrific problem in the United States. I do that because that's where my heart is. I do politics because that's where my name is.

George Green: It really seems like your heart is in that one, almost more than it is in politics.

Michael Reagan: Well, I'm in politics because my last name's Reagan.

George Green: I'm really delighted that you're doing so well. I presume Colleen and the kids are well.

Michael Reagan: We're still above ground, which is good.

Peter Ueberroth

A 're-potter' with many mountains to climb

Peter Victor Ueberroth was born in Evanston, Illinois, in 1937. He grew up in Northern California where he attended Fremont High School. During high school Peter excelled in football, baseball and swimming. After graduation he was offered an athletic scholarship at San Jose State University.

In 1956 he competed in the U.S. water-polo trials, but unfortunately did not make the team. Peter then graduated from San Jose in 1959 with a degree in business.

At the age of twenty-two-years-old, Peter joined Trans International Airlines as both a shareholder and the vice-president. Roughly four years later he formed his own travel company which is known today as the First Travel Corporation. When he finally sold this business in 1980, it was the second largest travel company in North America.

Peter Ueberroth first came under the spotlight for his role as organizer of the 1984 Summer Olympics held in Los Angeles. Under his management, the first privately-financed Olympic Games resulted in a surplus of nearly two-hundred-and-fifty-million-dollars, which was used to support youth and sports activities throughout the U.S. For this role, Peter was named Time Magazine's 'Man Of The Year' in 1984. He also received an 'Olympic Order' in gold; the highest award given by the Olympic Movement for distinguished contributions to the movement.

Also in 1984, Peter became baseball commissioner, succeeding Bowie Kuhn. Under his authority the game of baseball saw numerous positive changes.

But it was not always only about sports for Peter Ueberroth. He followed many other paths, too, including running for governor of California in 2003, becoming director of the Coca-Cola company in 1986, becoming co-chairman of the Pebble Beach Company, and a director of Hilton Hotels among numerous other business ventures. He commonly refers to himself as a 're-potter'; fixing things, creating, but never hanging on to one thing for too long.

Along with his wife, Virginia, he also founded the Sage Hill School. On a humanitarian level, the couple created the Ueberroth Family Foundation with the intention of giving back to the Orange County community. Organizations that focus on children, education and cancer are the primary beneficiaries. In 2011 the Ueberroth family granted in excess of two-million dollars to over seventy-five non-profit agencies. Today Peter and his family live in Corona Del Mar, California.

Interview with Peter Ueberroth

George Green: Tell me about the different areas of your life.

Peter Ueberroth: Everybody approaches life differently. I think that too many people in life get stuck. Some have no choice. My father moved around. He was in the radio business. He was in the advertising business. He was in the farm-equipment business. He was in a lot of different things and he moved around. We moved around the country and that was exciting as a young person. I think that if you do anything well, you probably do it well for maybe a maximum of about ten years. From college, my first responsibility is; I found myself. My wife and I were going to have children, and we had no money. The intensity is you have to make a living for more than yourself. So, I've always been a re-potter and an entrepreneur; those are the two labels! I'm best at taking something and either fixing it, or taking it and creating it. I'm not the right person to just be the steward. I'm not a good steward. I wouldn't be a person to keep something for ten, fifteen years and operate in the same environment.

George Green: How did you know that you were a re-potter?

Peter Ueberroth: Early on, my interest span would go only for a few years. If there wasn't something new and exciting, I'd want to kind of change and get out. The first ten years I was trying to get an income base. The second ten years I built a business. Third ten years I was involved in the two best jobs in sport. The fourth ten years I've been trying to be an 'incubator of businesses' and try and make a significant amount of money which all goes to charity anyway. And then I'll have to figure out, in a couple of years, what I want to do in the next ten years.

George Green: Having a lot of accomplishments; was it important to get the applause or the recognition?

Peter Ueberroth: It was never important. The Olympic committee controversy; I was locally in the limelight very negatively. Every headline was a negative headline. We were going to 'bankrupt the city'. We were going to 'cause the worst terrorism'. We were going to 'ruin the economy'. Those kinds of things forced my position into the limelight. I didn't like it. In Major League baseball; I think I was a less visible commissioner and a very effective commissioner. I'm pleased with my five years in baseball.

George Green: Some people need it, don't they?

Peter Ueberroth: Those who seek it. I didn't join things. I didn't participate in things, other than anonymously on the charitable side. We still do all of our charitable things anonymously.

George Green: What made you so secure that you didn't need the recognition from other people?

Peter Ueberroth: I don't think I was more secure than anybody else, I just didn't find it something very attractive. I don't enjoy a crowd. I don't enjoy a cocktail party. I like an evening of no more than eight - six is about perfect - have a quiet dinner and listen to the intellect, the ideas and the passions of six people. But you can't do it with forty. Publicity is of no value. Yes, the Ueberroth name was fairly well-known. The combination of events, getting your face on the cover of Time Magazine, that causes a big spike in recognition. But if you'll think about it, if you want to keep that up, you've got to go to events, do interviews, be out there. We always went the opposite direction. In the media, the local media or the national media, I just never participated. If I had to do something I'd make an announcement.

George Green: Even when you became Man Of The Year in Time Magazine, that was of no value?

Peter Ueberroth: It was a recognition of the seventy-seven thousand people who worked on the Olympic Games. There's no nicer story ever written, that I've ever read about anybody, than Time Magazine wrote about me when I was Time Magazine Man Of The Year. Now, the opposite side of that. There was one paragraph that made it a very unpleasant experience. My stepmother raised me because my mother had passed on. She had a son of her own, my half-brother, and she kind of focused on him. But then when I came in the limelight she focused more on me. In the Time Magazine article, they went back and interviewed people I'd gone to high school with. Evidently, somebody I went to grade school with said I left home because I had a 'mean and wicked stepmother.' Well, my retired stepmother read it. That paragraph was devastating. So the balance of publicity is; I don't know what the value is.

George Green: Something made you secure. That internal satisfaction, that happiness is something that is from within, not from without.

Peter Ueberroth: If you didn't eat Italian food until you were forty-five-years-old, and you liked it, and you couldn't have it anymore, it probably wouldn't be the end of the world. Well, it's not much more difficult than that. It's not much more sophisticated than that. I had no interest in notoriety. It's better for your kids. It's better for everything. It's safer. I think a positive part was access. I was able to access interesting people who can make impact. I maintain the relationships and the friendships; I don't find one better than the other. The hardest thing that anybody does in life is to be married and raise a family. Business is not hard. Running Olympics is not hard. It's also the most pleasurable. You get the most fun out of your kids and your grandkids. Our offspring are now in their thirties. They're all doing well and we've got interesting and challenging grandchildren. And that's more the focus.

George Green: So there really has been no transition?

Peter Ueberroth: No.

George Green: You don't have any adjustments to make.

Peter Ueberroth: No adjustment. Never had an entourage. We never got out of line. We never rode in limousines. We didn't all of a sudden change lifestyle. The five years in the Olympics and the five years in baseball, that ten year period; if anything we went backwards economically. Those were expensive years and we didn't invest any money.

George Green: What advice do you give other people who are going through transitions and they need the action.

Peter Ueberroth: Get everything from within and those you love. I worry about people getting enwrapped by the environment that they work in; the power-base you get used to. But if you move... it was easy. I could choose my own timing. The problem with most people is they give someone else their timing. I think I would advise somebody, 'Always look ahead, always jump ahead to what's exciting.' Three or four years from now, I'll be doing something else, and I'm exploring what that is.

Brief Update Interview with Peter Ueberroth, May 2014

George Green: I wanted to close the chapter on Peter Ueberroth, and wanted to know whether you're still a re-potter?

Peter Ueberroth: I continued to do that and I think that until they cart me away, that's my skill set. We bought Pebble Beach. I wanted to be sure that it wasn't resold because it was a commercial business, but at the same time it was kind of a global treasure and I didn't want it to be mistreated. I was able to buy it in a way that it would be held by us for three generations. That's about all you can legally do in this country. But three generations take you over a hundred years, so that'll be good. Some things don't deserve to be kicked around. Some things are assets or have prestige. It's five-thousand-seven-hundred acres, four golf courses, three hotels and the coastline; one of God's best works. It deserves to be in American hands, so I bought it from the Japanese with my partner.

George Green: I presume that you still have an aversion to publicity.

Peter Ueberroth: Oh yeah. I don't seek that or want it, and I just don't think it benefits anybody to get that. If you can walk around the streets and not be recognized, that's always a good thing.

George Green: Reading over the fascinating interview that we did way back, you said, "Business is not hard, running the Olympics wasn't hard. But the most pleasurable thing that you get the most fun out of; your kids, your grandkids, being married and raising a family is the most difficult part." I hope your family is well?

Peter Ueberroth: They are! I've recently taken on Chairman of the Board of a New York Stock Exchange company that was going through one of these buy-out firms. Our charitable foundation is really being run by the next generation, and they've done some wonderful things; they've established a new high school here in Orange County. I still serve on the board of the Coca-Cola Company and a couple others. We're making real progress with the investment in cancer research, and we're at the company called Stem Centrx. We helped a company go public, called Marrone, which is in the pesticide business, but all natural so it's not polluting our water supply, our drinking water and everything else.

George Green: It sounds like you're still going strong and it sounds to me like you're still interested in all the various things you're doing. Of all the things you've ever done in your life, what was the most important?

Peter Ueberroth: I haven't done it yet!

Gary Brill

Life is a roller-coaster, be sure you're on track

Gary Brill grew up working and learning the basics through his family-owned business, a tuxedo rental company. At the age of five-years-old, Gary's father decided to name his business after Gary, hence Gary's Tux Shop was born.

After graduating from high school he went on to serve in the army. On returning from the army he was married and began to work in his father's new store, in the San Fernando Valley, in 1960. After a year it was clear that working together as father and son wasn't quite panning out as well as they'd hoped. He never left the family business; instead his father remained supportive but relocated him to another store in Encino. Gary worked extra hard in what was now his own store, and soon managed to double its size when his neighboring tenant moved out. This of course, improved his relationship with his father and onward and upward they moved together.

Gary ran the store in Encino for ten years. Then, seeing a need for growth, he and his father purchased a piece of land which they converted into a warehouse, enabling them to now branch out and distribute their clothing to stores in areas of Northern California, Nevada, Arizona and Utah.

Gary excelled in the industry and became part of the National Association. In 1973 he was placed on the steering committee that created the National American Formal Wear Association. After a few years he went on to become President of the organization, in 1977. With no college education, he certainly proved that hands-on experience often gets one further than books do.

In 1978 Gary's father passed away, leaving all business operations to be run by his son. Gary then went one step further. Not only was his company exceeding in distribution, he began focusing on acquisitions, too, purchasing whole companies (usually competitors) and running them with perfection.

At the age of fifty-seven-years-old, having been in control for so many years, he decided it was time to slow down, but not by much. He sold some of his company, on the terms that he remained CEO, kept a small portion of the company and be in charge of future mergers and acquisitions.

All seemed to be going well. Gary believed he had time to concentrate more on a few specific projects in the business, now that he didn't have to go in to work each and every day. However, without his supervision, the company failed to reach its projections soon after the deal was made. Gary's partners then asked him to leave. They took with them everything he had spent over forty years of his life building.

Not only was his lifelong passion for his work removed from him, the company itself (no longer in his hands), went bankrupt. Gary tried to bid on the company at this stage, but was outbid. He describes the experience as devastating and stressful, one that left him not knowing 'where to next'.

Fortunately Gary had a hobby; boating. After a boating trip to Alaska he found the time to reconsider and accept all that had happened. He'd also acquired some real-estate over the years. So, in a small office of his own, he still manages his interests. Today Gary lives happily with his beautiful wife, Sera, in Rancho Mirage for half of the year, returning to Newport Beach during the warmer months. Although he feels he has a great life now, living at his own pace, comfortable with everything he has and does, he claims it took him as long as five years to come to terms with the loss of his company.

Gary's advice to those who are starting out in life, or striving to achieve their dream, is that they should realize that many important life lessons, and lessons in business, cannot be learned through books. Experience that comes from facing ups and downs is what gets one to where they need to be. He also suggests that one should always have something to fall back on, because they never know when that spotlight that shines so brightly could suddenly be dimmed.

Interview with Gary Brill

George Green: Talk about your early beginnings.

Gary Brill: My father was in the men's formal-wear rental business, more commonly known as tuxedo rentals. I grew up in that small family-owned business. I learned to count by packaging the shirt studs and cufflinks in little bags. I learned to count to five; three studs and two cufflinks! Through high school I was a bright guy but a lazy student. After one semester of junior college, I enlisted in the army. While I was in the army my father purchased a small commercial building in the San Fernando Valley. This was 1960. He purchased it for income purposes, but when I came back from the army a couple things happened. I was quite young but I decided that I wanted to get married, and then I had to earn a living. The easiest way was to go to work for the old man. I did that for a year or so. We had our father-son conflicts, which you always have in a family business, and we found it difficult to work together under the same roof. My father suggested that in order for us to keep family unity it would be a good idea for me to be out. So, we took one of the locations in this small commercial building in Encino, in the San Fernando Valley, and we opened a third tuxedo store. It was called Gary's Tux Shop. When I was five-years-old my father had opened an additional location and he named it after me, so that's how Gary's was created. At the age of twenty-two-years-old I had my own little store-front, renting and selling tuxedos in the San Fernando Valley. Now I had something to prove to the old man. Fortunately for me he said, "Go ahead and do your thing. I'll be there to back you up if you fall." There were ups and downs and tough times, but after a couple of years we were able to expand. The tenant next door moved out. I doubled the size of my store. At the time I became active in the local service clubs. I was in the Optimist's Club of Encino. I was in the Chamber of Commerce. I was married at that time.

George Green: So you had a family to support, you had to make a living, and you had to prove something to your Dad.

Gary Brill: Exactly. We had some great times and some not so great times. It's pretty much a seasonal business. During the period from around right after Easter through the end of June, we used to call that 'the season' because of proms that would take place in mid-April through May. In those days I was doing almost everything by myself. In other words I would wait on the customers; I would prepare the orders every week. I wouldn't do the sewing, I had someone that did the sewing for me, but I did do the pressing and the finishing. During the season you'd be working from 6:00 in the morning until, sometimes, midnight. If you had a couple hundred garments going out on a weekly basis, for one or two people to process all that from start to finish; it's a lot of work. The good news is that as the business grew, we began to grow geographically. The season took on a different dynamic. In different areas things took place at different times.

George Green: Tell me about the expansion now that things are working for you.

Gary Brill: I worked in this single store in Encino for ten years. At the end of that it was one of the highest volume tuxedo stores, maybe in the country.

George Green: Can you share the approximate value?

Gary Brill: I think it was about two-hundred and fifty.

George Green: 250, 000 dollars a year in gross, just for the one store?

Gary Brill: Just for the one store. And that was a lot in our industry at the time. My father and I now were working much more closely together, since I had matured dramatically through the trials and tribulations. During the course of the ten year period he allowed me to acquire the store from him. So I actually paid for it as I went along and then I owned it one-hundred-percent. My father had his own store in South Central Los Angeles. Even though it catered on a retail level to the community, the crux of that business was what we call a 'distribution business', where he had a network of dealers, mostly in Southern California and a few out of state, that would rent tuxedos via a catalog to their customers. For example, a men's wear store or a bridal salon that wanted to rent tuxedos did not have to carry their own inventory. They had no cost; it was a pay-as-you-go, rent-as-you-go. So, they would rent the garments from Gary's and then they would put a markup, and re-rent those same garments to the consumer. When the consumer was done they'd just bring the garments back to the dealer, the dealer ships them back to us, no muss no fuss. One of the issues in our industry is that you had to continually stay ahead of the fashion trends, which meant buying new styles and new inventory. As you buy new inventory, and you still have demand for the older inventory, nothing ever gets thrown away. So you have to continually have these larger and larger facilities to house the stuff. I had been bugging my father that we need to get a bigger building, a bigger facility. So, my father and I together found a piece of industrial land near the Van Nuys Airport which we purchased. It had an old house on it. There's a legend that said that Norma-Jeanne Baker/Marilyn Monroe lived in that house as a young girl!

Anyway, we did knock the house down and we built an industrial facility that was going to be our new corporate headquarters and main distribution center. That was a major expansion, in 1972. We started construction on the 6th of January, 1972. I remember that date like it was yesterday because my son, who was six-years-old at the time, dumped the first shovel of dirt. Symbolic! A little more than four months later we opened for business, which was a miracle. My father was overwhelmed by the magnitude of what we had accomplished. It was fifteen-thousand square feet at the time. I transitioned out from working on the customers individually, into running the company and running this facility, expanding our distribution network in Northern California, Nevada, Arizona, somewhat in Utah. I became more involved in our industry, in the National Association. In 1973 I was put on the steering committee to create our National American Formal Wear Association. My father was scheduled to give a talk at this national meeting. He got sick, so I went and filled in. The group seemed to be impressed with my knowledge of the industry. The next thing I'm nominated to be on this steering committee. A couple of years later I become President of the organization, in 1977. I didn't have a college education but I sure had a street education in how to make it all happen!

George Green: Some of the most important business people in the world...

Gary Brill: ...Do not have a college education.

George Green: From fifty-thousand dollars, now you're close to a million dollars.

Gary Brill: In volume, yeah. Our distribution business was going along well, but the trend was now back to individual retail locations. Malls were becoming more and more important in the retail environment nationally. I started pushing for us to open additional retail stores. Now one of the reasons for maybe not opening retail stores is you have to deal with all the employees. You have to have a management team. In 1978, literally a week or two after we opened up our fourth location, in the Promenade Mall in Woodland Hills, my father passed away. It was a very difficult time. I survived it by pouring myself into the company. By that time I was married to Sera, who put up with quite a bit from me but supported me in everything that I was doing, and allowed me to continue to create and do what I was doing. By the early 80's I think we had about seven stores. I made one major leap. I leased a store on Wilshire Boulevard in Santa Monica, California. It was a major corner, a signalized corner. It had a sign that you could see for a mile in each direction, and it was probably the most expensive non-mall location in the United States for a tuxedo rental store. The amount of money I was paying was ridiculous. The size of the store was ridiculous. But from the day we opened that store, it took off. In about 1990 the store literally did become the largest volume formal wear store in the country, doing one-million-dollars.

George Green: But you still have the big warehouse, the headquarters out there?

Gary Brill: Yes. We doubled in size. We grew the company organically by opening up our own locations. We also grew the company through acquisitions. Our first acquisition was done in 1982. We bought a company that was based in San Diego. They had twenty-one locations. I bought their stores, their dealers. Not the real-estate, just the business part. That one was very difficult to absorb because I didn't have the infrastructure in place, and we had a lot of issues. We had employee issues, we had management issues. We didn't have any operational issues because we already knew how to move merchandise, but it was getting the newly acquired people working in our methods, which is always tough. The next largest acquisition that I did was in 1992 when I literally did buy our largest competitor. They were the ones that had the Sears concessions; we took over all of that. Now, in order to do that acquisition I had to go into debt for the first time, and it was significant. It was a nightmarish time because with that acquisition being much bigger than the one I had done several years earlier, we had the same kind of problems but they were magnified. And there were many, many more employee issues because that was done in the early 90's when the advent of employee stress claims was very prominent in the workman's comp arena. But we finally got through it and we worked out our financial issues. We had some serious financial issues at that time but I worked them through, and after a couple of years we found a new bank to finance us. They not only refinanced the current debt, they actually gave me even extra cash to work with. With some of that cash we were able to bring in some high-level marketing people that really helped me turn the thing around.

George Green: So now, from fifty-thousand dollars...

Gary Brill: Double digit millions. So now I have to decide, "What am I going to do for the rest of my life?" I think I was fifty-seven-years-old. I didn't want to stop working. I decided to sell the company because neither of my children had an interest in taking over. I would have liked them to, but they had their own lives and they just weren't interested. So I said to myself, "Am I going to be doing this for the rest of my life? I don't think so, although I do want to continue to do it some more!" So what I did is I negotiated the deal with the private equity people that I would sell them a majority of the company and retain a small portion of it myself for the future, and that I would continue to be the CEO and be in charge of the future mergers and acquisitions.

George Green: So now you're out from under the major responsibilities, but you still have a role.

Gary Brill: I still have a major responsibility because I'm still CEO, I'm still running the company. My eye goes off the ball a little bit and business dropped off slightly. The first month we missed our projections. The new owners, now they get antsy. Now they want constant reporting. I mean, on a daily or almost hourly basis.

George Green: They're pushing you.

Gary Brill: It was beyond.

George Green: They're pushing you, they're stressing you and you're saying to yourself, "I don't need all this."

Gary Brill: ...But I'm going to try. There were some very unpleasant conversations back and forth. One day, just before Christmas, I get a call. They came down and basically say, "You're out." They said, "Step down as CEO, we want to make you Vice-Chairman of the company and we want you to still handle the MNA." So they wanted to have their cake and eat it, too. I consulted with my advisors, and thinking back on the way they'd treated me I said, "I'm not going to work for these people." They locked the doors and threw away the keys. I'm still the landlord. They're still paying me rent! What they were trying to do is get all of the employees to shift their allegiance from me to them. So they had to cut me off completely.

George Green: How did you feel at that time?

Gary Brill: I was devastated. I didn't know what hit me. I had no idea what I was going to do, where I was going, what I was going to be? What good is the money going to do me; I've got nothing left. My whole life was that business. I mean, I sacrificed a lot for that business, including my family the first go round. With Sera there were some things that went on that weren't as happy as they could've been, because I was so obsessed about making this thing work. I was extremely stressed.

George Green: Give me a quick transition; you decide you've got to go ahead.

Gary Brill: Yeah, you've got to go ahead. I was pretty fortunate. This is kind of a fantasy. My hobby has always been boating and boats. At the time I had a very nice boat and I had always wanted to go to Alaska on my boat. I left the company, or I was thrown out of the company, in February of '98. I didn't know what I was going to do, but then I made a decision that summer; "Okay, let's take the boat to Alaska because now I've got nowhere to go. I've got no work I have to do; I don't have to do anything." So, the first thing I did after I left the company, I rented an office in an office building in Encino near my house. I never had an office in the house, I never worked from home. I always worked from the office, my own office in the company. I had a controller, I had a bookkeeper; they took care of all of my stuff. I had some real-estate investments. I had some other issues and things, so I had an office that I was using. Part of what I was doing was planning for my summer trip to Alaska. Anyway, we took the boat up North and we spent several weeks in Alaska. It was sort of a healing experience for me because I was away from the business. I went in May. That was the first time I'd ever been away from my business during the month of May. It was weird but it was great. When I came back from that trip I was more enthralled with the boating life than ever before, and now I had the wherewithal to be able to do something more about it. I went through a series of large yachts. We did a tremendous amount of traveling over the course of ten years, and that saved me. That saved me because I didn't have to think about what had happened, and after three or four years, maybe five, I got over it. Also, I had a brief opportunity to re-enter the business because about either eighteen months to twenty-four months after they threw me out, they were in bankruptcy court. I wanted to make a bid to buy the company back out of the bankruptcy. I was outbid by a division of May Company department stores. Their division wound up with my company. They happened to be affiliated with another tuxedo company in the Southeast.

George Green: So now you're finished. Tell me what you're doing now, how you feel.

Gary Brill: First of all I want to say that I don't think you ever get over it. You never get over it. But you need to get over it and you need to move on.

George Green: What replaced the anger? The new life?

Gary Brill: Well, yes. So my life now, or my business now, is... over the years I acquired some real-estate, so what I do is I manage that real-estate. That real-estate provides for my income currently and it's quite comfortable. We made a couple of physical moves of our homes. We live six months a year in Newport Beach on the water. And then the other six months of the year we live in Rancho Mirage in the desert, and we have a very lovely life. We think we have the best of all worlds. We have a lovely social environment, a great group of friends. I play a little golf, I'm not sure you could call it playing! I manage my investments, I do my work. I'm still the one that's doing my own bookkeeping because I like it that way, and I work on the computer and do all that sort of thing, and that's kind of it.

George Green: Sounds to me like I'm looking at a happy Gary Brill, happily married and happily involved in the things that you want to do. What advice would you give to young people who are starting out? In addition to an education or working hard, what would you tell them?

Gary Brill: I would tell them that they're not going to learn everything they need to know out of books. That the practical ups and downs and mud-in-your-face of life is going to teach you a lot more than what you're going to learn in a book. If you're in a business or even not in a business but in a working environment, as you're going along and you get to a place where you think you want to quit or go do something else or 'retire' - have a life plan, don't get caught short like most of us did, where all of a sudden one day we're on top of the world and the next day we're like, underground and not knowing what the hell you're going to do next.

George Green: Gary Brill, you've had an extremely interesting life and that still goes on. You're healthy, and that's very important. You're married to a wonderful lady and that's really important. And everything's getting better. Your golf game's getting better.

Gary Brill: I don't know if I'll live long enough to get my golf game better!

Patricia Welch

Singing alongside Yul Brynner for over four years on Broadway 'aint a bad way to start

Patricia Welch, born Patricia Ann Carpico, was born in Steubenville, Ohio, in September, 1954. She grew up as a country girl in Colliers, West Virginia.

Her love for singing and performing started at a young age. During her years at school she'd walk home, three and a half miles, after rehearsals for school musicals. Her passion and outstanding voice led to her receiving a scholarship from West Virginia University where she majored in music and drama. Patricia was fortunate enough to study with internationally acclaimed, Francis Yeend; an American Classical soprano.

In 1980 she left West Virginia and moved to New York City to, hopefully, further her career as a professional singer. A few days before she was about to turn around and head home, she landed the role as Tuptim in the musical 'The King And I' with Yul Brynner. For four and a half years she played this role, until Yul's passing in 1985.

Patricia then performed other lead roles in theater, including the role of Maria in 'The

Sound Of Music', Marsinah in 'Kismet', Hodel in 'Fiddler On The Roof' and Maria in 'West Side Story'.

She met her husband in Los Angeles and together they moved to Las Vegas. It was there, at a party, that Robert Goulet heard her sing and asked her to join him on the road in his show 'The Man And His Music'. After Robert fell ill, she moved on and found herself featuring in the Wayne Newton Show. Wayne was known for his spectacular Christmas 'on ice' shows.

By this time she was well-known, admired and in demand for corporate functions and patriotic events. One such event was the 9/11 memorial in 2002. She also sang the American national anthem on two occasions for the former president, Bill Clinton, President Ford and General Schwarzkopf.

Patricia fluttered in and out of different roles in her later years, from singing for a number of children's entertainment shows and movies, to singing for Brittney Spears' 'Brave New Girl'.

After falling ill she decided to slow down ever so slightly and settle down at her home in Rancho Mirage. There she recorded a special album with songwriter/US soldier, Kevin Nevel, called 'Country Songs For Our Unsung Hero's'. The project and all proceeds were handed over to 'Dogs For Our Brave', a non-profit organization that provides service dogs to U.S. veterans. This she considers as her way of 'paying it forward'.

Having left the bright spotlight, not wanting to give up on her passion, she continues still today to perform at small events like cocktail parties and charity events. She also recently released a CD called 'Cocktails with Patricia'.

Her career in music has been abundantly fruitful, more so than this once-West-Virginia-country-girl could ever have imagined as a child.

Interview with Patricia Welch

George Green: Patricia, tell me about you.

Patricia Welch: I was born in Ohio but raised in West Virginia, and I was a country girl. I lived way out in the country. I had a love and passion for music probably since I was about six-years-old. I started singing. I had a very mature voice as a child and I actually did quite a few school things. But the activities bus didn't go where I lived; it was three and a half miles. After school they had the musical rehearsals. I wanted so badly to be involved, I begged my mother, "Please, let me walk home. Let me be involved in this." Back then it was pretty safe so she said, "Okay." So, I would go to the rehearsals and walk three and a half miles, singing all the way home every single day. That kind of started my roots of music. From then on I was a scholarship winner for West Virginia University. I studied with the Metropolitan Opera soprano, Francis Yeend. She's gone now but she was a wonderful Metropolitan Opera soprano. Because I was raised in West Virginia, I also was introduced to a lot of other things like country music. That's how I developed my range; I had an operatic voice but I also had a voice that I could do country music and pop and so forth. Later on I took a big leap and went to New York City. I went with fourteen-hundred-dollars; It was gone within fourteen days. I was at the bank, my mother was wiring me some money; I said, "Just wire me a little bit of money. If this doesn't work

I'm just going to leave." As I was walking out of the bank I actually bumped into a college friend. I started telling her that I was going back to West Virginia and she says, "We have a two-bedroom apartment. You can stay with us for a while." That was the breaking point because I stayed with her and two weeks later they had an open call for 'The King And I'; the Broadway musical with Yul Brynner. I didn't have any real experience as a professional singer/actress. They would see all the equity people first and then they would see the non-equity people. There were six-thousand people.

For three or four days I sat there with this little bag lunch in the hall. Finally I got my chance. I walked in, I sang a song from the show, and they called me back. They said, "Yul Brynner is in Japan. We want him to hear you when he gets back." I went for that final call-back. There were ten women; we all got up to sing on stage. Yul Brynner actually physically came out of the audience, walked up on stage, came up to me, and said, "I want you to sing that again, but I want you to take your shoes off and work the stage and do it one more time." So, I did. When I got back to my friend's apartment, I get a call from Mitch Leigh, the co-producer with Yul Brynner. Mitch offered me the role of Tuptim. Mitch said, "We're offering you fourteen-hundred-dollars." I'm thinking fourteen-hundred-dollars for the month. I went to sign my contract and it was fourteen-hundred-dollars a week, much to my surprise.

George Green: So you became an equity member right away.

Patricia Welch: Right away. I went from being a young girl from West Virginia, not knowing anything about musical theatre or being a professional actress, to just diving right into it. Within a few weeks I was in rehearsals in New York City and then we were on the road. I did four and a half years with Yul Brynner. He passed away in October of 1985.

George Green: After Yul dies, after the show closed, what happened?

Patricia Welch: After the show closed, I settled in California. I went back to Los Angeles. I got an apartment and just started working. I did other shows and I worked quite a while. Then I met my husband and we moved to Las Vegas. I was at a birthday party and a friend of mine asked me, "Would you get up and sing?" I got up to sing 'Summertime.' Robert Goulet was also at that party. I finish the song; he went, "Wow." He came up to me and he said, "I really loved your 'Summertime,' it was beautiful." We started talking for a few minutes and then I thank him and I left. The next day Vera Goulet calls me up. She had called the host of the party and got my phone number, and wanted to know if I would be interested in singing with Robert Goulet in his show 'The Man and His Music.' So that's how I ended up with my relationship with Vera and Robert. We performed at the Venetian and then we performed at some other venues, and then on the road.

George Green: Was that as exciting as Broadway?

Patricia Welch: It was different.

George Green: A different spotlight.

Patricia Welch: It was a different spotlight. Robert had his orchestra and his main players. He gave me two solos in his show, and two duets. The rest of the show was his, of course. We worked together almost a year. He ended up with pulmonary fibrosis. We thought he had pneumonia and then it turned out to be something much worse. Up to the very end, Robert had his voice. When he was speaking on stage he was a little winded, a little out of breath. But his voice was there even though his lungs were going.

George Green: So that show closes. Now what happens to Patricia Welch?

Patricia Welch: A friend of mine was an ice skater in the Wayne Newton show. Wayne did this wonderful show with ice skating, and his little penguins came up on stage. So my friend said, "You really should be with Wayne." She gave him my promo kit and his wife called, just like Robert. In Wayne's show I had a couple solos but I also was backup which I'd never done before. I didn't know how to do backup at all. Frances Lee, a great gospel singer, took me under her wing. All of a sudden we were on tour singing backup. If I didn't get a note right Frances would give me the starting note and help me along. Then I finally got it. It kind of takes a knack, learning to do those harmonies. Before I knew it I'm singing my solos in Wayne's show. They had a full orchestra so it was really beautiful; to have this wonderful instrumentation behind me.

George Green: Before you wrapped up your major singing career, and you're still signing today, there were all kinds of appearances at Dodger Stadium, before the Presidents. Give me a brief of little things that you've done that you've enjoyed.

Patricia Welch: A lot of corporate conventions, a lot of patriotic openers. I was invited to sing for the 9/11 memorial and I've sung for Presidents. I'm very patriotic. I had a health issue a couple years ago. As a result, I did a CD called 'Country Songs for Our Unsung Heroes,' all written by a U.S. soldier, and I donated that entire project as a 'Pay it Forward' to 'Dogs For Our Brave', for the soldiers. It's my Pay it Forward, because when you get a second chance at life like that, I think we need to do that.

George Green: When did you decide that you don't need the intensity; 'I'd prefer something else'?

Patricia Welch: I decided when we moved here to the desert. The lifestyle here is so wonderful and it's a very social community. I got involved with a lot of the things, socially, singing for charities and that's fulfilling in itself. Another thing that I've been doing recently that is so much fun for me; I actually do in-home private parties like dinner parties and cocktail parties. I'll do a thirty minute show between dinner and dessert, or at cocktails, or before dinner, or after dinner. I am meeting the most interesting people. That is a different kind of thing. I was so used to, in the past, being onstage with the spotlights in your face, and you can't really see the audience past the first row. Well this is different. This is in a house where there might be twenty or maybe ten or twelve people sometimes. I'm loving that. I think I like that better than being on a big stage because I'm right there. I see the reaction. I can see them humming along, their heads bobbing along, their hands or feet tapping. It's a whole different thing. I have a good life. I'm very, very blessed. I feel very fortunate to have this and I wouldn't trade it for the world. And I'm so glad that I ended up in Southern California and I'm married to my husband, because had I gone on with the career I probably wouldn't have the life that I have right now.

George Green: What advice would you give to young people trying to make it?

Patricia Welch: The biggest flaw that I see in our young music scene today is people like to clone themselves after others. The individuality is being lost. I think it's important for them to have their own sound. You've got to work hard, you've got to be multi-talented, you've got to be diversified, you've got to learn. Performers nowadays need to know how to act, how to dance; they have to have it all. I think being educated and having a fallback is also very important, because a lot of people are out there striving to become a professional, and only a handful make it to the top. Strive to be creative, but creative within their selves; their own, unique creativity.

Barbara Sinatra

Life without Frank; it goes on

Barbara Sinatra (born Barbara Blakeley) was born in October, 1927, in Bosworth, Missouri. Her family then moved to Wichita, Kansas, where she was raised, and then on to Long Beach, Los Angeles, where they settled.

Barbara spent most of her younger years as a model, despite her claiming to be 'shy' and 'a little gangly'. She started out by modeling for department stores and even a few car shows, but soon landed a contract with the Eileen Ford agency in New York. At the age of twenty-one she moved back to California where she opened the Barbara Blakeley School of Modeling and Charm.

During the 1940s she met Robert Harrison Oliver, an executive with the Miss Universe beauty pageant, and soon they were married. Together they had a son whom they named Robert, after his father.

During the 1950s she moved on to Las Vegas where she featured as showgirl. During this time she met Zeppo Marx, the youngest of the infamous Marx brothers. After divorcing

Robert Oliver she was remarried to Zeppo in 1963. Zeppo soon retired to a country club in Palm Springs where Barbara enjoyed horse-riding, tennis and golf. However, she considered Zeppo too 'reclusive' and they were divorced a few years later. Zeppo died of lung cancer in 1977.

By 1976 Barbara had met Frank Sinatra. He, too, had been through a number of marriages (his ex-wives include Ava Gardner, Mia Farrow and Nancy Barbato). In July, 1976, Barbara and Frank were married; this being Barbara's third marriage and Frank's fourth. Barbara even chose to convert to Catholicism in order to have the Church recognize their marriage. She remembers their wonderful years together.

Since Frank's passing in May, 1998, Barbara has placed all of her focus on the Barbara Sinatra Children's Center, which was founded by herself and Frank in 1986, in Rancho Mirage, California. This center for abused children stands on the Eisenhower Hospital Campus.

During the year of Frank's passing, Barbara was awarded her own star on the Palm Springs Walk of Stars. In 2011 she released her first book titled 'Lady Blue Eyes, My life with Frank'. Barbara is noted by many, including Frank's children from his previous marriage, as being his rock, his guide; always in control, always in charge.

Interview with Barbara Sinatra

George Green: What was life like during the twenty-two years of marriage to Frank Sinatra?

Barbara Sinatra: Very exciting. I was born in Missouri, a small town; a farming town. My grandfather had the store that has everything in it, feed for animals; everything. So, from a small town background, to be thrown into that life was really pretty marvelous. I was impressed and I just loved it, and him.

George Green: The life you had with him must have been extremely exciting.

Barbara Sinatra: Yes. I've written a book, too; 'Lady Blue Eyes'. That's what everyone called my husband, 'Blue Eyes.' He was probably the greatest singer of that century. You were in the spotlight every moment, from the time you get up to the time you go to bed. Some of it was exciting, some of it wasn't. My husband wasn't a big fan of the press, he really didn't like it.

George Green: He had so much of it. I would think that at some point you want some privacy. I think one of the biggest complaints that a lot of entertainers and stars have, is that there is no privacy.

Barbara Sinatra: I enjoyed every moment and I enjoyed being with Frank. He was a remarkable person; very generous. I can't say enough nice things about him. We went together for four years before we were married, and we traveled the whole world, every place. I don't think we missed any place.

George Green: Was there any place special that you guys adored?

Barbara Sinatra: I enjoyed Italy, and I loved Italian men and women. He was very Italian. His father was from Palermo in the South and his mother was from the North.

George Green: And you never got tired of traveling?

Barbara Sinatra: No, I am now. I don't want to travel ever again. I had the best of everything. I had private planes. I lived like a queen. I loved it and was spoiled rotten. I'm still spoiled! He left me very well fixed, as well as his children and his ex-wife. He was just a very generous man; warm, sweet, charming, great singer, of course. I met people that I never dreamed I would ever meet.

George Green: What is your life right now; still under a spotlight, but not quite as bright or hectic?

Barbara Sinatra: Not bright at all. I consider myself very fortunate that I've taken up the cause of children who've been abused.

George Green: I want to know about the Barbara Sinatra Children's Center. That is probably your pride and joy?

Barbara Sinatra: I was living here in the desert doing one charity a year, sharing one charity, and thought I was doing my part. We had a doctor here in town at the desert hospital, Doctor Kaplan, and his daughter-in-law was on my board. I formed a board when I first met some of the children.

George Green: In 1986 you founded the center.

Barbara Sinatra: Yes. We had a tea at a theatre in the house where we lived before. I invited everyone; Betty Ford, Lee Annenberg. When I formed the board, when I met the children, they were taking therapy group lessons in basements of banks, churches, schools, any place we could find. We'd have the therapist come in and work with the abused children. I got to know some of the children, which really hooked me. That's when I decided we have to have a place for them to meet and congregate, where they can get therapy. I could see that it was really helping. They'd come in and they'd be hiding behind a skirt or something with their heads down. After they were there for a while, to watch them blossom and to smile...

George Green: I know it costs about four-thousand-dollars to counsel one child. How do these people find you?

Barbara Sinatra: The police department. I work closely with the schools, the churches, with different groups of people. It's very gratifying.

George Green: That's just one of the great accomplishments that you've done and that will continue on.

Barbara Sinatra: My husband used to go visit everybody in hospital. I visited with him. But no one knew this; he didn't want anything known about it. He picked up tabs for people in the hospitals. He was really quite a man.

George Green: What advice you would give to young people who are trying to climb that ladder of success in the entertainment field?

Barbara Sinatra: Entertainment is not my business. I have many friends in the entertainment business.

George Green: What is the 'Bosley the Bear, Good-touch, Bad-touch Puppet and Music

Presentation' about?

Barbara Sinatra: It is something that was devised at our center, the Barbara Sinatra Children's Center. When I decided to get into that business and try to build a place for the children, there was one man who came to my rescue. It was Walter Annenberg. At first I formed a board and among the members was Danny Schwartz. I told him what my plight was and he said, "You know, Barbara, I started this in London, something like this, and I started it here at Desert Hospital. They both went down the tubes. What makes you think that you can be a success at this?" I said, "Walter, I don't know. I don't know if I can and I can't guarantee it, but all I can tell you is that I'm passionate about it. I love the children and I'm willing to work hard on it." By the next morning I had the land by Betty Ford. Anyway, at the center we developed this theme because we go out and speak to all the schools and churches and police departments. It's child friendly, when they come in there they know that they're going to be helped. We have people here who helped with all of it. Frank, Sammy, Dean and all his group would do concerts here and that raised a tremendous amount of money. 'Bosley the Bear' was originated in our center by Rosemary Marta and a group of therapists. We'd train the women so that they know what it's all about. Then they go to the schools, the police department, and talk to all the children. They have the bear there. They respond to it and communicate with each other. It's just wonderful.

George Green: You'll enjoy my books. They're for children; if they have bad self-esteem, there's something else you've got to search for; that inner-strength, and everybody in this world has inner-strength, you just have to find it.

Barbara Sinatra: And use it!

MK Zordani

Always aim for a hole-in-one

Maria Katrina Thanopoulos was born to Greek parents in Crown Point, Chicago, Northwest Indiana. Her grandfather shortened their name to 'Thanos' after arriving in the U.S., and she became known by her friends as Mary Kay or MK.

Born with a disability that involved the underdevelopment of her legs, MK spent much of her youth in braces. However, as soon as she was freed from them, she did what most doctors had once thought impossible.

It was soon discovered that she was indeed a gifted athlete. To start with, going through therapy in a swimming pool, she discovered she was an excellent swimmer. MK went on to become a junior Olympic swimmer. After that she decided to try her hand at tennis, a game her father enjoyed. Once again she surprised everyone and went on to win the State Championships through high school. She was then offered a scholarship through Franklin College, outside Indianapolis.

MK gives all the credit to her father who believed in and supported her every step of the way. After her mother passed away due to kidney complications, she and her father became close. As she grew older she placed great importance on achieving everything she set out to.

Although her father was proud and extremely supportive of her sporting achievements, he suggested she study to earn a degree, so as to have something to fall back on bedsides sport. She chose to study law at Valparaiso University Law School in Indiana. Being a top achiever there she went on to do a second year in London. During this time she also earned her pilots license.

Once she'd graduated, she found work with a small firm. However, MK soon decided that she'd prefer to run things her own way and ultimately opened her own firm. Starting out, all she hoped was to be able to cover her overheads. However, after an intense case, she suddenly found herself in the public-eye and was considered 'as tough as nails'; invincible.

During a vacation where she'd taken time off to play tennis with a friend, she met her husband, Gerry Zordani. Even though they connected instantly, MK wanted to continue with her law firm. Ten years later they got together again, and before long she began to wind down her business due to the fact that she and Gerry were married.

With her law firm out of the picture she took up the game of golf, one of Gerry's favorite sports. As with everything else she did in her life, she took the club by the handle and aimed for a hole-in-one. MK went on to win numerous championships including the Women's Trans National Senior Amateur Championships and the Illinois State Women's Amateur Championships, to name but a few.

Today MK lives in Palm Springs with husband, Gerry, and continues to play golf and live a life driven by self-motivation and personal achievement. Although she walked out of a few bright spotlights in her life, it never took too long before she'd find herself directly beneath another.

Interview with MK Zordani

George Green: Tell me a bit about you.

MK Zordani: I was born in Northwest Indiana in a small community called Crown Point, which is considered a suburb of Chicago. To Greek immigrant parents, I was born Maria Katrina Thanopoulos. My grandfather shortened the name to Thanos. As I was growing up my name became MK. I started out as a normal young girl. We quickly found out I was a tomboy. I was a gifted athlete, after having some unfortunate health problems as a young child where my legs didn't develop properly. I was in braces, and they didn't think I would be able to walk. I overcame that with very supportive parents, and went on to become a junior Olympic swimmer. Then I picked up a tennis racket because my father was a tennis player, and they found that I was gifted in that area. I went on to win State Championships through high school and college. I was the only high school athlete to ever win State in two sports in the same year; swimming and tennis. I then was lucky to go on a full tennis scholarship to college. But as a backdrop, which really formed my youth, my mother got very sick when I was young. She lost her kidneys and was on dialysis when we were at home. My father ran her as his patient. My Mom ultimately died when I was young. My father raised me and was super supportive, and told me all of the positive things about how 'you can do whatever you want.' This was in the day that women were coming out in equality.

George Green: What did your father do?

MK Zordani: He was in real-estate; a big business. But when my mother passed he became so sad. So, it was he and I most of my life. I went to Crown Point high school where I graduated with thirteen major letters, which no one ever did in the country. Tennis, gymnastics, swimming, and cheer-leading; I was busy constantly. I went on a full-ride scholarship to Franklin College, a small private school right outside of Indianapolis. I did really well as a tennis player and became one of the top five ranked women college tennis players in the country. When it was time to graduate I got a sponsor, 'Head', which is a tennis company, sponsoring me to play professional tennis. My father told me before he passed away, "You're a great tennis player, but you have a brilliant mind." His family was too poor to send him to law school or college, so he went to college at night. He said, "You should focus on your education; you can always play tennis." He always held lawyers in such high esteem. So, I applied and got into law school and went to Valparaiso University law school in Indiana. After your first year of law school, if you are one of the top academic players, you can apply to second year program in London sponsored through Notre Dame, which I applied for and was awarded. I did my second year of law school in London and graduated. Between law school and undergrad, I took a year off. My Dad was mourning the death of my Mom still, so I had to go home and attended to his affairs. I spent several months in Greece just traveling around. I got my pilot's license. There were a few things I really wanted to do during that time. So I did them, then I started law school. When I graduated from Valparaiso, because my name was so well-known in the sports world, I was recruited by a lot of my home town law firms. I was recruited by Goldsmith, Goodman, Ball and Van Bokkelen. I went to work for them and I saw how the business world worked and how much business I was generating. I realized I was in the wrong place. I felt like I should be running the law firm instead of just generating the business. So I had a meeting with my bosses, and I said, "I don't think that this is a fair arrangement." They said, "It's as fair as you're going to get. You're a first-year out of law school." I left that firm with one file; a friend that had slipped and fell at a wedding reception. I was on my own. I didn't have family; no relatives. I was alone.

I took an office at the top of a new building in our area. I decided I would deck the office out as spectacularly as I could and then I sat there and worried about how I was going to pay the electric bill. As luck would have it, one of my close friends got a divorce and she retained me. It became a media blitz, where I was being televised constantly because of what had transpired between the two of them. All of a sudden, I became well-renowned and known as being as tough as nails. It was mainly because I was so desperate. I just wanted to do the best job I could because I needed to survive. I wanted to help people. I struggled for a short time. Then I had another friend that in Chicago got into an accident, and it was a federal case in Chicago. It was a severe injury. It was the first time I was in federal court. My client was awarded one of the bigger judgments at that time, in the late 80's, early 90's. So, I went from struggling to all of a sudden becoming pretty successful, and then I just grew and grew. I decided to be flamboyant. I had the most beautiful office; I had the most over-the-top home.

George Green: Were you single at the time?

MK Zordani: Single my whole life. I built a reputation just being as tough as tough could be. But I still had some friends in the tennis world. Vitas Gerulaitis invited me to come to Florida to hit with him, so I did. We were in Turnberry in Miami. Donny Soffer, who owned Turnberry at the time, came over and said, "You're a Chicagoan. I'm having a party." Chicago guys were betting in this big golf tournament. I go to the golf tournament and a guy walks up to me and says, "You see that guy across the room..." (he was so gorgeous), "...he's single; a real big shot in Chicago. He's got a ton of money. You should date him." I looked at him and I thought, 'This man is gorgeous.' So, I walked up to him and said, "You are so handsome. Would you like to go out with me?" He said, "Yeah, I would!" So we went back to Chicago and went out for a while. His name was Gerry Zordani. He was flying me here, flying me there, and I thought, 'This is good, but I have a business to run.' So, as wonderful as his life was, the timing was not right. I went about my own life. Ten years later, I have really built something of myself. I was single, earning my living and all of a sudden I became kind of a big shot. I was proud.

George Green: How big was the law firm?

MK Zordani: I couldn't have partners. I didn't work well like that. I had people that came in as independent contractors. They got the benefit of my entire physical plant, my entire staff. I didn't charge anybody rent, but I...

George Green: Took a percentage of their wins.

MK Zordani: Yeah, it worked well for me. We had as many as twenty-five lawyers at one time.

George Green: That's a big firm.

MK Zordani: It was way too big. So, ten years go by and my phone rings. My receptionist says, "Ms. Thanos, there's a Zor Dani on the phone." The guys at the Board of Trade only refer to themselves by their last name... she thought Zor was his first name and Dani was his last name. I pick up the phone and I said, "Ger?" And he said, "Yeah, I was wondering..." (this is when the Bulls were in the play-offs) "...I've got seats on the floor. You want to go to a Bulls game?" I said, "Have you looked at a calendar? I haven't heard from you in 10 years." I figured I'd do it. We went to the Bulls game and it was nice. He calls the next day. He says, "I've got a box at the Kentucky Derby. You're on the way; I'll have my driver pick you up." I thought, 'Okay, I'll try this.' So, we're driving down the 1-65 towards Kentucky, we're chit-chatting and I said, "You know, Ger, you have the cutest little lisp." He said, "I don't have a lisp." I said, "Yeah, you have a cute lisp. There's nothing to be embarrassed about. Hey, I got my nose fixed, did you notice?" He said, "You think I'm blind? Of course I noticed." I must have had a Greek nose, who knows? So, from that point on, we were never apart. They say timing is everything, and that was kind of our timing. Now, Gerry's twenty-three years older than me. He's done everything there is to do. He really hadn't worked in... forever, so after we got together he said, "I really think we should get married." I said, "Well, I'm not interested in kids." So, back track to the year I took off before I went to law school; I was sitting in Santorini, looking down and I said, "I don't think I'll ever get married. But if I do, I want to get married right here." That's where we got married.

George Green: And you rode the donkey up the side of the hill.

MK Zordani: Absolutely. Ger's life was all about playing golf with his buddies at the Board of Trade, and gambling and playing golf, and I kind of felt like I was getting left out a bit. So, he said, "Here, try hitting a golf ball." I never owned a set of golf clubs; I never hit a golf ball before in my life. I said, "Well, okay." I knew I had good hand-eye coordination!

Then he said, "About that law practice of yours... I want to go to Palm Springs and retire. You've made all the money you could make. We don't need anything. You need to wind this business down." Well that was no easy feat. It took years and I wound it down. In the meantime I learned that I could play this game of golf. I was only playing summer times because I was still working. Ger belonged to a bunch of clubs, and I was winning the club championship at every club that I played at.

George Green: And you really picked the game up quickly.

MK Zordani: Yeah, I started shooting in the 80's and then all of a sudden I was, from the women's tees, playing in the 70's. The guys wouldn't play with me from the women's tees. I had to play from the men's tees. So, I learned very quickly that it was important to hit the ball long, and how to hit the woods from the fairway.

George Green: You went from one spotlight to another. It went out on your law practice, but you immediately were in another one. You never had it down.

MK Zordani: At the end of my practicing, I have to be honest, I hated it. I hated everything that went along with it. I hated the stress of it all. While I was working to pay the electric bill it had a whole different feel to it, and then once it became everything and more, it was just too much for me.

George Green: So you're really looking back at the stress you endured while you were a lawyer, versus the kind of life you have now that is stress free and full of fun.

MK Zordani: Absolutely! I feel blessed and honored to have this life. As far as the golf goes, Ger did it, he taught me to golf. I picked it up, now I compete and I'm one of the top senior players in the country.

George Green: Your tennis, your flying; it seems to me that when you get interested in something there's an intensity to be the best at that event.

MK Zordani: Some people don't understand that. If you're not a competitive person, you don't understand. Now that I'm fifty I have the senior events. I want to be the best senior in the country. I don't want to be one of the top five best seniors, I want to be the best. And so I keep practicing, I keep living and making myself happy doing that.

George Green: You're so motivated all the time but nobody handed it to you, you had to work for it. What advice would you give?

MK Zordani: Well, what really propelled me is I try not to have negative people or negative feelings surround me. I like to have people that are positive; a positive reinforcement. Back away and leave any negative type of aura, and always think positively. Even in the face of some real negative things that have happened to me, losing family, losing parents, not having people... you just try whatever it takes, whether it's through your Rabbi or Pastor; find some positive place in your life. It's worked with me, having a positive place to look or a positive place to go has motivated me. Get rid of the negative, look at the sunshine always.

Dr. Nathan Sperling

A surfing accident changed this man's life

Nathan Sperling grew up in East Los Angeles then moved to Beverley Hills. For over twenty-eight years he was a popular and successful dentist in Beverly Hills with a large client base, some of whom were well-known celebrities and personalities. Nathan (Nate) was considered one of highest-earning dental surgeons in the country soon after he developed a unique practice in restorative and cosmetic dentistry. This practice allowed an estimated year's-worth of dentistry to be completed in a single day, under hospital conditions using light anesthesia.

Dr. Sperling was the President of the Association of Hospital Dentists. He appeared on television shows and attended societal functions held by his celebrity patients. He enjoyed a bright spotlight throughout most of his career.

At the age of fifty-years-old, Nate suffered a severe neck injury during a surfing accident in Hawaii. At first the injury was presumed to be only a sprain or strain. However, despite attempts to discover the nature of the injury, it did not improve. Soon he lost control over one of his legs. After a late visit with a neurologist, Nate learned he was moving into paralysis; a disc was pressing down on his spinal cord and had begun to cut into the cord itself.

There was a chance that the process could be halted by surgery, but doctors refused to predict the result. After the operation, it was determined that Nate would require at least six months of therapy.

In the meantime he sold an interest in his practice to a colleague, to keep the office from folding. He also understood that his physical condition would not allow him practice law (which he wanted to pursue), or teach dentistry ever again.

Through all this, he rearranged his life around his family now, instead of around his occupation. Although his accident had put an end to the spotlight he found himself under during his career, he did find a new perhaps more satisfying beginning. Today he lives with his wife, Elaine, in their home in Beverley Hills. They travel together and enjoy their lives to the fullest.

Interview with Nathan Sperling

George Green: You had a very big practice and it was successful. You were in practice for how long?

Nathan Sperling: Almost thirty years. I was in the top-ten dentists in the United States as far as level of income.

George Green: What kind of lifestyle did you enjoy?

Nathan Sperling: In Beverly Hills we had a lovely home. I structured my practice so that I took a week off a month, or if I couldn't I would save the weeks up and take two or three weeks off every three or four months. We traveled all over the world.

George Green: You took care of a lot of famous people in Hollywood.

Nathan Sperling: We took care of a lot of people in the entertainment industry. At the time these people wanted to be your friend. We were invited to social functions, weddings; sitting at tables with their physicians, plastic surgeons and dentists. I was interviewed on TV talk shows...

George Green: You got a lot of recognition for the job you did.

Nathan Sperling: Yes. I was the president of the American Association of Hospital Dentists. At the time I thought, 'This is great.' Then on one of our travels to Hawaii I went body-surfing, misjudged the depth of the water; I didn't realize it was as shallow as it was. My head hit the bottom and snapped my neck back. I remember feeling like when you hit your elbow and you get the electric shock. It seemed to go down my neck, down my arms, into my body. Luckily there were people around. I got up onto the beach but every time I moved I got an electric shock.

George Green: How concerned were you?

Nathan Sperling: I realized I hurt something but thought I had sprained. I didn't realize it was something that was going to be going on and on. I thought it would get better.

George Green: You had no idea that accident would change your life.

Nathan Sperling: No.

George Green: When did you first discover that you had a serious injury?

Nathan Sperling: After the CAT scans it didn't get better. I was on several methods of treatment. I tried to walk up three steps and my legs gave out from under me. I had no pain but my legs didn't work.

George Green: You weren't working at that point.

Nathan Sperling: I tried to go back to the office but I couldn't work properly. I couldn't function so I went to a neurologist. I was kind of dragged in. The neurologist finally said, "You have symptoms of paralysis." That shook the c--p out of me. Now I was taken everywhere by wheelchair to get these tests, more injections. It was all pretty bad. I had paralysis down into my arms. It got into my leg.

George Green: The doctor told you that you would be permanently disabled, is that correct?

Nathan Sperling: He said he wouldn't know until he went in and did the surgery. I couldn't move my left hand going into the surgery. I tried to move my left toe and I couldn't.

George Green: What was going through your mind?

Nathan Sperling: I broke down, cried by myself, prayed to God - not only for me but for my family. I was hopeless.

George Green: Now you come out of surgery. You had to start focusing on a different life, thinking about different things. You had to cope with your family. How did all of this happen?

Nathan Sperling: It took six months for me to reevaluate if I would be able to function in my capacity as a dentist.

George Green: You had no clue that you are going to have to stop.

Nathan Sperling: After the surgery I had to learn to walk again. The therapist tried to get me to pick up peas with my fingers. I could not pick things up with my hands. It took me six months to learn to walk and move. I couldn't really do what I used to do. I have to think about my practice. The doctors would stick needles down my neck to see if the nerves were there. There was a possibility they were never coming back.

George Green: At that point you decided you couldn't continue in that profession.

Nathan Sperling: Yes. I knew I would never be able to work again.

George Green: How did your family handle that?

Nathan Sperling: I thought about doing something else. I started in law school. It was very difficult. My hands didn't work. I couldn't write, I couldn't take an exam. I tried to do other things but I just couldn't get there. I tried to do dictation but I realized I wasn't going to be able to do it. People said, "Why don't you teach dentistry?" I was a doing person. I wasn't going to be able to do anything.

George Green: Were you emotionally down?

Nathan Sperling: My wife was livid because I was depressed. When the spotlight went out I realized a lot of my friends were friends because of my interactions with them in a professional manner. I realized they needed me in some way, in their professional lives. I realized that people that really cared about me where my immediate family. My wife felt good because, for the first time, she felt like I really needed her. I was always a person who didn't need anybody.

George Green: Now you're a dependent. That dependence brought you closer.

Nathan Sperling: Exactly. My wife said, "You know, maybe this is a blessing in disguise. This isn't when you wanted to retire, it's a little early." But I had enough investments. We changed our lifestyle a little. I decided I would live the rest of my life and try to really look at things and enjoy what I had as a person. We belong to a charitable organization where we are actually getting involved. The difference is I'm not in the limelight anymore. I don't know how many good years I have, but while I have them, I want to enjoy.

George Green: You've had twelve years of finding substitutes for the spotlight. How do you cope with that?

Nathan Sperling: It's different because you were in the limelight, almost like you were a celebrity. That's not there anymore. Some of my old patients say, "This is the guy that used to…" – it's more mellow, not those tremendous highs. I look at it and say, "I'm thrilled I can walk." Most people in this world get up in the morning and are grumpy and grouchy because they've got to do whatever they may or may not like. Hey - if you can't get up, if you can't move your feet over the bed, think of how great it is to go to the bathroom! Most people take that for granted. There was a long time I couldn't do those things; dress myself, tying my shoes. I'm thrilled that I can get up and function. I can drive a car. I can get places and do things. That is a whole different attitude.

George Green: Some parts of your life are better now than they were before.

Nathan Sperling: I definitely have a better relationship with close friends, with family. My wife and I have a relationship that is great because we're able to spend time and do things we couldn't do before because I was too busy.

George Green: What happened in law school?

Nathan Sperling: When I realized I couldn't do dentistry, I didn't want to give up the limelight. I was spending sixty or eighty hours a week trying to get through law school. The students would look up to me and call me Dad; they thought I was a genius!

George Green: So you were getting recognition then.

Nathan Sperling: I got the Book Award for being top of my class. But I realized I was killing myself. With my disability, I would've died one way or another. I thought, 'When I do graduate law school, I could be sixty years of age. Who is going to hire me…'

George Green: You were clinging to the spotlight and couldn't let go.

Nathan Sperling: I couldn't let go. I had to have something. I finally had to drop out of law school with the realization that it wasn't going to work. I would have lost my physical abilities because I was putting in so much time that I didn't have time to stretch, to exercise. I dropped out of law school and changed my life along with my family and friends, and started to structure and work on my body. That's when everyone turned around. To let go of the spotlight was really difficult. I was unhappy in my former life, I was looking to retire between fifty-five and sixty. I would slowly phase down - kind of a little dream - and then it short-circuited. I truly believe it was a blessing in disguise.

George Green: What would be your advice to someone who was thrown out of the spotlight and endured some personal trauma?

Nathan Sperling: For me, it's finding a circle that you do have; your immediate family? There has to be something that motivates you, that makes you feel good about the fact that you're here. For me, I think it's the fact that we give. We give and feel good about whatever little thing it is we are doing. If you feel good about something, if you are helping, there is a reason for you to be around. You got to have a goal. I get up every day and if I can move my feet and my hands and go to the bathroom, I'm ahead of the game.

An Update Note From Nate, August 2014

"Even though I am considered totally disabled and cannot practice in my profession, I've been very fortunate that I can function and live a fairly normal lifestyle. During my work years, I invested in assets that gave me passive income. Fortunately, that took the pressure off of how I would support myself and my family.

I exercise routinely to keep in shape physically. I can walk fairly well and, if necessary, I use a cane when I need to walk up or down steep inclines or long distances. I have had the time to share in much of my family events and therefore have developed a much closer relationship with my wife, my three daughters and my four grandchildren. We have a number of close friends that we socialize with, and we enjoy going to Palm Desert several times during the winter to be with our friends from out of town. I look forward to every day that I wake-up, and I enjoy the life I have!"

Clancy Imislund

Intoxicated by the Holy Spirit

Clancy Imislund was born in Eau Claire, Wisconsin, in 1927. His early years were troubled and he spent most of them alone. At the age of fifteen he ran away from home, wanting to join the merchant marines. After lying about his age, claiming he was sixteen, he was accepted. However, on a personal level, he had to 'pass the test' with the other marines. "To be a man," they'd say, "you have to hold down your drink." Clancy couldn't hold down any liquor at first, but 'sheer determination' helped him 'knock back a few' without them coming up again.

After the war he returned to Wisconsin where he attended the University of Wisconsin. Unfortunately, Clancy had chosen to stand firm with his new friend, Liquor. Consequently, a moment of misguided frustration led to him being expelled from the university and never graduating. Alcohol led him on a downward spiral that even landed him in jail on numerous occasions.

At the age of twenty-one, Clancy met Charlotte Koehler whom he married. Throughout their time together they brought six children into the world.

After pursuing a number of jobs, including sports-writing for his local paper, he went on to work in advertising with Tracy Locke in Dallas, hoping to earn more to support his family. However, due to his drinking problem, as with his other jobs Clancy was inevitably fired. When he returned home, Charlotte had taken their children and left without leaving a forwarding address.

Clancy attempted to take his own life at the age of twenty-nine after his son died, and ended up in an asylum as a result. After he left the asylum he slowly made his way to Los Angeles, where he ended up on Skid Row.

He discovered The Midnight Mission (an organization dedicated to serving and providing for the homeless, as an independent social service agency), but after rudely 'demanding' a breakfast from an employee, he was asked to leave. Clancy soon realized that no one really cared whether he lived or died, and that he needed serious help.

In October, 1958, Clancy was told about a small rehab center in LA where he may be able to receive the help he needed. Indeed, actor Bob Bailey was there and he agreed to sponsor Clancy's rehabilitation. Bob did everything necessary and told Clancy each day to change his actions. He said, "If you change your actions long enough, your attitude catches up."

Clancy found stability and began working in odd jobs, sometimes against his wishes yet under Bob's advice. Once Clancy had found a job he could hold down, Bob suggested he reconnect with his family by sending them money at first. Clancy didn't know where they were until, one Christmas, he received a card from his daughter and on the back was a return address.

After five years of being sober, Clancy was able to start at a great job as director of advertising for a medical corporation. At that time he reunited with his family in Los Angeles. Clancy then moved on to become a highly-paid executive in a Beverley Hills publishing company.

In 1973 the manager of The Midnight Mission passed-away. Clancy felt drawn to the position and, with Charlotte's approval, he interviewed for the job. He was awarded the position which meant leaving the publishing company and receiving far less of a salary. Clancy never looked back and still works with the mission today.

Charlotte sadly passed-away in their home in September, 2012. In March, 2014, Clancy celebrated forty years of working with the mission.

Interview with Clancy Imislund

George Green: I have told you about the purpose of the book. I need you to give some advice on what you would say to young people.

Clancy Imislund: It seems, to me, the greatest problem in stepping out of the spotlight is depression and the tendency to quit. I think so much is bracing yourself, going through the bad days, doing what you have to do to survive. When I had difficult times, every fiber of my being just wanted to go to bed and pull the covers over my head. But sooner or later you have to get up and get something going.

George Green: How important is it to regain a goal?

Clancy Imislund: There are not a lot of long-term goals. Just get through the day.

George Green: How important is having a partner in your life?

Clancy Imislund: I wondered if I did the right thing by getting together again, because we had grown apart significantly. My children began raising hell. In my life my parents' divorce caused me to run away at fifteen, and I didn't want that to happen to my kids. So I said, "We'll get settled."

George Green: Before you graduated, what happened when you went on to several jobs?

Clancy Imislund: I enjoyed drinking as a young man. For years I controlled it and then it started getting a little out of control, especially at University. I was doing quite good. I won some trophies and so on, but I got a blank diploma. My English history class was first thing in the morning; I didn't get to it very often, so I received an 'incomplete'. I had to go to English history in summer school. Then I was hired to teach journalism at the Duluth Denfeld high school in Minnesota. I got a job working nights. I would go to bars at night and drink until they closed. One night, this woman came in. I was explaining how the University had screwed me around. She didn't quite believe that I had won all of these trophies. So I said, "I'll show you." We went down to the University and I kicked in a pane of glass to the administration building. She was amazed by it. I thought she had slumped to the floor in surprise; I thought she had a flat tire! I was trying to pump her up when a policeman's flash illuminated us and he arrested us. We had to go to court the next morning. Before court started, this guy brought in a box from the University with all my personal effects, with a note from the Dean that said, 'I told you, you can't handle your alcohol. I begged you to keep it under control but you can't. You have made it impossible for me to retain you. You are expelled from university.' So, I got a job at the newspaper as a sportswriter. I married a charming young lady. We had a girl. I couldn't afford to be out of work, so I got a job with a company in the advertising department. For the next few years I fought to control my drinking.

George Green: You always thought you could quit.

Clancy Imislund: Yeah. I didn't want to quit because quitting made it intolerable; sobriety seemed unattainable. I had a bunch of kids, all born in different states, in different places. I had some good jobs and some bad jobs. My last job was with Tracy Locke in Dallas.

George Green: That was the seventh job you got fired from, because of drinking.

Clancy Imislund: I either got fired or quit in a rage, or 'emotional explosion'. I was a walking time-bomb. I got fired in Dallas and my wife and children left me. They took my car.

George Green: Talk about the suicide attempt.

Clancy Imislund: That was before. I used to go to jail once in a while because I found it necessary to counsel police officers, pointing out their deficiencies! I came out one morning and a neighbor told me my son died while I was in there. I quit drinking that time. I put my head on his casket and stopped drinking. Drinking will never replace the bad feelings. One day I parked my car in the garage and tried to commit suicide out of desperation.

George Green: And somebody saved you.

Clancy Imislund: They pulled me out, beat on my chest and sent me to hospital where they determined I was mentally ill. They put me in an insane asylum in Texas. Then I got a good job in advertising and spoke at the advertising convention. I blew up there and they fired me. By this time, this 'guy' had given me this car to drive to Los Angeles. I got as far as Phoenix and lost the car and went to jail. The guy kicked my front teeth out.

George Green: You finally end up meeting the right man who straightens you out.

Clancy Imislund: He explained the nature of my problem to me. He said, "You're an alcoholic." I said, "No, my problem really isn't alcohol." He said, "An alcoholic isn't a person whose 'problem' is alcohol; it is a person whose 'answer' is alcohol. I began to understand. Quitting drinking does no good unless you have something to replace it with.

George Green: You had ups and downs for all those years.

Clancy Imislund: I would go into terrible depression. That is long gone now.

George Green: Your life changed when you took that job at The Midnight Mission.

Clancy Imislund: My life changed long before this. I worked around, I had good jobs, I had a pretty good advertising record because of my background. I wanted to help people who were in my situation. I found it gratifying and, so, I have been here for a long time.

George Green: You look back only to demonstrate what 'hell' is.

Clancy Imislund: Right! I find people living in those same situations; absolute confusion and loss. I can sometimes guide them out if they believe that I know how they feel. My greater role is trying to help a crowd of people to just learn how to exist in the world; to survive.

George Green: What makes you happy these days?

Clancy Imislund: When I see people change and they start to get a life; watching the light come out of their eyes.

George Green: How important is it to be busy every day, like you are?

Clancy Imislund: Very important! It seems the busier I am, the more I can do. There is that old saying, 'If you have something to be done, give it to the busiest guy you know. He'll get it done!'

Brief Update Interview with Clancy Imislund, May 2014

George Green: Fill me in on what life is like for Clancy Imislund right now.

Clancy Imislund: Well, since we last talked, my life has stayed pretty much the same. The last few years I've been a little more active in my speaking schedule. I've been to such exotic places as Bali, Bangkok, Rio de Janeiro, Scandinavia and Canada. I'm still basically doing the same things. I go to work every morning at The Midnight Mission.

George Green: You're speaking to AA chapters around the world, are you not?

Clancy Imislund: Yes. My life has changed in one way, rather significantly. About a year and a half ago my wife suddenly passed away, which is not terribly unusual because she was in her eighties. The fact is that it makes me have to adjust to living alone, which is not as easy as I thought it would be. But I have some dogs. We hold fort out there, and do the best we can.

George Green: I lost my wife about eight years ago, and I have two dogs. As you know, life does go on and we do the best we can.

Clancy Imislund: That's right. I must say it is always a pleasure when I come in from the store at night, to have my dogs there wagging their tails and saying, "Welcome home!"

George Green: When you speak in front of AA chapters, do you find any differences now?

Clancy Imislund: No, I don't think so. Alcoholics are rather all the same in the way they look different on the outside, and they act different. But you get down to a certain level of humanity inside of all of them, and you see they're all the same. They respond to the same stimuli and they respond to the same aspects of recovery, which I try to talk about to make the recovery a little easier, and guide them into recovery to help them. So that's what I do every day.

George Green: How long have you been at the mission now?

Clancy Imislund: I've been here just over forty years. I didn't think I would be here all this long, I thought it would just be a while. I may be bound and hog-tied to get out of here.

George Green: What turns you on at this age?

Clancy Imislund: I enjoy reading a great deal. I enjoy music. I enjoy sports. I don't enjoy a well-turned ankle as much as I used to! Just the usual ramifications of life have always been pleasant to me. Let me send you off with this wonderful story. Early in January I was getting up early in the morning, 6:00am, still dark, going to get the paper off my front porch. I tripped over one of my dogs who was sleeping in the wrong place. I broke my finger in a couple places. It was such an unsatisfying story to say, "I tripped over my dog." I finally had to create a more impressive story, which I just told to my confidants. I said, "I was in the elevator at City Hall, coming down from the top floor. The first few floors I was riding down by myself in the elevator and, suddenly, the elevator stopped. A woman got on who had the largest bosom I'd ever seen. So, I tried to avert my face so I wouldn't gawk. We went a few more stories and she said, "Would you mind pressing one for me?" So I leaned over; I said, "No, not at all." She hit me with her purse!

George Green: Well, you keep pressing number one, because that's the floor to get off at.

Clancy Imislund: You bet, George. You take care of yourself now!

John and Judy Bedrosian

Keep it in court until you win!

John Bedrosian was born in Troy, New York, and moved to California in 1948. He graduated from UCLA in 1956, and then enrolled in the USC School of Law where he received his LL.B in 1959. At USC he served as the Student Bar Association president.

John first came under a major spotlight in 1969 when he cofounded 'National Medical Enterprises' with Richard (Dick) Eamer and Leonard Cohen. The aim of the company was to develop and own hospitals and healthcare facilities. Richard had previously worked in a law firm that belonged to Leonard, hence their connection. Richard and John's practice (the Law Firm of Eamer and Bedrosian) was one that operated in the medical field, and so they had an existing client base to work with. The company grew rapidly and, in a short space of time, entered into the New York Stock Exchange, being worth a whopping 5.5-billion dollars. They expanded further, eventually covering nursing homes and psychiatric facilities, operating three-hundred medical facilities with over ninety-thousand employees. In the company, John held the title of Senior Executive Vice President.

As they expanded, however, new faces came to the company via acquisitions. One of the companies moved in a direction that placed NME in a negative spotlight. The move was likened to fraud, and before long NME nosedived due to the negative effects caused by media. Changes were made throughout which included both Richard and Leonard taking their retirement. Not long after that, John received his marching orders and was given only three days to pack up his belongings and leave. John had built the company from very little and had worked hard at it for twenty-four years; it was all he loved. The comfortable life he and his family knew slowly turned uncomfortable. Having to file law suits related to wrongful termination and breach of contract, among others, everything began to turn upside-down. The case went on for as long as seven years, through appeal after appeal.

Fortunately John had a wonderful family and wife, Judy. The timing couldn't have been worse for them, either, as it was at this time that they were experiencing hardships with their son. They were forced into making decisions they'd never considered they'd need to.

John and Judy luckily had a few investments that helped them through this time, however, and John still held shares in NME. Although they lost a great deal, they managed to survive. Before long, John was approached with a business proposition which would become the internet's largest 'new and used car buying service'. The business took off almost as quickly as NME had, and they were back on their feet again. John served as 'Auto-by-tel's' chairman from 1995 to 1999. He claims that although it wasn't the same as working with NME, it was equally satisfying with one of the perks being that he didn't need to drive into work each day!

Seven years after the first court case regarding John's wrongful termination started, the California Court of Appeals finally gave him the winning decision. Due to the position he'd held, he was granted monetary compensation. Considering he'd kept his shares in NME for ten years, the monetary reward turned out to be more than 160-million dollars.

He began to focus on his personal business investments and a number of charitable endeavors, and thus became a philanthropist. John claims that his success came through understanding, living and working in an open and democratic society. Since 1983 he's been a member of SPPD's (School of Policy, Planning and Development) Board of Councilors. In 2005, John and Judy endowed the Judy and John Bedrosian Center on Governance and the Public Enterprise at the USC School of Policy, Planning and Development (recently renamed the USC Price School of Policy). The purpose of the center is to examine the nature of democratic governance and learn how to improve it at every societal level. Also in 2005, John joined the board of directors of Oaks Christian School in Thousand Oaks, a position he still holds.

In 2006 the SPPD presented him with the 2006 PPD Guardian Award for vision and leadership, an award which honors alumni and supporters who have shown dedication and leadership toward the betterment of their communities and the world around them.

John has also served as president of the Federation of American Health Systems, as well as on the boards of the Los Angeles Chamber of Commerce, the California Business Round Table, the Healthcare Leadership Council and the American Hospital Associations board of directors. He still serves on the board of NIT and the NIT Foundation. The name of these changed recently to Mendez National Institute of Transplantation (MNIT) and Mendez National Institute of Transplantation Foundation (MNIT Foundation).

Both John and Judy remember clearly the transitions they went through together, and how crisis brought them closer as a family. At the same time, they developed their faith and became stronger this way. Ultimately this led to John having a strong presence in the Bel Air Presbyterian Church. He consequently served as the Chair of the Personnel Committee for more than a decade, and as President for more than ten years.

Despite their many ups and downs, some that veered in the direction of financial crisis, some that involved personal family crisis; John and Judy continued to find new mountains to climb and move from one spotlight to another. They certainly got what they deserved in the end and, being who they are, chose to give much of it back to the community. Today they live happily in Bel Air, still participating in the church and working at what they love. John claims that even at his age, he has never been busier. All he hopes to find time for now is the book he wishes to write.

Two interviews are included below; the first being John's story and second, Judy's.

Interview with John Bedrosian

George Green: Tell me about NME and the spotlight you had. What was going on in your life at that point?

John Bedrosian: How to condense twenty-four years into a few minutes? NME was a company, National Medical Enterprises, that was an idea of a friend of mine that I met in Law School at USC, Dick Eamer. We got out of school; we were practicing law. Dick had some clients who wanted to build a hospital and he got the idea to put together a company to develop hospitals; to own and operate hospitals and healthcare facilities. His practice was heavily oriented to that area when he was practicing law after graduation. When he got close to doing something with that idea, he came to me and he came to a third fellow, Leonard Cohen, for whom he used to work. Essentially, long story short, the three of us put the company together. The way we created it was to take our existing clientele, the Law Firm of Eamer and Bedrosian, and be heavily oriented to the medical side. We had clients, hospitals, doctors, partnerships and so on. We literally cannibalized the practice to put together the company. The company was created in May, 1969, starting with four acute hospitals, three convalescent hospitals, some parcels of property upon which we were later to develop buildings, and we started off doing business. The company, over the years, was in the right place at the right time. The growth was significant. We became a New York Stock Exchange company, at one time employing as many as ninety-thousand people. We grew to about 5.5-billion dollars. We got into home care. We got into nursing homes. Got into psychiatric...

George Green: You said 5.5-billion.

John Bedrosian: Billion with a 'b'. It was a wonderful run in terms of opportunity, development, growth. I got to go all over the world meeting all kinds of interesting people.

George Green: What was your job?

John Bedrosian: My job was primarily the outside person for the company. I was responsible for all of our industrial relations programs, our government relations activities, and public affairs issues, public relations. I also dealt with administrative matters of the company. I was on the Board. I was on the Executive Committee of the company. My title was Senior Executive Vice President. I spent a lot of time with Dick as CEO, getting involved with a lot of operational issues and matters. But officially I was the outside man. In fact, I was involved in all the major decision making of the company. Dick had a hearing problem, still does, and I think it was helpful to him because he trusted me. We go back a long way. We had a trust. So, he knew that I was his ears to a degree.

George Green: Once you started expanding from `69, when did life really start to become good for you?

John Bedrosian: You're talking economically.

George Green: Economically, image-wise, position-wise, possession-wise...

John Bedrosian: I would say in the early 80's; `81, `82, in there.

George Green: Those were big years.

John Bedrosian: Yeah. In the 80's a lot of things happened. We matured as a company. We had acquired significant size. Our stock was always a good buy. So, yeah, I was on top of the world in the 80's, traveling around, ultimately in a G-4. I never traveled commercially for twenty years.

George Green: For twenty years you had your own airplane; your own pilot.

John Bedrosian: Yep. We had two airplanes, a whole aviation department, three/four pilots and we went everywhere by means of that corporate aircraft, including vacations for which we paid to keep the IRS happy. It was a very enjoyable way to live. We lived and moved hard and fast. It was a lifestyle that, being a guy whose parents came to this country on a boat; you would never dream that you could reach that level. Home in the desert. Home in Aspen. Home in Bel Air... and a lodge in Alaska.

George Green: So life was really good. The family basked in your protection and glory, did they not?

John Bedrosian: They surely did. A family with three kids, they had a wonderful upbringing because they had a lot of opportunity. They learned to enjoy that lifestyle, which is not always good. Trying to teach them values is not always easy when they're flying around in a private jet, going to wonderful places. That was the challenge to us, as parents. But Judy and I did the best we could. It was a very wonderful time. I never really hit a bump in the road of life until just before the NME experience, where I was chairman of the board of a bank and it got into trouble because the president was doing things we didn't know about as a Board. Long story short, that cost me some money but the real bump in the road came when the problems began at NME. I never had setbacks of any significant nature.

George Green: Tell me about the bump.

John Bedrosian: One of the acquisitions we made in the 80's was a company that ran psychiatric hospitals called 'Psychiatric Institutes of America', and for ten years they were a wonderful addition to the company. At the beginning of 1990, 1991 that whole psychiatric hospital industry, it became apparent, was engaging in practices that were not ethical in my view. Managed-care was starting to cut inroads into the profitability of the operation, and management at that subsidiary level was on a bonus structure. The whole thing was not pleasant, particularly for three guys who thought they were as honest as anybody could be; starting a company, and growing it. We were also a company that the Wall street Journal, a year prior to that time, said was the white knight of the industry. We had a good reputation. A lot of flack came out of that.

George Green: Why the flack?

John Bedrosian: About the headlines of chasing after patients, billing for services not rendered. It was accusations of fraud. It was not pleasant and to compound it, the media picked up on it big time. There was a great big story, starting in Texas and running through the country. Oprah picked up on it. Business Week picked up on these accusations. Everyone did. The reason the government got involved, Medicare and the Justice Department; they said, "You are a lightning rod. We want to send the message to the whole industry. You're a big player in the industry and there's nobody better to throw a message out than to go after a big player and send out a statement about the practices that had grown in the psychiatric hospital industry." I'm not talking about legalities, I'm talking about perceptions. It was ugly. It got to the point where the insurance carriers, who paid our bills after all, filed a law suit that in essence squeezed on the company to the degree that you had to make peace or you would go out of business. They would stop paying you, or get involved in litigation forever. It was a very tough time; '91, '92, '93. Very hard years on the company. Obviously the stock took a beating and the shareholder institutions were unhappy and, of course, the classic solution to a problem of that type is to change the management. Our Board, which was made up heavily of 'friends'; our Board upon advice of outside counsel picked up on that theory and idea, and they asked the two senior associates of mine, Dick and Leonard; they negotiated a settlement package with them and asked them to leave. After much discussion, the Board asked me at the same time to stay on, and I agreed to. My thinking was that I was fifty-eight-years-old. I wasn't happy about the blemish on our reputation. I thought if I stayed a few years I could help fix things and then I would move on to something else. We brought in a new CEO who was on our Board. He was an old time former banker of ours, investment banker from Merrill Lynch, Jeff Barbicow. We brought Jeff on. He came on June 1, 1993. Dick and Leonard left in June. To make a long story short, Jeff gave me a notice of termination without cause, meaning I did nothing wrong under my contract. He wanted to terminate me and that was in September of '93. So, beginning September 24th, I guess, I was on the street, so to speak, and I was given all of three days to vacate my office.

George Green: Had you given any thought to retirement?

John Bedrosian: Never once. Many times Dick and I would have conversations about; "This company has been so good to us and we've benefited and we've grown, and we're going to be here until we're old men and they'll walk us out the door." Never once thought about it.

George Green: You loved what you did?

John Bedrosian: Absolutely. I was surprised that he gave me three day notice. I knew it was coming during the summer of '93. You could tell. All of a sudden people who normally reported to me were avoiding me. It didn't really affect me a whole lot because at the same time we were going through a personal crisis with our son, and that had my attention. I knew what was happening. I knew that Jeff was not wanting to involve me in the discussions and meetings. I wasn't anticipating the termination as such, but I knew I was being left out of stuff. I even talked to him once or twice and he just put it off. But I was so focused on the personal problem we were dealing with at home, with one of our children.

George Green: What was the first thing that went through your mind?

John Bedrosian: Well, the first thing that went through my mind was anger, obviously directed at him. When I had a conversation with him in my office in August, a few weeks before he gave me the notice, I said, "Jeff, the FBI visited the offices in conjunction with these investigations and they left." The day they came, he wasn't around and I was upset that he wasn't around. I thought he should be there. We had a conversation about my situation. I said, "Jeff, why are you creating a problem for the company. Dick and Leonard had a contract. You gave them a settlement package. Give me the same package and I'll go away." He said, "The shareholders would be very upset if I gave you the same economic package I gave them. Also, I don't want to be criticized by anybody for doing something at this point in time, when the company is under such attack." Those were his reasons. I said, "Then you're inviting a law suit or something like that because it's not fair. I put my whole life in this thing. I certainly expected to retire here, and you're taking that opportunity away from me for no reason." He didn't answer me. That was the last one-on-one conversation we had. Three weeks later, almost a month later, I was gone.

George Green: When you walked out of the building, do you remember how you felt?

John Bedrosian: I felt out of touch with reality. I felt like I was off in a fog somewhere, like it was happening to someone else, not me. It's not real. It was hard to believe that it could possibly happen.

George Green: What was the reaction of your family?

John Bedrosian: The three kids, they didn't verbalize much to me. I found out later that they were really shaken because the rock had been jarred. Judy was terribly shaken but she carried it very well. I'll tell you, the two years following the departure from the company, she got stronger as time went on to where she was a big help to me in processing all of this. She was madder than hell at the people responsible for this action. She wanted to get even. She wanted to get revenge. I thought that way, too, for a while. But she stayed strong for me and it sort of bonded us even better than we had been.

George Green: When you left what was the response from the people in the company, your close associates, your so-to-speak friends?

John Bedrosian: Are you talking about the people who came to court to testify against?

George Green: Against you?

John Bedrosian: That's what happened; the closest ones. A guy I traveled all over the world with, going to the banks in Europe and U.S., and the guy who really gave me all the lip service in the world; all of a sudden there was no communication there. I found out that all of my friends outside the company didn't waiver an inch. They're still there today. I didn't lose one. The people I thought were friends at the company all pulled tail. That's understandable. They were all scared. In many cases they were all afraid for their own existence. I was angry at first about that. Then I came to think about it. What would you do, John? Well, I might be a coward, too. I would hope I wouldn't be. But it is sort of cowardly... and on the other hand it's survival. It's a tough world. These guys, two of them, when they testified, things came out that I know they volunteered, which really made me angry. They didn't have to volunteer conversations I had with them, criticizing Jeff for things he had done. The only way they found that out was by volunteering it. I've never talked to them since. One of them gave me a phone call and said he would be out next week, can we talk. I said, "Sure." He never called. Never showed up.

George Green: But there are still some close friends over there that you still are close with?

John Bedrosian: Yes, there are some good people at that company.

George Green: Are there any lasting hurts or anger?

John Bedrosian: Nope. Nope. In all honesty it's gone. I don't know when it went, but it happened sometime. Don't live in the past, only in the future.

George Green: After you left, how long did it take you to create a new mountain and a new spotlight?

John Bedrosian: I think that I never lost any confidence in myself and my own abilities. I never felt that I was a failure. Ever. What happened when I left the company in September `93 was, all of my time was consumed in the lawsuit that my lawyer said I had to file. I agreed with him because he said we had a good case of Wrongful Termination and Breach of Contract. So, for six months I was living with my lawyer in the office and I was busier than hell just working on all that stuff. Then we went through the trial. It wasn't until the following August that I sort of had time to catch my breath and take a look, and take stock, and say, "Who are you and what are you doing." I shared office space with my niece's husband in Culver City. It was a terribly distasteful experience. He was in a construction-related business and I just didn't fit. But I was going down there, I had my desk there and files there and whatever. I was doing all personal stuff, pretty much. Then I moved to an office in Westwood and all I was doing was taking care of my personal affairs.

The thing that hurt me was the action the company took and the Board and everybody was backing out on me. But the other thing that hurt me was that I never got a call from the health industry; from anybody in the health industry to offer me an opportunity to get involved one way or another. I was the president of the association. I was on the board of the American Hospital Association which represents all non-profit hospitals in America. I think the reason was because of the negativism that the company had gotten and the press release when I was released. The innuendo in that press release was that I was somehow involved in the problems the company had. That was one of our counts for libel. I wasn't involved. I wasn't involved in the operations there at all, and I knew that... so I slept at night. Health industry is a tough business and I don't want to be anywhere near it.

George Green: What did you do to get emotionally well?

John Bedrosian: Well, I just started to network with people that I cared about and knew. I was not doing anything substantive at all. The real strength for my process was my faith. I got stronger in that instead of weaker. And so I was really okay. But I did think, 'What are you going to do. You have some assets, but you don't want to deplete your assets... if you want to continue to live the way you live.' I had a couple of business opportunities that I looked at that weren't very exciting. I invested in a small health company, and I still have the investment. As a passive investor I helped them and counseled them sometimes, and it's coming along nicely and slowly. I talked about another project, which is ongoing, with two guys where I was an investor. So I became an investor of sorts, to a limited degree, until I got to talking to Pete Ellis about Auto-by-tel.

George Green: When did you realize that you didn't have to stay busy every second; that it was okay to have a calendar that wasn't loaded with things every half hour?

John Bedrosian: That only happened within the last six months, and only in the last month or two have I gotten totally rid of the concept of feeling any guilt about playing golf on a weekday, or going to the golf course instead of sticking around here to do something else, or pick up a phone and talk to somebody! It's a work ethic that you and I were raised with. It's inbred. It took a long time. I realized that, 'Hey, you earned the right to not work like that, but you still want to keep your mind busy. You still want to be active.' Thank God I have this other opportunity that has kept me perfectly happy with the car business. It helps to be financially secure. No question about it.

George Green: If you weren't financially secure, if you had to work, emotionally it would be a little bit different?

John Bedrosian: It would have been tough. At one point I went to a counseling outfit who approached me. They called me, cold. I forgot the name of it. It's an interesting company. They work with higher-up executives, both in placement and in helping them start their own businesses if they want to, or whatever. I thought the company had referred them. But coincidentally she called me thinking I was still with the company, and was going to ask me if I knew of any executives who might use their service. I said, "Yeah, me." I worked with them and their people. I had an interesting conversation and went to a couple of their workshop sessions. But the more I did that the more I realized that it was not me, because I'm my own man. Even though I was the number three guy in a big company, I'm on the top of the shelf. So, I didn't want to look for a job. And, again, I was fifty-eight-years-old; where are you going to start? They're not going to get you in the health industry where you know everything. Where else are you going to go? Then I realized that the only pressure on me was recognizing that we had resources but they were limited, to the extent that I had no new income coming in. For a long time after I left, the company was holding on to what stock I had. I couldn't sell it. We were able to work that out about a year and a half after I left, so that eased a lot of economic pressure.

George Green: Give me a brief picture of this new spotlight, Auto-by-tel.

John Bedrosian: Auto-by-tel. The idea; it was the brainstorm of a friend of mine, Pete Ellis who used to be a very successful car dealer in Southern California. Peter had this idea. Peter had been through a rough time himself. He had to file bankruptcy in '94 and he hit bottom and went through a worse process than I did, because he was economically devastated, I wasn't. Long story short; we were skiing up in Aspen. We took him and his wife up there. He said, "I have this idea for a company." He showed me what he had and he said, "Do you have any interest in this?" I said, "You know, that's an interesting idea. Yeah, let's give it a try and see what happens." When we looked at the original projections, it looked like not much of an investment was necessary to find out if it was real or not. I said, "Okay." The whole concept is to create a network of dealers who would offer to sell cars at or very near their invoice cost to consumers who would put in an order on their computer through us. We market the request to the dealer. He calls up the customer and quotes a price. It's a very consumer-friendly concept. No charge to the consumer.

Charge the dealers a monthly fee, etc. It took off like gangbusters. I wound up putting a lot of money in it; a lot more than I could afford to put in, but luckily we got some capital infusion from folks like GE Capital and AIG Insurance. These are big companies who love the idea and they are involved with us as strategic partners. I have a new hill to climb; a new ride! But I'm chairman on this one and I don't work every day down there in Irvine.

George Green: Compare the two spotlights.

John Bedrosian: The one I have now I appreciate a lot more for what it is, because I have had the experience of what it represents; the opportunity for growth, the challenge of building something. The first time around you get up, you go to work, you work your tail off. You see it growing but you don't really step out of it to look at it. I didn't. This time around I can step back. The company is down in Irvine; I don't go down there every day. It's really a perspective I didn't have before. I was more of the 'financial background' for this one. I'm not involved in the middle of the operations on a day to day basis. I'm not the key decision maker. That bothered me for a while; that's the hard part - letting go of your decision-making authority. I've got people down at that company who are so grateful to me for funding it, and the knowledge that these people really do appreciate what I was able to do; it's very comforting. And so, where I am today, this is the second mountain that I've climbed. This is the third career. I was an attorney. I was in the healthcare business, and we were on the cutting edge of the healthcare business. We're on the cutting edge of changes in the automobile industry, big time. We're getting more attention from the manufacturers down the line; it's unbelievable.

George Green: You recently bought a spot in the Super Bowl.

John Bedrosian: We did. We are the first internet-based company doing commerce on the internet to advertise in the Super Bowl. It had amazing results. The ad really tripled our purchase requests in the first week. It was Pete's idea, again. He's a great marketing guy. I said, "You've got to be crazy to spend this kind of money. We can't afford this. We're a new company." Looking back on it; it was smart as hell. It worked!

George Green: So, the spotlight's becoming more intense.

John Bedrosian: It's not on me, individually. It's on the company and on Pete Ellis. We've got about one-hundred employees right now. It's great. I'm looking for the next hill after this one.

George Green: So there's always another mountain?

John Bedrosian: There's always another mountain.

George Green: What advice would you give to other people, not only executive types like yourself, but people that go into emotional transitions. What things would you suggest?

John Bedrosian: Number one, they should never lose faith in themselves. They should recognize that circumstances put them where they are; that they didn't do it to themselves. If you lose your self-esteem, you're in big trouble. You can't do that. Number two; they should know, and I used to hear this through my years of experience but I never really related to it... you should know that when you get through the chaos and look back, you'll find there was a reason for it and that you're in a better place than you were before, in one form or another. Not necessarily a better company, or bigger company, but you're going to be better off for the experience. I really believe that. I am happier today. I'm my own man for the first time in my life. When you're part of an organization, much as you think you're independent, on top, in charge; you're still surrounded by that organization. Now I'm dealing with things on my own, fully making my own decisions, fully responsible to myself and my family, alone. And that's a different place. It didn't scare me, but it was different. The experience of the ride of building this second company has been so much fun.

George Green: How about the rest of the family and Judy, how do they feel about you being the way you are today?

John Bedrosian: You'd have to ask the kids. I can't speak for the kids, really. I think Judy loves having me around more. We actually go to lunch together once in a while. Never did that in twenty-five years.

George Green: I think you found out your best friend is your spouse.

John Bedrosian: Big time. I never ever thought that before. We were married for a long time. We've been married thirty-six years. We are better friends today than we ever were. This crisis brought us closer. Crisis won't make you or break you. It will reveal you.

Interview with Judy Bedrosian

George Green: We've just heard a wonderful story about John and how he started. From your side, what was life like between `69 and `91?

Judy Bedrosian: It was a very good life. I hesitate to say that I ever acknowledged the fact that we were rich. That was not a word that I really like to use, but I think we were. John tells me we were rich and my kids used to say, "Are we rich?" I would say, "No, but we're comfortable." That's how I always looked at our lifestyle. But we did have wonderful perks. We had the airplane. I remember my mother once asking me, "What's it like to be rich?" I said, "It means that I can hire a limousine instead of taking a taxi." That's really... I had that luxury. We lived very nicely. But, again, I never thought of it as rich.

George Green: When the bumps started occurring, what was your reaction to that situation?

Judy Bedrosian: Well, all of a sudden the stock started to drop and I remember John was fishing and I was with my daughter. She had just gotten married in June and this was August, and she and I were watching Prime Time, and watching this whole story unfold.

John was out of town and he was not reachable by telephone, so I couldn't even ask him about it. They had done all these investigations into these nursing homes in Texas. It was just awful. However, I don't think I took it terribly seriously at that point. It was the following year when the stock really started to go down; it was down to about four-dollars. I wasn't frightened, but I was uneasy.

George Green: You were concerned about the future.

Judy Bedrosian: I was concerned a little bit about the future, but I had no idea that what ultimately happened was in the offing until perhaps the next year. As soon as Dick Eamer and Leonard left the company, that March, then I didn't really feel secure any longer. I thought the writing was on the wall and ultimately something was going to happen.

George Green: At that point you felt that maybe the security of the family and this great lifestyle was going to be threatened.

Judy Bedrosian: Yes, but I also knew that he had a contract, so I wasn't horribly concerned. I never really thought that he's going to get fired. We were having all the problems with our son so, you know, that was the main thing that was on our mind. But when it actually happened and we found out that the contract really was not going to be honored, and we were going to have a law suit, then I really did get scared.

George Green: How did you support him during that transition period?

Judy Bedrosian: I wasn't dealing with it in any manner up until Jeff took over. Then John was coming home with all these stories about what things were like at the office, and I kept trying to encourage him and trying to being his friend, help him out, do anything you can to make yourself as accessible and invaluable to him as you can. But, I guess it was really obvious to John, although he didn't want to say it to me, that Jeff really didn't want him there, had no use for him and really wanted him out so he could run things his own way. That I didn't have any problem with. It was the manner in which it happened, where not only was he terminated but he was the fall guy; this man who had never done anything untoward, and has an impeccable reputation... that hurts the most. It was just shock and yet we're trying to find the bright side of everything. We figured we had a great law suit, not that anybody wants to file a lawsuit, but we figured we had a great law suit. We were also fortunate enough to have two other houses. I kept telling John, "Do you think we should list the Bel Air house?" And he said, "No, we're okay for six months." I'd say, "I don't want to be okay for six months, I want to know that I'm okay forever or else I want to list this thing before we have to give it away. Let's give ourselves at least time to sell it at a good price."

George Green: So you felt financially threatened.

Judy Bedrosian: That's right. When you're not getting much in... we did get salary for one year because there was two years left on his contract. So, we got salary for one year and the second year they somehow used our salary to pay taxes. They arbitrarily did this, so we did not have that money coming in. If it wasn't for a really good investment that we have on some property, I don't know what we would have done. John's secretary always handled all of our financial stuff, and all of a sudden we didn't have a secretary and I got the discs and I started paying the bills. It gave me something to do. I also had a man living with us who had leukemia, and I think that was my saving grace because I concentrated on him a lot, so I didn't have time to think about everything else that was going on. I was able to keep sane for Tony and for John. I made up my mind that John had been through a lot of stuff with me. I've had a lot of problems. He has always been there for me and this was one time when I could be here for him, and not go into my role as being the needy, whimpering wife. I would look at my yard and I would put bird feeders out, and I would watch the birds in the morning. I think that was the most calming influence. It was like God was in my yard. When I saw those birds it was like I hadn't been deserted by the Lord; he was here.

George Green: You probably felt pretty good about being able to be there for john.

Judy Bedrosian: I felt good about being strong for him. I thought that this guy doesn't need a wailing wife in bed when he's got to get up every day... This has got to be harder for him than it's ever going to be for me. His ego is shattered. He has nowhere to move his stuff. To be told to get out of your office in three days and have to decide where all your stuff is going to go. It has to be packed. It has to be inventoried. It's got to go somewhere. He didn't need to be managing me, too. Yeah, it was time for me to grow up.

George Green: So, the experience was helpful?

Judy Bedrosian: It was the best thing that ever happened to us as far as our relationship and our marriage is concerned. I couldn't have said this three years ago.

George Green: So, out of adversity came strength. If you could have the old times back, what would you say?

Judy Bedrosian: I would say, "No! I couldn't do that again." This is good; it's great now because we have another mountain to climb. If we didn't have the new mountain to climb and we were still waiting to get a judgment, then I'm not too sure where I would be.

George Green: What other things did you do for emotional support and for strength in the family during the transitionary period?

Judy Bedrosian: Well, John and I started praying together. God became more important. He's always been important, but, we would share it together. John was always sort of uncomfortable with prayer even though he was raised a Christian as I was. We attended church and he had been an elder and all that stuff. But when the problems started with Chris and then accelerated into this, I mean, we just had nowhere else to turn. We turned to God. Let me tell you, it's the most wonderful thing that has happened to us. We pray for our friends who are going through stuff. We prayed for you when you were going through your stuff. We pray for our kids, our families, our friends whose marriages are in trouble or who are having financial difficulties, and we just sort of keep a mental list of who needs it, and it just helps us to feel good.

George Green: In conclusion, what advice would you give other spouses going through this, so that they could help their mate get through it?

Judy Bedrosian: Well, I think what I learned was when one door closes another door opens. Don't ever feel that this is the end of the world, because there are other great things going on. I wouldn't want John to go back to that company for anything in the world. You just have to wait. Always look for the blessing in everything. There always is a silver lining to every cloud. And stick by the person that you came to the dance with. You're there for the long haul, for better or for worse and sometimes it's worse, but it always gets better.

Brief Update Interview with John Bedrosian, May 2014

George Green: What's life like now? What new things are happening for you?

John Bedrosian: As far as church goes, besides the eleven years where I was President, last year our pastor was moving on, retiring, and going back to Denver. They asked me if I would consider chairing the personnel committee, because there would be a lot of issues that would go on while we did not have a leader, a senior. And so I, at first reluctantly, was happy to say, "Yeah," I would chair the personnel committee. I did it last year and they asked me to do it again this year. We got the new pastor, new senior, and he's only thirty-three-years old, a good guy. I'm working with him closely. I'm happy that I stayed in. That takes a little bit of time, obviously, and so I am still active in the church. As far as everything else goes, it's just between my daughter taking care of a lot of stuff for me, and then I'm still busier than I ever dreamed I would be at this point. But I'm just looking at other opportunities and trying to learn how to say, "No." That's the biggest thing I have to learn.

George Green: Not only that, you're trying to learn how to retire, I think.

John Bedrosian: Well, I think I am. Psychologically I think I'm ready to, but in terms of the program and the calendar and so on, it's not that easy. What I do enjoy doing a lot of, and I don't do enough of it, is I love to talk to young people and give them counsel and advice. I've been able to do that a little bit. Everyone wants to have lunch with me so they can pick my brain, thinking that I know something, and I don't tell them otherwise! I enjoy the opportunity to share whatever I've experienced with people, especially younger people. People I've run across over the years, they don't forget. They show up and they say, "I have this idea, what do you think about it?" or "I have this plan and I want to get your reaction to it," that kind of thing. So, I've been doing some of that. Bottom-line, I'm busier, as I say, than I ever dreamed I would be. I'm trying to get my book done which is taking longer than it should because of me!

Author's note: *John also serves as chairman of the Star Parker's Policy 'think tank', C.U.R.E. (Center for Urban Renewal and Education), based in Washington D.C.*

Sheldon Good

If the Statue of Liberty was for sale, he could sell it!

Sheldon Good was born in 1933, in Chicago. Life wasn't easy for him as a child, or his family, due to the depression. His parents would constantly remind him of the importance of receiving a good education, even though they weren't sure which career he'd one day choose to pursue. He became friendly with a young girl whose parents' careers were in the educational field. The relationship with the family played a large role in directing him to the importance of education. He turned his attention to excelling in all areas of high school, from Student Council to President of his class and becoming an 'A' student.

He graduated from the University of Illinois with a degree in Urban land Economics, and then enlisted in the United States Army where he served two years in Japan.

Soon he was married and found himself working for an established real-estate business that was well-known with a good reputation. Although he was doing well, he wasn't making the money he'd hoped he would. This changed when he met a friend who told him he should be working on larger projects in order to make bigger sales. At the same time, he took an interest in the auctioning industry and often wondered why realtors didn't spend more time auctioning properties rather than try selling them at a fixed rate.

After learning the tools of his trade he opened up his own company; Sheldon Good and Company. Selling commercial real-estate, and the introduction of the auction as a means of selling real-estate, was the company's brand. Through hard work and a questioning mind, Sheldon Good became the 'Father of the Real-Estate Auction' and the company became the foremost real-estate auction company in America. Soon he was being contacted by names such as Donald Trump and became internationally recognized. Sheldon went on to become a property expert for the United Nations, and obtained the title of World President of the International Real-Estate Federation. His portrait hangs at the University of Illinois, as the recipient of the Lifetime Achievement Award.

Sheldon Good lives part-time in Palm Springs and Chicago. He consults, is actively involved in the United Nations as an NGO in real-estate and considers himself a philanthropist, all of which he enjoys. He is a firm believer in preparation; "When preparation meets opportunity, this is known as 'Good' luck!"

Interview with Sheldon Good

George Green: Shelly, the microphone is yours. Go for it.

Sheldon Good: I was raised in Chicago, born in 1933, during the Great Depression. We were a modest family suffering during the recession. I went to grammar school, high school and college in the public schools, and enjoyed my life. During the war, when my mother worked with my father, I had a young sister who I took care of. We learned to fend for ourselves. I was an athlete; not a great one but a good one. I wanted to play football and I needed an education. I was not a particularly good student. When I got into high school, this girl lockered right next to me. Her father was a teacher at the Roosevelt University, and her mother was the principal of our grammar school. She ended up being the valedictorian of our class. She and her parents taught me a lot of things that my parents didn't know. My parents always said, "Get educated," but they didn't know what I should get educated to. Like every Jewish family they would've loved me to be a doctor or a lawyer, but we couldn't afford to go. So, through this girl I learned about theater. I learned about going to museums. It made me inquisitive; all kinds of things that I would never have been exposed to. That gave me some motivation. Those earlier years I always worked. I remember the first job I had was selling the Saturday Evening Post out of a little envelope. I went on to college. I transferred to University of Illinois, and there I really got motivated. I had a number of teachers that took interest in me and helped me and kind of guided me along. When I graduated I was President of the counsel. She and I were voted the most popular people in the class, and I was selected by the Chicago Tribune, with others, as one of the outstanding public school graduates that year. I liked it. I liked the recognition and it motivated me!

George Green: You wanted more of it.

Sheldon Good: I wanted more of it. I wanted to go to business school to get educated so I could make a living. I walked to registration and I said, "What am I going to do to make a living?" When I went to class there was a big sign, a promotional sign that said, 'If you plan to own your own house one day, take a course in principles of real-estate.' And this was the first time the course was being taught at Illinois. I got in the class as a junior; just nineteen going into twenty. On my twenty-first birthday I went down to the state of Illinois. I ended up being a real-estate major. I had a degree in urban land economics and marketing. My fraternity, the University of Illinois; they taught me how to use silverware, how to dress. They had rules. When you went out you wore a tie and a jacket...

George Green: They knew how to polish you up at the university.

Sheldon Good: I graduated. I got married my senior year. The Korean War was just ending in 1955 and I had gone through the ROTC program, Air Force ROTC. They were drafting but it was taking a year and half to get drafted after you got out of school. I couldn't get a job because no one wanted to hire anybody for a year and a half. So, I went down to the draft board and met the people there, and they allowed me to go right into service. Now I had military training. I knew how to salute; I knew how to march. While I was in school we set up a college real-estate fraternity. We'd bring down speakers to talk about real-estate. I was also selling Pepsi-Cola in vending machines, making one-thousand-five-hundred dollars a month. I was making money. One of the firms sent down someone to speak to the University, and he talked about a career in real-estate. I knew I wanted to be a salesman. He liked me. I was always a great believer in good luck, preparation meeting opportunity, where you have to be prepared. I was a very organized guy; life without organization and discipline is havoc! After a while you get smart enough. When I got out of school I went to work for this company. I looked out the window and I said, "I own six-percent of everything I see."

George Green: Six-percent refers to the commission as a salesperson?

Sheldon Good: Yeah. So, what I did was I came up with a program to solicit owners of properties and I would go door to door; "My name is Sheldon Good. I'm with such and such a company. Do you want to sell your real-estate?" Most people shut the door on me, and a lot of them didn't. I was a young nice-looking guy, wearing a tie and jacket, and those were different times. I prospected and, every once in a while, I'd run into somebody; "Yes, I want to sell." I met a buyer, I met a seller, and I met fifteen or twenty people that looked at property before I sold it.

George Green: So now you're networking.

Sheldon Good: And I'm in business. Don Rumsfeld's father worked for the company in a suburban community, a very ritzy suburban company, and had been with them for about forty years. He took a liking to me. They used to have promotional sales, contests within the organization, and the first four or five years I would be one of the leading guys, and the guy that was the leader was Rumsfeld. I was working fourteen hours a day. The company had a quarterly meeting to recognize those people that were leading sales. I sat with him and I said, "You know, Mr. Rumsfeld, I don't know how you're doing it. I'm making deals, I can't work any harder." He said, "Well, what's your average sale?"

George Green: You've got to be selling million dollar properties because when you commission on a million it's a lot more?

Sheldon Good: If I want to double the size of my income, I have to double the size of the properties I'm prospecting. I started to develop concentration on certain communities. I was sending out fifteen-thousand mailing pieces a quarter, selling the seller on dealing with Sheldon Good & Company. That's when I discovered the use of the tax free exchange, 1031 tax free exchange. That's where you could change a smaller property for a big property, and I did develop a local reputation for being an expert on tax free exchanges. I'm solving real-estate problems for people who own real-estate that they don't want.

George Green: When you mentioned the word 'auction', they said, "Don't do it."

Sheldon Good: People looked at an auction as a fire sale. They looked at it as a sign of bankruptcy, as a sign of not having any money. That wasn't the case. It was just good business to run an auction. I canvased properties; properties that I showed in the paper were real-estate news. The real-estate section of the Chicago Tribune, Wall Street Journal, they got all the information. When I was making friends with the press I was working in the charities. I'd already built a reputation of being a good marketing guy. My ads were the best. It wasn't that I was so good. It was the rest of them were so bad. I hate to say it that way.

George Green: How did you decide you wanted to be an auctioneer?

Sheldon Good: I went to Ireland and to England and saw them doing auctions on the site. I said, "Why don't we do that?" So then I started to canvas the auctioneers. I could meet people in other communities that had a property they wanted to sell; they couldn't sell the thing or they're just not getting the activity they should and the cost to carry it is killing them. This guy calls me from New York. He says he's got a really good client that owns a property in Minneapolis, Minnesota. He says, "You think you can auction it?" I said, "I think so." Before that I talked to Winternitz and he said, "It won't work. People won't buy or sell real-estate through auctions." But the guy he had with him was his brother-in-law; the inside man. As he walked me out of the office he said, "You're a smart kid. Lester, Lester Winternitz says he doesn't think auctions will work for real-estate." Winternitz was the biggest auctioneer in America. He said (brother-in-law), "I'm not so sure he's right. I think given the circumstances, auctions could work for real-estate."

George Green: So nobody had done it before you?

Sheldon Good: There were auctions being held, but not to make a sale. They were to get good title in foreclosures.

George Green: So, you held your first auction in what year?

Sheldon Good: 1966 and '67. The question is why didn't anybody else do it? It's easy, right? So, I went to meet with these guys that owned a company (in Minnesota). I said, "What do you think it's worth?" They said, "We'd be glad to get 2.3-million dollars." So, I list the property. I ordered signs after they signed the agreement, and I went back to place the signs when they were ready. I get back to my office and there's a call. A guy calls and he said, "Just saw your sign go up. We could be interested in buying the property. How much is it?" I said, "There's no price on it. It's being offered for sale at auction." He said, "Do you think they'd sell it before the auction? Call the owner and ask him?" So, I call and he says, "We're not into running real-estate auctions. You get that guy to make an offer. We want to sell the building." So, I go back and I said, "He would consider selling it, but he'd prefer to go to auction. I suggest you make the best offer you want to make." He said, "We'll come in tomorrow. We're going to make it an all-cash offer." They come in; they offer 3.5-million dollars million cash. It was Tonka Toy. I submit the offer, he said, "I wouldn't take it. I wouldn't take 3.5-million." I said, "You said you wanted 2.4, 2.5, and you're turning down 3.5?" He said, "yeah, but not Tonka Toy. I wouldn't sell it to them." They paid another one-hundred-thousand-dollars to make the sale. But here's the point; we didn't have an auction - the auctions caused the sale! Then I got twelve Minnie Pearls; short-order chicken restaurants. The insurance company who owned it had made mortgages with a company who was a fraud.

George Green: So you put those on auction?

Sheldon Good: We sold them all; got way more than we even anticipated.

George Green: So, it turned out the auction was generating a higher price for the property than if they had listed it through a traditional real-estate sale?

Sheldon Good: Yeah, on some properties, depending on the circumstances. I would look at each piece of property. I would determine what I thought it was worth. If they knew what it was worth, they didn't need me. Every time we had an auction, somebody that had a similar property showed up, called us and talked to us about running an auction.

George Green: By 1980 you are the biggest real-estate advertiser in Chicago, is that right?

Sheldon Good: I would say in the 80's we were one of the largest, if not the biggest real-estate advertiser in the Wall Street Journal, nationally. We were very creative. We ran training programs for bidders at an auction; we sold Trump Towers to Palm Beaches.

George Green: Donald Trump came to you and said, "I want to do business with you."

Sheldon Good: His lawyer called me and then he called me, and I went to see him.

George Green: So, now you are really at the top of the real-estate pack in Chicago. You're being honored by Universities, you're being honored by the Real-estate Associations, you were President of the Real-Estate Association, and you were traveling around the world at one time promoting properties.

Sheldon Good: Property rights all over the world... and helping countries solve their problems in their communities over real-estate.

George Green: Why is real-estate sales important in the United States. Why do countries like France care to the point they even gave you a medal of Paris. What do sales in the United States have to do with the international market place?

Sheldon Good: In every country, their real-estate is the primary investment vehicle for people. The governments want permanent residents so they can swoon and woo those people to vote for them when they come up for office. If a guy lives in that town, he's interested in that town, he votes in that town. They want it stable. They want to know they can get many investors to build the kind of properties that they would like to have, to generate income, to generate taxes.

George Green: And so the information that you were able to bring foreign countries around the world is why you got so much recognition?

Sheldon Good: Yes.

George Green: The United Nations recognizes Sheldon Good & Company as being important enough to become part of the Federation and a Delegation, a representative of the United Nations in the real-estate area.

Sheldon Good: We're their experts. We have sixty-five countries that are represented. I was World President.

George Green: You've been One Of Ten Outstanding Young Men Of Chicago, the University of Illinois recognized you as one of the best alumni, or one of the most successful alumni they've ever had. The height of your real-estate career occurred fifteen years ago. You were at an intense spotlight. When did that spotlight start to dim?

Sheldon Good: After my son took over.

George Green: So you were able to pass your business on to a member of your family, your son. Describe the current spotlight that you're in today. Are you able to relax in a dimmer spotlight? Are you still consulting?

Sheldon Good: I'm consulting, which is not particularly profitable.

George Green: You're doing a lot of philanthropic work.

Sheldon Good: I do that because I'm good at it. I like doing it and I appreciate the recognition. I am a hard worker aiming for perfection.

George Green: What advice would you give to young people starting out?

Sheldon Good: What have they done to prepare?

George Green: That word 'preparation' is pretty important to you.

Sheldon Good: Preparation meeting opportunity. Most people go through life, don't even recognize the opportunity. People take jobs; they don't know what they're doing. I only did those things that I knew I could do. They're going to make mistakes. They're going to have problems. Problem-solving goes through every business. It's the same thing for your life. The most important move you're going to make in your entire life is who you marry. If you make a mistake it's going to cost you for the rest of your life. Think twice before you speak once. Life without organization and discipline is havoc, absolute havoc! And good luck is preparation meeting opportunity.

Sheldon Goldman

Life is magic!

Sheldon Goldman can be noted for being a great entrepreneur, one that moved his way from being a small-time sweater salesman to manager and part-owner of one of the largest clothing distributers in the U.S. known as Monarch Knits.

Sheldon first decided he wanted to be a dentist. Unfortunately, after serving as a dental technician with the army in Korea, this did not work out as planned. He then moved on to become the manager of a store, one of many in the Grayson-Robinson chain. However, the owner disagreed with some of his decisions and he was later fired.

He then began working for a small company selling sweaters. At the same time, his father was also in the sweater business, and after Sheldon agreed to sell a few for him, his uncle, head of the shipping department in his father's business, realized that Sheldon's skills would benefit the company.

Over time, Monarch Knits became one of the largest clothing wholesalers, selling to companies like 'JC Penney's' and 'The Limited', to name but a few.

But there was always another side to Sheldon, a magical side. Since childhood he'd always enjoyed watching magicians in action, and he in fact learned how to become one himself. Throughout his career he was known for performing his magic tricks, even in the office. He states that often buyers would request a show before any deals were made or papers signed.

As Sheldon grew older, the demands of running the company grew too strong for him. Complicated million-dollar decisions lay on his shoulders and became too much to bare.

After handing his business over to his sons, Sheldon retired and focused on his passion; one that wouldn't necessarily make him a millionaire, but would allow him to live the rest of his life doing what he loves the most; performing magic.

Sheldon is alive and well today, and lives with his family in Palm Springs. He may no longer be in demand from clothing retailers and fashion companies, but his magic tricks still keep many believing in the impossible.

Interview with Sheldon Goldman

George Green: Tell us a little bit about you.

Sheldon Goldman: When I graduated high school I went to college. I went to USC (University of Southern California) and decided I wanted to be an engineer. I found out that engineers don't work with wire-cutters and pliers, so I changed to become a dentist! In the middle of college, Uncle Sam invited me to go to Korea. I was a dental technician in the army, and I learned a lot about dentistry.

George Green: Was that around 1952?

Sheldon Goldman: Yeah. When I came back I went to the dental school and I told them, "I'm ready." He said, "You get one more year of all A's and B's and you're in." So, I came back that year with all A's and B's and he said, "You're in next year." I said, "What do you mean next year? I just spent two years in the army. Every night, in Korea, I was scared someone was going to shoot me; as far as I'm concerned you bullshi**ed me." I left, took my girlfriend, we got married and now I had to find a job. I went to a friend of my father who had a chain of stores, Grayson-Robinson, and he gave me a job as a trainee; a six month program. After about a month one of the managers got sick and they said, "You go out to that store. We need somebody we can trust with the keys!" I stayed there and managed that big store. I was involved with the Businessmen's Association and JC Penney across the street. I had gone to JC Penney and applied for a job and he told me, "It's about six years before you can become a manager." There was a store available where they needed a store manager, so I went and interviewed. I took over one store and spent a year with them. I was doing good. My sales were up and I saw an ad for another retail store, for a buyer and a manager. I applied and I got the job and he said, "I want you to organize my stores. I'm going to only have five." I decided at that point I was going to go into the retail business of my own. So I set everything up for him.

George Green: What did you want to sell?

Sheldon Goldman: Lady's/men's clothes. I set this whole computer system up for him. He couldn't understand it. He was used to his hand-written system. One day I'm in a store and there's no business. We got a new shipment of a brand-new style, and I put that right up front in the store. He says, "Who put that up front?" The manager says, "Goldman did." He says, "We don't put the new stuff up front. We put the old stuff up. Get rid of it." I said, "We've got to get customers in here." He's driving me home and says, "I needed someone like you to take over, but you haven't got it, Goldman. We'll end it."

George Green: He fired you?

Sheldon Goldman: He fired me. I went home that night and interestingly enough, as difficult as it was to accept being fired, my stomach didn't hurt. Every night I went home with this guy who complained about everything I did, my stomach was killing me. Now I was fine!

George Green: So you were happy.

Sheldon Goldman: Right. I had a new baby, a new home; I had to go to work. I got a job selling sweaters; a small company. I'd go visit my father who had a little company selling sweaters, but I wasn't interested in working with my father. One day he said, "As long as you're selling sweaters, why don't you take some of mine with you?" I took some of his and, lo and behold, I was selling ten-times as much of his stuff. My father never hired me, but one day my uncle, who ran the shipping department, said, "It won't be long until all the phone calls in here come for you." I was doing the selling.

George Green: Were you in your thirties?

Sheldon Goldman: Yeah. I became friends with everybody. One of our big accounts was JC Penney. I got very involved with them. One day we had a customer in; I had a nice order from them. My Dad walks into the room, they say to my Dad, "Shelly won't give us any kind of a deal, will you give us a better price?" So he does. I said to him, "You can't come in and overrule me in front of a customer." He said, "Okay, bigshot, you run the place." So that's when I became the President. I ran this thing pretty official. I said, "I've got to move out of this building. I can't be on the fourth floor, trying to get shipments of sweaters in; we spend a half a day unloading the truck." So I found a building. We buy it. I hired an architect; I wanted everything to look first-class. I gave him (father) a private office and me a private office, and my step-mother comes up and says, "Why did you put him in the back and you're up front?" I said, "The senior officer is always in the back." Then I put a window between my office and his room, so he could see where I am, but I still pretty much ran everything.

George Green: And the name of the company?

Sheldon Goldman: Monarch Knits.

George Green: You'd import the sweaters and then distribute them. How many years did you do that?

Sheldon Goldman: Forty-five.

George Green: Did you stay in that building?

Sheldon Goldman: No. I found another building.

George Green: During those forty-five years, what moment was the most exhilarating moment?

Sheldon Goldman: I was selling to JC Penney and we came up with Angora sweaters that were fabulous, and Penney's liked them. They said, "We want to buy yours. The New York office has some. But yours are better." So, I really felt like we were sitting on top of the world. We only dealt with the big stores now. I found it was much easier to handle a million-dollar order than a thousand-dollar order.

George Green: How many sales people did you have?

Sheldon Goldman: We never really had sales people. I did it. My father had done it but now I was doing it.

George Green: So you had maybe twenty or thirty major customers.

Sheldon Goldman: We had Sears, The Limited... these were all people who were very demanding in what they wanted, so I had to watch everything I was doing and be careful. The Limited was the worst in demanding quality and specs. One day they said, "The specs are off." I said, "It's a big, over-sized garment. They're only off half an inch." The President came in from Limited, with the General Manager. They looked at me like they were going to assassinate me and said, "We're not going to accept it." I said, "You have to accept it. These are not bad garments. I'm going to ship them into your stores and you'll see, they're going to sell, no problem." That was a big step for me. I did develop some confidence.

George Green: You spent forty years or so at that business. At some point you say, "It's time to slow down." What made you slow down?

Sheldon Goldman: I always had big contracts from Penneys. They kept telling us, "We've got to have it cheaper." I went down and down. Then I was in Dallas, where their headquarters were, and the new President said, "You've got to give us another quarter off." I said, "Not possible." He said, "Then we can't use it." I said, "You had given me an order for a million units and you haven't used that up yet. I've got the fabric." So the question is, 'what do I do now?' To sue them; you'll never sell to them again. I said, "I can't live this life. If that's what it's coming to in the retail business, I want out." We managed to get rid of all the stuff we could. It was not good for business. We were losing money and the bank was on my tail. I didn't like being interviewed by the bank, by the guys that are the 'executioners'. I said, "Goodbye, I'm gone."

George Green: What happens to the company when you say that?

Sheldon Goldman: Two years prior to that I started a swimsuit division. I turned that over to my son and his partner. I gave them everything. They got that business going, it was fabulous. They built it up to twenty-million-dollars in a short time. I decided I wasn't going to go into business. I said, "I have my hobbies, I've got my magic, I work on my computer a lot, I've got stocks that I invest in."

George Green: You decide to downsize and retire with your wife. You've got one foot in the entertainment business and one foot in manufacturing and entrepreneurial. For the record let it be known that Shelly Goldman loves performing magic tricks. Tell me about the magic business and why did you choose that?

Sheldon Goldman: When I was nine-years-old I saw a magician at a show and I said,

"You've got to teach me that." I did it all through high school but stopped. Then I met one of the professional magicians, took lessons from him, and I got pretty proficient as an amateur magician. By the way, I used it in my business! Whenever I worked with customers, I did magic. It was almost a necessity that I do it because they'd call me; "Don't forget to bring your magic." One day I went to New York and the merchandise manager said, "I want you to show the buyers." He had a whole auditorium full of buyers. I made everybody happy. I think that actually helped my business. I've always enjoyed it. To this day I'm always learning new magic, to keep my brain going. A lot of things I don't remember, but I can remember the tricks I do.

George Green: What kind of magical advice would you give to some young people who are just starting out in a day where jobs are hard to find?

Sheldon Goldman: Well, if you have customers that are happy, you're off on the right foot. I always have something in my pocket to do a little magic. But you have to do it well. You have to have the personality that you can get up in front of people at the drop of a hat.

Bill Kaplan

Living the tenacious lifestyle

William (Bill) Kaplan was born and raised in Brooklyn, (Flatbush) New York. At the age of six-years-old his father left the family (consisting of Bill, his sister and mother), never to be seen again. He and his remaining family including his aunts, grandmother, uncles and cousins, lived together in the same building. He remembers his late mother as being very devoted to him, helping him learn the necessary life skills as he grew up.

Bill's first job was given to him by his neighbor who paid him to deliver bagels four days a week. At the age of fifteen, he joined his mother at work in a sweater and bathing-suit factory as a factory worker. He recalls how his boss worked him harder than any other employee, claiming that this was how he would ultimately get educated for the real world of business.

After that he began working at a local restaurant where the chef highlighted his skills in the kitchen. After two years there he decided to further his education. Having no money for college, he joined the School for Hotel and Culinary Arts and graduated with flying colors. He then served two years in the Army, only to decide afterwards that he wanted to further his education. Bill enrolled this time and finally graduated with a Bachelor of

Science degree from Pratt Institute.

Bill then started working for the Food Division of Greyhound Corporation and, over six years, became Group Senior VP of the Midwest Region. After a chance meeting with a real-estate firm wanting to venture with Greyhound, everything changed. The leadership team of the real-estate firm recognized qualities in Bill that would complement their organization, and they pursued him. They offered him a Partnership and he took the opportunity.

Bill recalled the initial experience as being similar to the 'blind leading the blind'. However, they learned together and their aggressive style soon led to great success. Years into their venture, the idea of converting a portion of their residential properties into condominiums was clear to Bill. He headed up the conversion of two large buildings with proportionately elderly residents. His days were spent in close contact with an older population. As time passed, he visualized a lifestyle that would address the needs and concerns of this segment of people. His idea was to congregate seniors in an environment that met their every need. With Bill's endless curiosity and enthusiasm, he was ready to launch this concept.

Bill believed firmly in his project and, with his wife's consent, went on his own to establish William B. Kaplan Limited, which later became known as, Senior Lifestyle Incorporated. His small company quickly excelled beyond what Bill had anticipated, and soon he partnered with Goldman Sachs, selling fifty-percent of his company to them. Unfortunately, this partnership did not work out as well as hoped. Their plan was to go public, but Bill believed that doing so would damage their reputation as people who care; one he'd spent so long developing. Their partnership ended shortly after.

While taking a time out, Bill considered whether retirement was an option. At sixty-years-old, he decided it wasn't. He turned back to his business and built it up to become of the most successful. Through his leadership, Senior Lifestyle grew to be nationally recognized with over 170 communities throughout twenty-eight states. Today Bill lives with his wife in Chicago and Palm Springs. Bill is still active in his company, but after passing most of the business over to a professional leadership team, including his son, he now has time to balance work with family. This, to him, is extremely important and being able to do so is what led to his success. Bill's story is clear indication that following a dream can most certainly lead to that dream becoming a reality, regardless of whether others believe in you or not. All it takes is a little tenacity and a whole lot of focus.

As of Footnote: Some of Bill's accomplishments include: President of Meals on Wheels, Chicago. Chairman (2004-2006), Chairman of the American Senior Housing Association (2002-2003). Member of the Institute of Real-estate Management, holding their Certified Property Manager Designation. Member of the Board of Directors of Shelby Williams Industries, a New York Stock Exchange Company. President Emeritus and Member of the Executive Board of the Chicago Fund on Aging and Disability. Former Vice Chairman of the Board of the YMCA Lawson House, Chicago's largest single-room occupancy hotel. Recipient of the City of Chicago's National Council of Aging's Distinguished Achievement Award. Recipient of the City of Chicago 2001 Luminary Senior Award and Seniors' Hall of Fame.

Interview with Bill Kaplan

George Green: Bill Kaplan is an entrepreneur and there's a great story behind his entrepreneurship. I want to know a little bit about you, how you started, how you built this little empire in the seniors living industry.

Bill Kaplan: I grew up in Brooklyn, New York, and was raised by my mother. When I was six-years-old my father left my mother, my sister and I, and was never to be seen or heard from again. That was my beginning. My mother who was a homemaker was forced to go out to work. She was an unbelievable woman who was my mother, father and best friend. The one area she stressed growing up was that I get educated. Education was very important to my mother. She went to work fifty hours a week. We lived in Brooklyn. She took the subway and went into the city, worked her time, and returned home. It was hard, but whenever she was home she always devoted time to me. My sister was nine years older, so after finishing high school she went right to work. I grew up in an area called Flatbush of New York City, or Brooklyn, New York, where we all grew up the hard way.

George Green: Did you have a Flexible Flyer?

Author's note: *a flexible flyer or steel runner sled is a steerable wooden sled with thin metal runners.*

Bill Kaplan: I did have a Flexible Flyer, are you kidding? Those things are the greatest! I lived in a building with my two aunts, their husbands and their kids, all in the same building along with my grandmother and my step-grandfather. I had more love, more support and more fathers than I knew what to do with, because they used to argue about what I should or shouldn't do and no one ever agreed. As I got older, my mother and I would always spend time together. She introduced me to the opera, theatre, the arts and great restaurants. I remember we used to go to Radio City Music Hall once a month. She'd take me out and we'd go to a restaurant for dinner, seeing a movie or stage show. She'd say at the end of the meal, "Billy, you pay the bill. Let's evaluate the service. Was the service good? If it was good, let's leave fifteen percent. If it's really good, let's leave another percent more." My mother was very conscious of that, being in the field of business.

George Green: That was her way of showing you the value of a dollar, too.

Bill Kaplan: She'd hand me the money under the table, then we'd go out and I'd pay the bill. To this day I'm a good tipper! As I grew up, I always worked. From the time I was probably ten-years-old, I delivered bagels. There was this young couple that lived in the building across from our four-story walk-up. His father-in-law owned the bagel factory in Brooklyn, and he worked for his father-in-law. He took a liking to me; I played sports in the street. He said to me, "How would you like to work four days a week? You and I can deliver bagels then we'll pick up the money after we deliver. Then in the afternoons we'll go to the Brooklyn Dodger games when they're in town?" My mother didn't think it was a good idea. He said, "Do you mind if my wife and I come over?" They'd just had a child and they came over to convince my mother that it would be a good experience, it would be male companionship and he understood my situation.

So, I did that and delivered bagels all summer. I didn't go to camp like a lot of kids. I just stayed in the streets or went to the school yard while my mother worked.

Then in New York, when you turned fifteen you could get a work permit. I got a job in my mother's knitwear factory. It was called Regal Knit Wear and they manufactured bathing suits and sweaters. My mother was the head of Accounts Payable. I worked in the factory unloading merchandise off trucks, putting them on carts and taking them up to the factory. I worked there until fifteen or sixteen. I used to go to work with my mother, come home with my mother but have lunch with the older guys. I worked for a man who was a good friend of my mother's. He said, "I'm going to give you an education you'll never forget." He never let me stop working. He drove me hard all summer. At the end he said, "I want you to know, I worked you harder than anyone else because you needed that education; this is something you'll never forget." How right he was! I never forgot that lesson in my entire life! He also went on to say, "Just remember, whatever you do in life, be proud of what you do and never do anything dishonest. If you do anything dishonest, you'll hurt your reputation and you never want to do that. That's the one aspect of your life you'll have forever, a good reputation." This man was a strong influence on my work ethic. I worked harder than any other employee. I was out to prove that I would be the best worker there was, and it just stuck with me. Whatever income I made, half went to my mother to help with the household.

George Green: And then you went on from there to...?

Bill Kaplan: I took a job at the local restaurant, one of the biggest in Brooklyn. I was like a jack of all trades. The chef and I developed a rapport. He said, "You have a flair for cooking." My mother would leave me food and I'd finish it off or create a new dish. The chef asked the owners to allow me to work in the kitchen. I wound up working there for two years, and developed my cooking skills. I had visions of becoming a great chef. My hope was to attend college, but the financial burden was too great. So, I attended a two year School for Hotel and Culinary Arts. Then I went on to spend two years in the army and realized, 'I have to go back to college for my four year degree.' I graduated from Pratt Institute with a Bachelor of Science degree. Upon graduation, I went to work for Greyhound Corporation, in their food service company, for six years. I became very active and moved up the channel of responsibility quickly. I worked with the Divisional President who eventually became Vice Chairman of all of Greyhound. He took me under his wing and he'd send me all over the country. When he became the head honcho and established various regents, he made me the Group Senior VP of the Midwest Region. I was twenty-nine. I did that for a number of years. I ran various operations in college, industrial and hospital feeding, and we also had a division of bus station restaurants where we provided all the food service for the patrons.

George Green: Then there was a turning point in your life.

Bill Kaplan: I met two individuals that had started a real-estate firm. I met them purely by accident because they called Greyhound and were interested in putting a restaurant in one of their office buildings. They thought Greyhound would be interested. After several meetings, it was clear that the restaurant concept was not a good fit for Greyhound. However, the partnership team saw something in me that would enhance their company. They offered me a position that led to a partnership with their young real-estate firm. The year was 1971. Their real-estate firm centered on apartments, office buildings, shopping centers and hotel development. I gave it a lot of thought and talked to friends and advisors.

The two senior partners persuaded me that becoming a partner was an intermediate step in starting my own company. I partnered with them for fourteen years and became the Managing Partner. We grew to a fairly large all-purpose real-estate company.

George Green: Then you had another turning point.

Bill Kaplan: At the age of thirty-five my mother passed. When I was with the real-estate firm, I gave her a trip around the world for sixty days. It was the most incredible gift I could have given her. She was thrilled. Then I met my wife in 1977. A couple of years after, we were married in 1980. In those years our company really excelled and expanded. In '71 we expanded, and in '73 we acquired a large portfolio of over four-thousand apartments, followed by a recession. After the recession ended in '76 we saw the opportunity to convert apartments into condominiums. We set up a separate company of which I became President. 1977 and '79 were successful and very profitable years. However, the real turning point came during the conversion process, when the realization that thousands of sixty-five-year-olds (plus), were looking for rental apartments with multiple services. What was currently available were 'old-folk homes'. There were a few facilities around, but really nothing significant. I traveled to Florida and San Francisco where there were some up-scale retirement communities, and I introduced myself to the owners. I said, "Do you mind if I spend a little time here?" I was really interested and fascinated with the business because it's not readily available. Everyone was welcoming and invited me to stay as long as I liked. By 1980 we owned or operated seven-million square-feet of office space. We continued with the conversion process. We also owned several hotels and a shopping center. We were busy and profitable. At the next partnership meeting, I presented an innovative senior living concept firmly believing, 'This is the business we should get into.' We voted and it was six to one... no one wanted to be a pioneer in this new venture. That was the night I came home and said to my wife, "How would you feel if I went off on my own, because I believe in this opportunity?" I contacted my senior partner and let him know that I was moving on and they should look to replace me internally. By this time, we had 575 corporate employees who mostly reported to me. I gave them a year but, during that time, I would ease out of the organization. I set up shop somewhere else. I finally opened my doors on October 31, 1985. Senior Lifestyle Incorporation will be in business thirty years in 2015.

George Green: So you opened your first one where?

Bill Kaplan: Well, I hired a team of nine employees, including myself, to do what was necessary to get the job done. We were going to learn the business together. It took me about three years to fill our first building up. A year into construction, I broke ground on the second senior building. I knew that this was an opportunity of a lifetime. I even did all the financing myself because I was a 'Jack of all trades and a master of none.' In 1990, I had three developments and three that we acquired. I learned when I was in real-estate, how financing markets can make you a hero or a failure. In the late 70's, early 80's, the interest rates sky-rocketed. When rates returned to reasonable levels, I refinanced everything we owned and decided to aggressively acquire because rates were lower and you could get some great pricing. In 1995 the company was growing and very successful. I chose to bring in a financial partner to leverage our positions. Goldman Sachs bought fifty-percent of my existing company. In six years we built the company to become major players. The 2001, the industry (as it was) was in a state of flux with many changes occurring. Goldman had a different philosophy in dealing with people. They had a more institutional approach. My objective was to nurture my people while providing innovative services to our residents, to improve their quality of life. We finally reached a point to go our separate ways. But I'm in the people business, where we provide a family culture for America's elders through the finest and most dedicated employees. From the start I knew every person's name. I visited all the properties. I made sure that we kept that culture which was so important. At sixty-years-old I asked myself, "Do I want to retire?" I headed out to Vail and spent the summer reflecting on the choices before me; 'Do I keep the status quo or do I rebuild the company?' It was such a critical point in my career. I hired a professional consulting firm to evaluate the company and me, as an individual. I realized I still had another mountain to climb. I was not satisfied with where I was, and I knew it was time to take our company and grow it to be the best in the entire industry. I brought in all new talent in 2003. I took the company from two-thousand-eight-hundred units, and today we're approaching twenty-thousand units.

George Green: You're still going strong.

Bill Kaplan: Because I hired the right people. I delegate and allow them to operate the business and only get involved when it's strategic. I'm involved in the strategic decisions, but not in the day-to-day running of the business. I have a son who is a super-star, who is talented and loves the business. I have phased out of the spotlight; I'm not involved like I used to be. At one time I was involved in every single detail. I have worked my whole life to build this business. How can I balance both business and my personal lifestyle? I've been married thirty-five years now to an unbelievable woman. We have the best time together. I had a little health scare about six years ago and realized I wanted to do a good balancing act.

George Green: Give me sixty seconds on the Heart of Caring; a program within the company where they pick out six outstanding employees who have given their heart to this business.

Bill Kaplan: It's an award that is given to anyone in the company, no matter what position; housekeeping, CNA, a food-service employee, an executive, an administrative person or an accounting person that goes above and beyond their job description. Any employee can be recommended for the Heart of Caring Award. Then there's a process and judges. We take one individual out of every six regions in the country. Six people make the selection. Winners are brought in, with their families, to be presented this special award at the Heart of Caring ceremony. It is a moving and touching experience. The end result; employee recognition will result in a positive impact on everyone in the company.

George Green: What advice do you have for young people?

Bill Kaplan: A couple of years ago I won the Man of the Year Award. Young people were surrounding me, asking me how I'd achieved my success. I said, "I had an idea and I followed my dream. I was tenacious. I wouldn't give up. If I believed and was willing to work hard, I was going to make it successful. There was nothing that was going to change my mind. If you believe in something, don't think that it's just going to happen. You have to work at it. The harder I worked, the more successful I became. Just do what you think will make you happy. If you want to be an entrepreneur, go after it." Then they asked the big question, "If you had to do it all over again, would you do it?" I say, "There was a lot of struggle, but when I think about it I wouldn't change it for anything. There's less competition at the top, so go for it!"

Edward Schwartz

Insure your tomorrow

Edward Schwartz was born in 1926. He grew up in Illinois where he attended the University of Illinois and Roosevelt College, studying accounting. His father owned a small insurance business which Ed had first hoped to join once he'd completed his studies. However, his father decided it'd be beneficial for him to learn the ways of the trade through working at an insurance company first.

The company he chose to apply with, on his father's recommendation, told him that he should find somewhere else to work, due to the fact that they had no Jewish workers in their company; they believed Ed would find it difficult not having anyone to talk to there. Fortunately, his father spoke to the President of the company and, based on Ed's skills, convinced him to allow Ed to join them.

Ed began working in the company, the largest in Chicago at the time, and after some time was recognized for his good work. However, he chose to leave and together with some of the other agents whom he'd befriended, he began his own operation within his father's business.

His father passed away in 1950. At this time Ed was married and started a family of his own.

Before long he had numerous clients and large contracts, some due to his love for tennis; a sport in which he excelled. While playing tennis, or golf, folks would ask him what he did for a living. One thing would lead to another and, before he knew it, he was handling their accounts. Ed went on to recruit some of the country's top employees in the field, and it didn't take too long for his company to become ranked one of the highest in the country.

Ed prides himself on his ability to interact with his staff, always ensuring that they're happy.

Over time he found great pleasure in giving-back whenever he could, often helping those starting out for the first time, without even asking for a written agreement on loans he'd grant.

Edward, now eighty-nine-years-old, retired from the insurance industry not long ago. As he moved into retirement, he chose to make his outstanding employees part-owners of the business; each having a ten-percent share. He believes they are hard-working, and wanted to give them the best he could. Even though he is retired now, he still remains an active part of the company, visiting the offices in Chicago frequently to talk with employees and help them to feel at home. The company has offices in Scottsdale, Arizona, in Wisconsin and in Charlotte, North Carolina.

Edward lives in Palm Springs and although he's out of the intense spotlight he once found himself under, he still feels its warmth by remaining communicative with those working under the company name.

As A Footnote: *In the 1960's, Edward and several of his friends formed the Chicago Youth Centers. The organization eventually had fourteen centers, and a summer camp, for under-privileged children. This organization is still helping the young children in the City of Chicago. In 1983 the A.I.G General Counsel, Robert Ungerleiter and Edward, formed the Financial Risk Underwriting Agency. They issued bonds guaranteeing the unpaid installments of limited partners in large real-estate transactions. They wrote over one-billion dollars in premiums, and were the largest firm to write this type of insurance in the country.*

Interview with Edward Schwartz

George Green: I'm talking to Edward Schwartz. Ed, over to you.

Edward Schwartz: When I was very young my father had a small insurance agency. Every Saturday I would help him deliver calendars and daily datebooks to his clients, and to people who he would try to write their insurance. I didn't learn anything about the insurance business; we only delivered them in the winter. But I learned that you had to do something in life and accomplish something. I went to the University of Illinois and took up accounting.

Then I went to Roosevelt College at night to take up more accounting. I decided I wanted to go into my Dad's business. The first day, I drove him to the office then waited in line to park the car. I got into the office about ten after eight and my Dad said, "Do you know what time we start here?" I said, "Around 8:00am." He said, "Do you know what time it is now?" I told him the time and he says, "I'd like you to go work somewhere else if you can't get here on time." I said, "But, Dad, I drove you and I parked and..." He said, "I know the whole story, son. You're going to go to work somewhere else. You'll put a couple good hard years in and then you'll come back and we'll do business."

George Green: That was on the first day?

Edward Schwartz: The first morning. I couldn't understand, so I decided to go and get a job. I said, "Where do you think I should go?" He says, "I would go to Continental Casualty Company. It's the largest company in Chicago. You can learn the property and casualty business there, and then after that you can learn the life insurance business there. They have the Continental Insurance Company also." I said, "Okay, that sounds reasonable." So, the same day I walked over to the Continental Casualty Company and took an application. I wanted to apply for a job there.

George Green: Were you angry at your father for putting you out on the street your first day?

Edward Schwartz: Then I was. But looking back I thought he was pretty smart. At the time I couldn't understand it, but I figured, "Okay, I'll just make the best of it and go learn the business." I got the application and I started to fill it out. The first question they asked was, 'Are you Hebrew?' I thought to myself that's a language, not a religion. The second question; 'Are you Jewish?' I said, 'Hebrew, no. Jewish, yes.' I turned it in to the gentleman there. He looked it over and says, "I don't think you'll be very happy here. I suggest you go because we don't have any Jewish employees here." They didn't want any Jewish employees.

George Green: What year was that? Do you remember?

Edward Schwartz: 1947. I went back to my father and said, "This company discriminates." He says, "You've got a lot to learn, son. They'll let us be agents, but they don't want us to work there. I'm going to call the President because I am an agent." He called and said, "I want you to meet my son. He'll show you the application. They told him to take it back. And then you can tell me whether or not you are willing to let him become part of your executive training program." He said (president), "The kid is not going to be happy here. Nobody will have lunch with him. I don't know why... you should find a different place." He says (father), "No, I think he'll be very happy there and I'm an agent there. I do a lot of business with you. I'd like him to learn there." He said, "Send him over." I went over and talked to him for about five minutes. He says, "Okay, I'm going to let you be part of this executive program that we have, but you are going to have a tough time. You won't be fired because of your religion. You'll only be fired if you don't do the work or you don't have a decent attitude." I said, "I accept." The pay was about twenty-five-dollars a week, which was okay. The next day I came into work and they sent me over to a different building about seven or eight blocks away on South Michigan Avenue. It was an old building, bad lights, no air conditioning. I was put in the sub-basement to look over old claims. I don't know why they wanted the old, closed claims but I didn't ask why; I just did what they asked me to do. I stayed there for ninety days. That was the deal. Then they let me go on a program of six weeks in each department. They offered me a job in management; they said, "You really did a good job. You worked hard. I told your Dad that we would like to keep you." I decided to leave. I didn't like the fact that there were no Jewish employees there. I made many friends there and years later we became the largest agent.

George Green: You wanted to be out on your own, to start your own agency?

Edward Schwartz: My father died. I came in there and decided to have my own operation inside his agency. I would build my own accounts. We weren't wealthy people, so I would manage my father's business for my mother and not take any of the commissions. In school I made some wonderful contacts playing tennis. The first week after my father passed away, a good friend said, "Dad, can you give my friend some business?" He said, "On the basis of merit I will give him business. On the basis of friendship, we don't do business for friends." I went to one of the larger agencies because I knew we didn't have the means to handle an account that big. They worked with me. I ended up writing the largest hotel in Chicago, Morrison Hotel, and ended up being able to make a living. In the meantime I had been married five days before. I decided that I would join an organization called Young Men's Jewish Council. We ran youth centers, a summer camp, and would help the very poor Jewish people. As the years went on, the neighborhoods changed and it became one-hundred percent black; previously one-hundred percent Jewish. The years that I spent on the Jewish Council introduced me to the many nice and wealthy family people, big businesses, and I was able to get some very prominent accounts.

I played tennis with all these people, never asked anybody for their business. I just felt that when you're out playing tennis or golf, you don't want to be bothered with an insurance salesman. But that only made them say, "What do you do for a living?" after you played with them! I got to meet some very wealthy people.

George Green: So you were playing tennis; your business was going. You had a lot of expansion, other agents working for you...

Edward Schwartz: The first thing I did when we got that very large first account; I realized that I have to have inside people that know the business and know how to handle it. So, I re-invested a lot of money into hiring top people. Nobody, in my opinion, had a better team. Then I switched all of our new business, to try to get new construction accounts. When we started I had none, and when I ended up I had about six of the big ones. People in that business would leave and start their own small construction companies, and they would come to us because we were always in sight. We always were out there. We ended up becoming the fifty-fifth largest agency in the country... from zero. There were 135,000 agencies in Illinois alone, and at that point I said, "I have enough. I have everything that I need. I want to have some time to spend time with my kids, to travel, to do other things."

George Green: You had taken forty or forty-five years to build probably one of the premier insurance agencies in the country. It sounds to me like you were very comfortable.

Edward Schwartz: My brother, Bob, joined me in 1956. He still got fifty-percent of everything. Along the way I ran into a young man who I hired as my attorney when he graduated law school. His name was Sam Zell. I was his only client. After one year he came into the office and said, "I don't want to be in the law business anymore. I want to be a developer. Right now I don't have any money and I want to build a five-thousand square foot warehouse." I said, "Okay, I'll be your partner." He says, "You put up the money and I'll do the deal." Sam made a fortune! He's a genius. I did seventy-two real-estate deals with him. I never read one of the deals. Every one of them, except one, worked out to be good. But fourteen years after that one deal went bad, he sent me a check for the full investment. He said, "Now you can't say I'm a bad real-estate man." He was fabulous.

George Green: At this point your brother is running the company while you're playing tennis, investing, making a lot of friends. At what point are you going to start to slow down?

Edward Schwartz: I bought a house in Aspen and took up skiing. I bought a house in Florida at Longboat Key, took up more tennis and started to play golf. I started giving back and helping friends. Anybody in need, I would help them. They would say, "I'll give you a note so you have a record of it." I said, "Do you intend to pay me back?" They said, "Yeah." I said, "Then I don't need a note. Your word's good." I loaned to a lot of people and helped with their businesses and I enjoyed it. It was a great life. My brother separated from me since he had three sons that are in his business, and they are doing fabulous. In my end of it I decided that every year I would give ten-percent away to the people who were working and building the business. They got ten-percent more each year. At the end of ten years, which was about three or four years ago, they owned the business.

George Green: The employees?

Edward Schwartz: Yes. They would end up as partners owning ten-percent more each year, and nobody had to write a check to buy me out.

George Green: They're still keeping in touch with you just to keep you advised about what's going on with the company.

Edward Schwartz: They feel I can be of help to them on the larger accounts that I brought in. I still see them socially or know them, or play golf or tennis with them. Still, if anybody asks me about insurance I put them in touch with my office and I get nothing for it but the pleasure of seeing the name continue and grow. These people were with me for so many years.

George Green: So this spotlight, though it's not as intense as it was in Chicago, it's still shining as far as you're concerned, because you're still able to see what is going on in your past life and enjoy your current one.

Edward Schwartz: Absolutely. They're friends; I made every employee a friend. The first thing I would do when I would go to the office; I would walk around the office and say 'hello' to each one, thank them for the nice job they were doing, and ask 'do they have any problems they want to talk about?' I tried to make them happy. We had a program where we put their children through college if they were willing to get good grades, at least a B average.

George Green: What advice would you give to younger people that are starting out or people who have been thrown out of their job?

Edward Schwartz: Find an industry that you would be happy in. Start at the bottom because you have to learn the business. Make friends along the way where you are not pushing them but you are their friend, and they'll want to do business with you. If you can't be honest, don't go into business. You just must be sure that you do everything the right way. I never got a speeding ticket. I never got a parking ticket. I never had a problem with anything or anybody, and that's what I would suggest. Learn the hard way, work hard and you'll be a success.

Jack Feinberg

If you're gonna' gamble, let me show you around

From The Author: *Jack Feinberg has one of the most interesting jobs of anyone that I interviewed. I have never met anyone like him. Imagine the kind of perks coming to him, his family and his clients. His gambling clients are some of the richest people in the world. He determines what Casino's these billionaires should be playing poker in, with fifty-thousand-dollars a hand in Blackjack. The suites, the food, the service these people get are not given to many other people coming to Casino's from around the world. He is so personable, so smart and witty; I can understand why the gamblers loved him and Casino's catered to him 'because of his contact list, for forty years. It doesn't get any better!*

Jack Feinberg was born in San Francisco. After attending Berkley and graduating in Economics, he worked for his father in his shoe-repair business. Believing it would be a profitable business, Jack asked his Dad if he could partner with him in the business. His father then offered him some 'start-up' financing, which enabled Jack to progress to a point where he owned fifteen shoe-repair stores in The Bay area. His business became the largest in its field, in California.

At the age of thirty-seven-years-old he sold all of his stores, wanting to move on and into a different career. He wasn't too sure what he wanted to do, but after a friend suggested he interview with Al Rosen from Caeser's Palace, he accepted a job as PR in their offices in San Francisco.

Shortly after, a culinary strike led to him being relieved of his duties, but not without an outstanding letter of recommendation. With this letter he was offered a job at the Sands Hotel (Park Place Entertainment). Striving higher, in 1999 Jack finally went out on his own; working as... *THE HOST OF THE RICH AND FAMOUS GAMBLERS OF THE WORLD!*

Today, even though Jack still maintains contact with his clientele, he considers himself semi-retired and lives with his wonderful wife between Rancho Mirage, Lake Tahoe and The Bay area.

Interview with Jack Feinberg

George Green: I'm interested in how you started your world. Where were you born? Where did you go to school, what transpired in your life?

Jack Feinberg: I was born in San Francisco. I lived in the Bay Area my entire life, went to Berkeley, graduated in economics. My father owned a shoe-repair store on Montgomery street. He purchased it from my uncle, a physician. I worked there a while endeavoring to get a Master's degree in Economics. I saw this little cash-register with all the money in it, and I said, "Dad, I want to go into the shoe-repair business." He gave me ten-thousand-dollars and I ended up opening fifteen shoe-repair stores in the Bay Area, and was the largest in that business at the time in California. At the age of thirty-seven I sold all the stores. My friend, whose father was a friend of the President of Caesar's Palace, Billy Weinberger, was looking for a job in Las Vegas. So, he went down to interview for the job. He interviewed with Al Rosen.

Author's note: see interview with Al Rosen

Al said, "You're really not cut out for this job. Do you have any friends that might be more appropriate?" He said, "Jack Feinberg." So, I went down and interviewed for the job. He was at Caesar's Palace, in charge of outside offices. I said, "The only thing I really have as an asset is my name, and I'm concerned about getting into the gaming business because I've heard of mafia ties, etcetera." He said (Al), "No large corporations are involved." He hired me to work as a PR person in their office in San Francisco. Six months later they had a culinary strike and I was let go. But I guess I did a pretty good job for them because they wrote a nice letter of recommendation which I took to the Sands Hotel, and they opened an office for me. I started with about twenty fellows that I played poker with; I'd invite them there. They would tell me, "If a person loses five-hundred-dollars, go to his office and take him out to lunch then collect the five-hundred-dollars; send it to the casino." They paid me, at the time, seventy-five-dollars a person to do this. I said, "I can't make any money doing it this way." So I did it on my own, in my own way and shortly thereafter, in the first eighteen months, I had four-thousand names on a bi-monthly mailer that I sent out. I represented more and more casinos around the world. Currently I'm still licensed with about forty casinos, domestically and internationally. You have to be licensed to do what I do.

In 1999 I resigned from Park Place Entertainment and I was their number-one producer in the country. They were the largest gaming casino in the country; Harrah's, Caesar's, etcetera. In the last fourteen years, I've been an independent rep, and have handled some of the largest casino customers in the world; people with million-dollar lines, five-million-dollar, ten-million-dollar lines. That means they're not only credit worthy for that amount, but it means that they probably will win or lose that amount on a trip basis, three or four nights. Those people were betting; they were allowed to bet at some places up to fifty-thousand-dollars a hand in blackjack. My job was basically to be concierge for them. I would set up their credit, suggesting lines that casinos give them. I would provide the private planes and all the bells and whistles. It's a service business, it's very important that you watch details. If you do, and if you really do it almost fanatically, it puts you a cut above anyone else who might be doing my same job. In that period of time I built up rapports with many of the Presidents of many of the casinos. I worked with the Presidents because many of the Vice-Presidents were hesitant to make good business decisions, because if it were 'out-of-the-box' and didn't prove to be financially successful to the hotel on that particular trip, they felt they might be chastised. So, I went right to the Presidents and also I negotiated with those people for my commission. I wasn't interested in the standard commission that was given. I was interested in the commission that would be representative for the amounts of profit that the casinos had made from my clients over a period of time. Now that's not to say that people lose every time. They really don't. If you take ten people there, six usually lose on that trip and four win. Without that win, people wouldn't be continuously going there for the last umpteen years.

George Green: How much attention was being paid to you and your guest?

Jack Feinberg: I wasn't cognizant of it. Obviously all my expenses are covered by that casino. But the best thing that casinos do is they know how to feed an ego. If you go there, they don't call you 'Mr. Green'. They call you 'Mr. G'. If you're smoking Camel cigarettes, it's my job to make sure there's a pack of Camels every single place you go in that casino. So the suite that you get, and it might be a fourteen-thousand square foot suite with a private pool on the top of the Hilton Hotel, that cigarette or your type of wine would be at every table you turn to. I knew what your wife or lady-friend liked. I made sure they were happy. I made sure, if they were to bring children, they would be happy. There would be private movie theaters where they would see movies to keep them occupied. The wife; we might give her mink coat so she would be happy with the trip. That's all done when they get there, not after a person were to lose a million or two-million dollars, but when they walk in the door. So you must cater to the egos of these people. Now the people that I brought there are really interesting people. The majority, by far, were successful business people. You wonder to yourself why a person doing so well in business would go to someone else's business and lose this type of money. It basically is just that their ego is so catered to that even these people would go through fortunes of money, and I do mean fortunes. One fellow, unfortunately; eighty-four-million dollars.

George Green: Lost?

Jack Feinberg: Lost eighty-four-million over a period of three or four years.

George Green: Was it exciting or did you finally take it as 'a job'. You had hundreds of trips to casinos all over the world, people catered to you in such a great way. Were you in a spotlight?

Jack Feinberg: I don't know if the term is 'spotlight'. I actually, humbly speaking, made it rain! I made it happen. I never took advantage of it. When I would sit down at the table with a couple, they may order six-thousand-dollar bottles of wine, I'd say, "Please, you drink the wine. I wouldn't know the difference between that wine and Morgan David." They'd laugh! That was me. I wasn't going to say, "This wine is delicious," because I don't have knowledge of wines.

George Green: You were married at the time?

Jack Feinberg: I still am. My wife went on ninety-nine percent of the trips. She played a very important part of my job. She would entertain the ladies. She would take them shopping and she would say, "Oh, you like that watch?" She'd call me and, "Yes, they liked that watch."

"How much is it?"

"Thirty-thousand-dollars."

"Tell them to charge it to the hotel." It would be a gift to the lady. So she played a very important part in our business.

George Green: You had permission from the hotel to be able to spend money.

Jack Feinberg: I don't think I ever asked for something from the hotel that they didn't say 'yes' to. The hotel realized that there has to be a profit at the end of the rainbow. I don't think they ever said, 'no'.

George Green: And then what happened when you and your wife got home? Were you able to make the transition?

Jack Feinberg: It wasn't even a transition. It was a way of life. It was a wonderful job.

George Green: When was it that you decided, 'it's time that we start slowing the engine down a little bit?'

Jack Feinberg: I do have a clientele that still goes places, but I no longer go with them. They're people that I've known for a long period of time and I set them up in these different places, and have an on-site host do what I used to do. In the last two or three years, that's really all I have done.

George Green: Do you miss the excitement?

Jack Feinberg: I don't miss it at all. We're fortunate; we have three sons all of whom have done financially nicely, so they don't need any help from me. I guess I just didn't feel like doing it anymore. I just kind of lost my interest.

George Green: What advice would you give? What do you think is one of the keys to a youngster's success?

Jack Feinberg: I think the primary key today is education, as it has been for so long. If monetary success is a goal, schooling is a must, is just a must. I think the majority of guys with decent intellect really need a college education, and possibly further than that to become successful today.

George Green: There are not many people in this world who have had the kind of excitement that you've had with so many exciting people. Are you in touch with any of these people?

Jack Feinberg: Yeah, the relationship I've had with these people has allowed me to do many other things. During the last forty years I've had other businesses as well, and I've had some limited partnerships, which many of my clients invested in as well as I did. I've had a business in Mexico that a client and I went into. So these have been lifelong friendships that I've been fortunate to have, and still have to this day.

Stuart Markus

Work hard, play hard, enjoy life

The story of Stuart and Ellen Markus is not 'just another story' about people who experience failed businesses. That happens to many individuals in our world. The bottom line to their story is *RECOVERY*.

Stuart Markus was born in Cleveland, Ohio. In 1941 he and his family moved to California where they lived in San Fernando Valley for a short time. During this time his father worked as a sound editor at 20th Century Fox and Warner Brothers, but in 1946 decided to go back to being a clothing salesman on the road. Living in Los Angeles now, Stuart attended Beverley Vista grammar school then Beverley Hills high school, after which he served in the army. On his return he went to Santa Monica City College but soon realized he didn't want to study, so left college and joined his father instead.

Enjoying the clothing industry he soon started his own small business which did well. In 1962 he was hired by the well-known clothing company, 'The Villager'. Over twenty-five years he worked his way from salesman to a top position as National Sales Manager and Executive Vice-President of Sales. When the company was sold, Stuart left and then joined another company, Paul Stanley. There he actually bought twenty-five percent shares in the company, and it seemed all was going well. However, after a few years his partner wanted to expand, a decision that Stuart did not agree with. He consequently sold his shares to his partner, and the company went under a short while later.

Feeling determined and confident, he took the money from his share and decided to open his own business. He hired a great designer, but things didn't work out as planned and he had to close down. With little left in savings at this point, he went to work for a company called 'Jones'. There he succeeded again, running three divisions within the company, raising the value of the company considerably.

Having married a wonderful woman, Ellen; when his daughter fell pregnant he decided to move the family back to Los Angeles, where he again met Paul Lewis (Paul Stanley) whom he'd worked with previously. They formed another partnership without Stuart having to put any money towards the project. They did well together, second-time around, but in 1998 Stuart decided that forty years in the clothing industry was enough.

 He ventured into a different field entirely, working in travel with Ellen who was an agent for Rich Worldwide Travel. They opened an office in August of 1998 in Sherman Oaks, and within five years built the small business up to be worth a small fortune. However, after some complications years later, Stuart dissolved the partnership. In 2005 he worked with New Act Travel as Director of Operations. Not long thereafter, he felt it was time to slow down and consequently moved his family to Palm Desert.

Stuart Markus went down a few times but recovered time and time again, never giving up, always trying to be successful. This is indeed a part of the American Dream: work hard... if you fail, dust yourself off and try again in the same field of endeavor that you failed in, or another. He failed in his primary business, manufacturing clothing. But this wasn't entirely his fault; his partners certainly had something to do with the failure.

The positive side of this story is the ending; his moving to Palm Desert, getting involved in Ellen's business of travel, and succeeding. Happiness surrounds the Markus Family today, as does peace of mind. Memories of great success are still with Stuart, but his memories of abundant financial comfort don't get in the way of his family life, health and many friendships they've made over the last dozen years living in Palm Desert. Good health, a roof over their heads, successful children and financial comfort to live in a country that is free, are only a few of the blessings that now surround Stuart Markus and his family.

As A Footnote: *Stuart and Ellen have phenomenal memories! They can recall names of people and places in the world at the drop of a hat. As travel specialists they can talk, in depth, about almost any country in the world and how to get there. They'll even include names of hotels, sites to see, restaurants and what's on their menus, without so much as opening the first page of a travel guide! Pretty amazing!*

Interview with Stuart Markus

George Green: Tell me about your background.

Stuart Markus: My family included my mother, father, brother who was eighteen months older than me, and myself. We moved from Cleveland, Ohio, by way of Greenville, Mississippi, and landed in California in August of 1941. A few months later WW II broke out. We lived in the San Fernando Valley at that time, which was North Hollywood and Sherman Oaks, and Studio City. I grew up there until second grade. My Dad worked at the studios; a sound editor at 20th Century Fox and Warner Brothers. We moved into the city and my Dad decided, in 1946, that he would go back on the road as a salesman. He started representing several different companies out of the East, which he did for a number of years. In 1949 we moved to New York. My Dad took a position as sales manager for a company called Moore Love Blouses. We did not like living in New York. We were there for about eight months then moved back to Los Angeles. My grandparents had purchased an apartment building in 1946. They both passed away. We moved to New York, leased out the apartment building. When we came back we moved back into the apartment. I went to Beverly Vista Grammar School then graduated Beverly Hills high school. After high school I went into the army under the RFA Act of 1955, which was six months active duty and seven and a half years reserve. It was very interesting because we went in with a group of fifty guys from Beverly Hills high school. We were all in for six months. When I came out it was in between semesters, so I didn't go to college. I worked at the Bank of America. I worked at Brussels Men's Store, and parked cars at the Beverly Hills Hotel every Saturday night. In September of 1958 I went to Santa Monica City College for a year, and realized that I didn't want to continue my education. I went to work for my father who was a multi-line sales rep in the lady's apparel industry. I did that for two years.

In 1961 I took on my own company which was a tailor-pant line, for women, out of Philadelphia called Norman Davidson. It was a very small company and I built the business as a salesman on the road, to about a million dollars within a year and a half. In 1962 I was hired by a company called 'The Villager', which in those days was a four-million-dollar company. I saw a lot of potential in it. I had a partner and we had the thirteen Western states. He traveled Northern California, Oregon, Washington, and I traveled the other ten. I built that business with Villager and became National Sales Manager and Executive Vice-President of Sales. I was with them for twenty-five years. I built the business up to ninety-million-dollars. It became a public company and then was taken over by Jonathan Logan. I was on the board for Jonathan Logan apparel. It was the largest apparel company in the industry next to Levi Strauss. I left Villager in 1985 and joined a company called Paul Stanley. I knew the owner, Paul Lewis, very well and we formed a partnership. I bought in and owned twenty-five percent of the company. When I bought into the company it was doing three-million, making very little money. Within six years we were doing twenty-six-million. It was very profitable. In 1991 he decided that he wanted to go a different route and expand the business. I did not agree because with the caliber and the quality of merchandise that we were making, you could not sell to everybody. We also owned Daphne Swimwear, Sheila Raymond, and we owned a couple other small companies. The total corporation was doing about thirty-million.

George Green: He wanted to expand it further?

Stuart Markus: Right. I said, "If you're going to do that, you have to buy me out because our product is not for all the market." He wanted to be in all the branch stores. I totally disagreed with that. He bought me out and eighteen months later he was bankrupt. What happened was we were in twelve Lord And Taylor stores, but he wanted all of them. They hit him with a markdown allowance of six-hundred-thousand dollars and he didn't have the money.

Macey's also went bankrupt. They owed us, but we never collected, over a million dollars.

George Green: You got out in time. Did he buy you out with cash?

Stuart Markus: He bought me out over two years. I got my money and then made a very foolish mistake. I felt that I was good enough to open my own business, which I did. I brought in a designer by the name of Norman Todd. We were open for two years. He cost me a million and a half dollars. I closed up the business. In 1993 I took a position with Jones in New York.

George Green: You lost money in all directions on that one mistake then went to Jones.

Stuart Markus: We were in New York. I went to work with Jones. I was running three divisions, and we did extremely well. About that time our daughter, who had gotten married, was about to have a baby. We decided it was time to come home, back to Los Angeles. In a conversation I had with Paul Lewis, who was Paul Stanley, he wanted to go back into business. He wanted to know if I'd go back into business with him. I said 'yes' but I would not put any money into it. We came back here in November of 1987. I started a business with him, November, and we were doing pretty well. Then I decided in March of 1998 that I did not like the garment business anymore. Forty years was enough. It's a changed business; it's no longer what it was. So I retired. My wife has been a travel agent now for thirty-five years. While we were in New York she worked for a company called Rich Worldwide Travel. When we moved back they wanted her to open an office. She said she was an agent and did not want to get involved in the business. She asked if I would do it. I said, "I can run that kind of business." We opened the office in August of 1998, in Sherman Oaks, with myself, my wife Ellen, and one assistant. Within five years I had built the business to sixteen-million-dollars and we had eighteen sales travel agents working for us. We had a couple issues come up. I said, "I'm dissolving the partnership." In 2005 we went to work with New Act Travel who had been after Ellen and I for a while. I was Director of Operations and built a very nice business with them as well. Then we moved to Palm Desert.

George Green: Looking back at your career now; the spotlight, the fun, the enjoyment of the business itself, making money and being very successful, that was a very intense part of your life.

Stuart Markus: I would think that. Twenty-five years with Villager was extremely gratifying.

George Green: Working your way up.

Stuart Markus: I went from a salesman on the West Coast to being Executive Vice-President of Sales and Marketing. I had been offered the Presidency but, at that time, my kids were in school and we did not want to uproot them and move to New York.

George Green: That spotlight, which was very intense, became a little dimmer as you went from spotlight to spotlight, emotionally.

Stuart Markus: I looked back for a short period of time only because of two things. The gratification of having a lot of money and then going all the way down, having no money. I never let that hinder my ability to make an income. It bothered me a lot because our social life was the same people when we had money... and when we didn't have money. We could not really maintain the same status. We had to take steps backwards.

George Green: There was a cutback period in your life, and all this time you've been married to a wonderful lady.

Stuart Markus: Fifty-two years.

George Green: Ellen was your rock then and your rock now.

Stuart Markus: She still is! She's very supportive. During good and bad times I supported my mother for a number of years. I've always taken care of everybody.

George Green: How important was a good marriage during these stressful periods of a cutback?

Stuart Markus: It was very important because Ellen was very supportive. She did not come from a lot of money and I did not come from a lot of money. We had to regroup and go backwards. Instead of going out and buying a purse or something like that, we did other things. We changed our whole lifestyle.

George Green: While you were changing lifestyle, you were still finding new successes.

Stuart Markus: Oh yeah.

George Green: You enjoy your work.

Stuart Markus: I love it! And my golf!

George Green: Now you're in a semi-retired position.

Stuart Markus: I work three and a half days a week.

George Green: You're working a little, you're playing a little, and you're enjoying your children, your family; life is good for Stuart Markus.

Stuart Markus: I have no complaints. The most important thing to anybody is that you have your health. I don't care how much money you have or you don't have. I've enjoyed being on the top of the mountain. I didn't enjoy being on the bottom, but I'm a fighter and I never stayed on the bottom long. We have a very nice life. We have a beautiful home. We live in Palm Desert, what could be better? We work hard when we work, and we play hard. I had a boss at Villager who was my mentor and he said, "If you work hard, you play hard and enjoy life."

George Green: What advice would you give to younger people, or older people, who are caught up in this consolidation today, where there's a lot of successful people that were downsized, out of work; they've had success and all of a sudden the light went out. What advice would you give them?

Stuart Markus: We've had some friends who lost everything. They've had to do what they've had to do to maintain a life. If they have to work and be a greeter at Walmart, they're a greeter at Walmart. You can't sit around and feel sorry for yourself. If you do that, you're not going to accomplish one thing. You have to go out every day with a positive attitude, and that's the best thing I can say.

Bill Chunowitz

We're not clowning around!

Bill Chunowitz was born in Chicago, in 1940. As a youngster growing up in Albany Park, he attended Volta Grammar School and Von Steuben high school. He also went to Hebrew school on a scholarship, where he became president, despite his family not being religious. Having little money, Bill worked in the U.S. Post Office at night to pay for his schooling. After that he went on to spend two years at Wright Junior College, and then Roosevelt University where he studied accounting. During this time he also served in the army.

In 1963 he was married and working for a CPA firm, Checkers. In 1967 he was offered a position with McDonald's Restaurant which, at the time, consisted of roughly eight-hundred restaurants around the world. By 1970 he was handling accounts for McDonald's franchisees throughout the Midwest.

One thing led to another and soon he purchased the only McDonald's in McHenry County, which also included the franchise rights throughout the county. He partnered with the previous owner's step-son, and together they ran the restaurant successfully. Before long they owned fourteen McDonald's Restaurants throughout the county.

Bill also went on to graduate from Hamburger University in Illinois! There he was taught how to make the perfect hamburger... and how to run a successful McDonald's business, of course. After some time, an organization for all the franchisees in the market place, in Chicago, was formed. It became known as the Chicagoland Operator's Association, and Bill was elected president.

Wanting to be active in the community, supporting different charities and organizations, he became inspired by a franchise in Philadelphia, where the first Ronald McDonald House was established. Fred Hill (Philadelphia Eagles), Doctor Audrey Evans and others in the Philadelphia association, first came up with the concept for 'Ronald MacDonald House' (named after the infamous Ronald McDonald clown). The purpose of the house was to serve as a place where families could stay and eat (for free if they had no funding) while their children were seen to in the nearby hospital. This has helped hundreds of families, preventing them from having to travel each day to see their children, or spend exuberant prices on motels.

Amazingly, Bill funded the purchase of the first house in Chicago by selling... the Artic Orange Shake! Indeed, Bill had no funds to buy the property himself, but promised to raise the funds through promotion. And they did! Today there are 338 Ronald McDonald Houses around the world.

In 2002 Bill and his partner sold their restaurants. Throughout his career, Bill also ran his own accounting firm, with most of his clients being McDonald's franchisees.

In 2007 Bill lost his first wife to a Glioblastoma brain tumor. Fortunately, he met Joanna who had lost her husband also to a brain tumor, due to Leukemia. They were there for one another and consequently got married. Bill never had any children.

In 2008 he went into semi-retirement. He is no longer as actively involved but still oversees operations and progress in Chicago. He lives with Joanna now in Rancho Mirage, California, and often visits his family when tending to business in Chicago. He states that he looks back at what he has achieved, feeling secure in the knowledge that he did everything he could to 'give back'. Bill will always be a legend when it comes to the name 'McDonald's'. His caring heart and contributions to those less fortunate, through creating Ronald McDonald House, can never be overrated.

Interview with Bill Chunowitz

George Green: I'm anxious to find out about Bill Chunowitz.

Bill Chunowitz: I was born in Chicago. I lived in Albany Park. We lived in a one-bedroom apartment on Ainslie. I went to Volta Grammar School and, in those days, my Father was in the army. I was born in 1940. He was in WW II. When my Father came back from the army, my sister was born, in '48, so we were eight years apart. He worked at the U.S. Post Office, as a post man, and he also worked for his brother who owned a printing company. When I was a kid we basically played outside. I went to grammar school and I had a lot of friends. Our area was pretty much Jewish, and so most of my friends went to Hebrew School. My parents didn't have any money; weren't religious or anything, but some of my friends were. When I was a kid I became Orthodox. I had a scholarship to Hebrew School. I was President of the School, and it became very simple to me. The Rabbi wanted me to go to New York, to college, and be a Rabbi. I did continue after I graduated grammar school. I went to a public high school (Von Steuben high school), in Albany Park. As I got older I continued to maintain the Jewish culture. I was not necessarily the smartest guy, but I had the ability to get along with people. I was considered a popular guy; played a lot of sports. I played junior basketball; fresh, sophomore, and varsity. I graduated from high school in '58. There were about eighty-five or ninety people in our graduating class. I then continued on and went to junior college for a couple years, and I worked while I went to school. I worked nights at the post office to pay for my school. I would've loved to go on and away to college, but I couldn't afford it.

My Mom was terrific. My Dad made ends meet. After I finished two years at Wright Junior College, I went to Roosevelt University. Again I went to school during the day time, and at night I worked at the Post Office. In 1962 there was the Berlin crisis going on. I got lucky enough to join the army reserves, six months active duty and six years volunteer reserve. I was in transportation. All I had to do was drive the General. I went ahead and got into a control group in 1966. After that I was on the south side of Chicago, in a unit, and it was a long ride because I was on the north side and I worked downtown for a CPA firm at that time. I graduated college and became an accountant. At the same time we're still going into army reserve units. I was a chaplain for a while. From there, I said, "This is too far South to go. I need a nice unit on the North side..."; found a nice little medical unit, I became a general assistant. So, I went from a general driver to chaplain to general assistant. I got married in 1963. We never had any children; it was just my wife and I. She was busy working and I was busy working, but we saved our money and, in 1967, I got involved with a man that was representing McDonald restaurants and he offered me a job. I went to work for him and we did the accounting for franchisees throughout the Midwest, and all over the country.

I used to travel every month. The franchisee had to submit a financial statement to the company, just so the company could keep tabs on them. In the earlier years McDonald's had passive investors, it was all about quality, service, and cleanliness was the whole philosophy. Doing the accounting I met one of our clients who franchised in McHenry County. That one restaurant, only one store in that town, was the only store in all McHenry County. But that restaurant held the franchise rights for the entire county.

He was looking to sell his restaurant, and he was going to sell this restaurant to us. We were getting approved; his step-son would be the operator. So, we went ahead and we were able to purchase the store in 1970. We had first right of refusal, an exclusive, which meant that McDonald's could not put in another store in that area unless they first offered it to us.

So, long story made short, we went ahead and over the years we were able to get fourteen restaurants throughout that territory. The area started growing, population was growing, and we ended up with fourteen restaurants throughout McHenry County.

George Green: It took you about twenty years.

Bill Chunowitz: Twenty years. We had almost one-thousand people working for us. I went to Hamburger University, just like my partner did. Hamburger University teaches you basically how to operate a restaurant, in Oak Brook, Illinois.

George Green: Hamburger University?

Bill Chunowitz: You get a degree in hamburgerology! You go to AOC, Advanced Operators Course, BOC, the Basic Operators Course. They have an equipment operator's course...

George Green: That's kind of fascinating!

Bill Chunowitz: They teach you exactly how to make the hamburger, how to prepare it, where to buy the equipment, how to hire, how many people to hire, how to prepare it, how to clean the place, how to clean and take care of all the equipment, advertising, marketing, where to go for insurance...

George Green: And you got a degree from Hamburger University.

Bill Chunowitz: That's exactly right. Before you can go into Hamburger U. you must work almost two-thousand (hours) in a store, free. No one pays you.

George Green: That's fascinating!

Bill Chunowitz: So, when people decide to go into McDonald's saying, "I'd like to get a franchise..." you have to be willing to go anywhere, any place, any time, because franchises are not necessarily given in your locale. You have to be willing to relocate. But before you even do that, you have to be an approved owner/operator. To be an approved franchisee, you have to go ahead and take tests, you work in the stores, you work with other operators, you work with corporate personnel, and they basically judge you to see whether or not you would be a good operator for the system.

George Green: And you put in how many hours?

Bill Chunowitz: Two-thousand hours; almost a year's worth of work. For many people it takes them a couple of years because people who work there can't afford to just quit their job and do that, because they have to feed their family. So they do a second job. Before that time, in 1970, every market had an owner/operators association to do advertising and marketing and so forth. We had a co-op. Ours was Chicagoland Operator's Co-op. Basically it was an organization for all the franchisees in the market place, where we could consolidate our energies together. We had a public relations firm that did PR for us. We had an ad agency that did all our advertising. We'd meet once a month. I had committees. I become President of the association. We support a lot of different charities and a lot of different organizations. Special Olympics, diabetes; we represented the muscular dystrophy with Jerry Lewis, all different charities. It was the objective of our PR firm to come to us with programs that they thought were good for us, that we should be involved with in 'giving back' to the community. McDonald's knew children were our major market, which gave us Ronald McDonald the clown! The other one is called 'Judy the Elephant' at the Lincoln Park Zoo.

George Green: What was the name of the elephant?

Bill Chunowitz: Judy the Elephant.

George Green: Oh, Judy the Elephant.

Bill Chunowitz: Judy the Elephant at the Lincoln Park Zoo, to help sponsor the Lincoln Park Zoo. Well that didn't turn me on very much. I said, "Let me find out more about what the Ronald McDonald House is." Well the first Ronald McDonald house was established in Philadelphia, Pennsylvania, in 1974 through the hospices of a football player named Fred Hill. Fred Hill was a football player, wide receiver, for the Philadelphia Eagles. His daughter was diagnosed with cancer at a young age. The very first Ronald House, I said, was opened in Philadelphia. It was a small five-bedroom house, basically through the hard work of a lady named Doctor Audrey Evans who was an oncologist/hematologist at the Children's Hospital in Philadelphia. Fred Hill got the Philadelphia Eagles to get involved because he was with the Eagles. Between the operators in Philadelphia, they were able to do an 'Eagles Fly For Leukemia' where they sold Shamrock Shakes. The proceeds went to help build a house in 1974.

George Green: That's the first Ronald McDonald...

Bill Chunowitz: That's correct. The house would be located close to the hospital where the families could stay while their child is being treated as an out-patient at the nearby Children's Hospital. The patient was mainly in the cancer leukemia area, because normally hospitals don't have facilities to house the families because it's enough to take care of the children. There's not room for them. There aren't places where the families can shower or shave or get a couple hours sleep because most parents, when their child is diagnosed with serious illnesses, don't want to leave the child. They want to be as close as they can. Well, a similar situation happened in Chicago, where children were in hospitals located in the Lincoln Park area and pediatric care was taken care of at the hospital. Once again, parents come from long distances to come to the Children's Hospital because it was well-known and renowned for taking care of children's serious illnesses.

George Green: So that was the reason for the Ronald McDonald House; as a housing platform for parents of cancer children and other serious diseases.

Bill Chunowitz: Exactly correct.

George Green: So you decided that's the project that you wanted to get on.

Bill Chunowitz: That's correct. So I met with Doctor Baum (an oncologist at the Children's Hospital; counterpart of Doctor Audrey Evans from Philadelphia) and Charlie Marino (an attorney and the father of one of Doctor Braum's eight-year-old patients, Gage) and they pitched it to me, "Would you be interested?" I said, "I don't have any money, but I have a bunch of restaurants; 150 restaurants in the Chicagoland McDonald operating area." There were 150 restaurants. I was the President of the association. So, we went through the neighborhood to try and find a facility that would meet the needs of these families and parents that would still be close by to the hospital. We walked around and, a block and a half away, there was Saint Clement Church, about two blocks from the hospital. It was a very nice church. Right next to the church were three buildings, beautiful homes. One was a home which was the parish, which they were using. Another one was an empty lot, and then one was a convent. An eighteenth-century home, it looked like a sorority house. It had eighteen bedrooms; looked like a Victorian home, it was beautiful.

George Green: Perfect.

Bill Chunowitz: Perfect. At that time there were three nuns still living in there. But the Archdiocese Club, Cardinal Cody, was looking forward to possibly selling some property. We went through the house and looked at it. The sisters in the house, there were only two left; they were going to be leaving to go to Florida anyhow. So great! An empty and beautiful Victorian house! We went ahead and said, "Okay, how much does he want for it?" Well, he wanted 250,000 dollars. Back in 1974 that's a lot of money. I didn't have 250,000 dollars, but I said I did have 150 McDonald restaurants that I could use for our vehicle to help fundraise and pay it off. Lo and behold the Cardinal said, "No problem. I'll go ahead and sign a note with you from a bank for the 250,000 dollars, and we'll be able to buy it and then you guys can pay it off." So, myself and the Cardinal co-signed a note. We went ahead and then after that we decided to have a promotion; Arctic Orange Shake, all the proceeds from Arctic Orange Shake for one week...

George Green: A what?

Bill Chunowitz: Arctic Orange Shake.

George Green: Oh, an Arctic Orange Shake.

Bill Chunowitz: Instead of a burger and milkshake, we'll be giving an Arctic Orange Shake.

George Green: A-R-C-T-I-C Arctic?

Bill Chunowitz: That's correct, we sold Arctic Orange Shakes and the proceeds went for that. Lo and behold we had a couple more promotions in the period of about a year or two years. We were able to burn the mortgage. We paid off. Now we have to furnish the house. Now, what we learned to do was become professional beggars! How do you do that? Because we didn't have any money, we went to the merchandise mart in Chicago which has all the furniture and all the lamps and so forth, and we went to big corporations and said, "We have a Ronald McDonald house." We started telling them what our story is and what we wanted to do with them. Companies all over the place opened up their hearts. It was like Mages' Moment of Madness where everybody started working... picture frames and everything.

George Green: Was that exciting?

Bill Chunowitz: Oh, most exciting.

George Green: Was that more exciting than opening, or was it equal to opening your first restaurant?

Bill Chunowitz: Without a doubt, because this was an opportunity to give back to families who were in dire need in a time of their life. You could help somebody else who needs some help.

George Green: So this was a euphoric moment in your life.

Bill Chunowitz: No question. You have the chills as you saw the house opening and the families coming in there and staying there because these people came from all over. They didn't have a lot of money, most people, and most of the money was spent on medical bills. You could stay at our house for five-dollars a night, if you could afford it. If not, it's free. In the house we had day rooms. We had places where the families could stay. I went to Bob Abt. He was able to open up his heart and help us out with that, too. We came to him and it was fantastic. Charlie Marino, myself, and Doctor Baum felt that we could do this program in Chicago, in Los Angeles, San Francisco, Atlanta, Denver, Pheonix, Houston, Dallas, all the major cities wherever there was McDonald's. So, we started traveling and we had a road show. The three of us would talk to groups. In addition to that, I also had my accounting practice. We represented McDonald's restaurants throughout the country. I was still practicing accounting all the way until I retired in 2008.

George Green: Woah!

Bill Chunowitz: My philosophy was, 'How do you wear all these hats? How can you work with Ronald McDonald house, operate restaurants, run an accounting business...' I guess the theory is, 'If you take a busy man and give him something to do, he'll get it done. Take somebody who's not too busy, they'll never get it done.' So today, we started an international advisory board where I was accepted as Vice-President and Treasurer, and we had annual conventions. We just had a convention last year, over two-thousand people in Chicago. We now have 338 houses throughout the world. We just opened up in Russia last year. My wife and I used to run dinner dances in Chicago for fundraising events. We personally raised over seventeen-million-dollars for the houses. We just opened up the largest house in the world in downtown Chicago, on Saint Clair Grand Avenue. It has eighty-six bedrooms. The house is fifteen stories high and we serve over fourteen-thousand families every year. We have a kitchen in there where we serve meals every single day; 365 days, free.

George Green: You're in a different spotlight now at this age. With your semi-retirement you're still in touch with everything that's going on. There's a new enjoyment today at this age, and you can look at your life and say you've accomplished a lot.

Bill Chunowitz: Yeah, I sit down with Charlie Marino and Doctor Baum; when it's our time to go, we didn't do so bad! I lost my wife in 2007. I decided that life is very short. I was fortunate when she passed away that I met another lady, my present wife, who also had lost her husband. He had leukemia and died from a brain tumor. We were both married forty-three years so we had a lot in common.

George Green: What advice would you give to youngsters and other people that consolidation threw out?

Bill Chunowitz: Well, today's environment is so much different than what I had. At that time you could do things. Because of the economy and education now, because of all the costs involved with things going on, young people today are having a little more difficult time because of jobs and the economy and so forth. Go out and make yourself exposed as much as you possibly can. Keep going to people, don't give up, follow your dreams, do what you can do. I think it's giving back and spending time, get involved as much as you can with different organizations. Meet people. I think the other thing is, probably, promote your strongest asset, whatever that may be. I always felt I wasn't the smartest but I felt that I had the ability to get along with people. So, what you do is you promote your best asset and, if you do that and you're genuine and you care about people and life and giving back, I think you'll find your dream.

Walter and Esther Schoenfeld

Variety is the spice of life

Walter Schoenfeld grew up in Seattle and earned a B.B.A from the University of Washington. His father ran a necktie business, selling ties across four different States in the U.S., and did well enough to support the entire family. But, after serving in the Korean War, Walter decided his father shouldn't have to travel and sell at his age. So, he took over the business and helped him to retire comfortably. In 1955 Walter met Esther. They recall it was 'love at first site'.

Together they ran Walter's father's neckwear business, and even expanded further than the initial four states in which they were first operating. They then went the extra mile and began importing their materials, making their neckwear unique and original.

During this time they also got involved in their community, and Walter became chairman of the first Artificial Kidney Center in Seattle. This was when things began to snowball for the Schoenfelds, in a good way! At a lunch meeting where Walter intended to discuss funding for the kidney project, he met Senator Henry Martin 'Scoop' Jackson who offered to assist with the center. Walter and Esther became well-known in Seattle for their contributions to the community. When it was decided that Seattle would host the World's Fair, Walter was elected to the committee and 'Century Twenty-One' was born. This ultimately turned Seattle around, especially now that the NBA was coming to town. Before long Walter became vice-president and director of the Seattle Supersonics (basketball).

During this time Walter continued in his father's neckwear business, but also went on to become the director of the Reading Railroad, in Philadelphia, V.P. and director of the Sunshine Mining Co, and chairman for Anchor Post Corporation (Anchor Fence). He had the ability to take a company that was seemingly failing and turn it around to become worth a fortune.

Following through with his love for sports, Walter then became involved with the Seattle Mariners (baseball), and went on to be owner for some time. At the same time he partnered with nine others to own the Seattle Sounders Soccer club.

Aside from sports Walter continued in the clothing industry. He became known as the King of Jeans soon after he founded Britannia Sportswear, and was also elected chairman of the Vans footwear company in 2004.

The roles mentioned above are only a few of Walter's achievements. He is known for being a great businessman, having run numerous great businesses. His efforts in the area of charity are also highly noted. He has been an advisor to two presidents of the U.S. and humanitarian to others in need. He also served on the President's executive committee.

Esther believes that Walter's success is due to his being 'smart and personable', and Walter believes he could not have done it without Esther. The couple is dynamic, to say the least, with a family of three children.

They live today in Seattle, and in Palm Springs during the winter. Although they have sold all of their major businesses, Walter still serves on various boards including the Barbara Sinatra Children's Center. At the age of eighty-three, Walter faces some medical challenges and realizes that it's time to slow down. He and Esther have gone everywhere hand-in-hand during their marriage, and are extremely happy with the lives they've lived. Seemingly they have little or no regrets, rarely looking back at any wrong decisions.

With success after success, and the ability to work together to achieve such successes, Walter and Esther Schoenfeld enjoyed a bright spotlight. Although this light may not be as bright today, they believe it's certainly still shining.

Interview with Walter and Esther Schoenfeld

George Green: Tell me about you and the spotlight you were under.

Walter Schoenfeld: Well, the question is, did my Father leave me a million dollars before we started? No. My Father lived to be 108-years-old. Our family had a necktie business in Seattle. In 1955, when I came home from Korea, the business was doing about five-hundred-thousand dollars in the state of Washington, Oregon, Idaho, and Montana. It supported about four families. It was a business that I really disliked. My Father was seventy-five, packing suitcases on the road, selling neckties in Washington, Idaho, and Montana.

George Green: He was a traveling salesman?

Walter Schoenfeld: At age seventy-five. He was one of the most unbelievable people you've ever met. As much as I disliked the business, I knew I had to take the sample cases out of his hands. Shortening this story, we took the company from five-hundred-thousand dollars to three-hundred-million dollars. When I started the business, I met this young lady (Esther). In 1955, we fell in love on our first date! I knew that we could not ever survive with a little neckwear company in those four Western states. When we got California going I realized nobody would want to buy neckwear from Seattle and sell it in New York. All

American buyers love to go over to Europe and buy, but the Europeans didn't know how to manufacture.

Esther Schoenfeld: By 1960 Walter was going to New York. I was going with him, on buying trips to buy silks. That's when he came up with the idea of going to Europe and buying fabrics in Europe that would make him more distinctive.

Walter Schoenfeld: I went to Europe looking for something that was similar to Dacron. I looked in the yellow pages and found a fellow by the name of Theo Broglia who had something called Terylene... much better than anything here.

Author's note: from Memidex Dictionary – Terylene is an arbitrary blend of terephthalate and polyethylene.

We got the material and it exploded! In the meantime I was very involved in Seattle, and the Swedish hospital in Seattle. They asked me to be chairman of the first artificial kidney center in Seattle, which was also the first in the U.S. It was a very successful campaign. But things happened. People were dying. NBC did a program called 'Who Shall Live?' nationwide. We had a committee in Seattle of twelve people who decided who would get treatment each year, and any of those who didn't get the treatment died. It was a crazy thing. I called our Senator Magnuson to see if I could go to Washington to get money to help this program. I go to Washington and have a lunch date with him. During lunch he spoke about how Boeing lost the contract on the C5A. Bill Allen from Seattle, the President of Boeing, also joined us for lunch. Senator Magnuson had told me not to talk about the kidney center at this lunch meeting. I agreed not to. Soon, who walks in? Scoop Jackson and his assistant.

Author's note: from Wikipedia - Henry Martin 'Scoop' Jackson was a United States congressman and Senator from the state of Washington, from 1941 until his death, September 1983.

During lunch, Bill Allen is giving Magnuson the third degree for not getting the contract with Boeing, which ultimately turned out to be the 747. Magnuson replied, "The next time they ask you to build a Ford, don't build a Cadillac." While they're going on about that, Scoop asks me about the kidney center. He ended up becoming one of our closest friends. In fact he was due for dinner at our home the night he died.

Esther Schoenfeld: You also went to China with him.

Walter Schoenfeld: Yeah. Moving on... I was also a director of the Reading Railroad, in Philadelphia, and I was chairman of their real-estate division. I was the chairman of the Sunshine Mining merger and acquisitions committee, too; that was a very interesting experience.

George Green: All these companies; mining, a railroad... did they want your money, your brain, or both?

Esther Schoenfeld: He just was smart and personable.

Walter Schoenfeld: While I was with Sunshine Mining they bought a company on the American Stock Exchange which was called 'Anchor Fence, Anchor Post'.

Esther Schoenfeld: Chain link fence.

Walter Schoenfeld: Chain link fence. It was the largest fence company in America. When they bought the company it was losing a ton of money. Nobody could figure out what was going on. So they made me chairman of the merger and acquisition committee, and asked me, "Would you go down and see what you can do to straighten this thing out?" Because this was such a major company, Esther and I thought maybe we'd go down there for a year or two to straighten it out.

Esther Schoenfeld: In the meantime we have three little babies.

Walter Schoenfeld: I had a look and in about four days I had the problem solved. It was a simple solution, although everybody thought I was a genius. Now the NBA is coming to Seattle...

Esther Schoenfeld: Some leaders of the city, whom Walter was involved with in the kidney center, were also the ones that decided that Seattle needed to have a World's Fair. They invited Walter to be one of these men. At that time, Jewish men weren't involved in civic things in the city, so it was really a big deal. There was this real swampy, horrible area in Seattle. They wanted to take this whole gigantic area right next to downtown, and make it into something that the city really needs. We didn't have an opera house, we didn't have a stadium of any kind; we didn't have a science center. So, basically they put these ideas together and called it Century Twenty-One.

Walter Schoenfeld: They had already started and they asked me to come and help develop it near the end, but they'd already had the idea.

Esther Schoenfeld: He was in the meetings. Century Twenty-One was fabulous. It was a really, really bad area of town and so the guys decided, 'We're not going to be like other cities where everything is up, temporary, and destroyed. Everything that we've put into these buildings is going to be permanent.' So, we had the Coliseum which was then going to enable us to get a basketball team. We put in an opera house which was a permanent fixture and a beautiful building which still today functions as an opera house. We put in the Space Needle. Howard Wright built the Space Needle. It opened in '62.

Author's note: *from Wikipedia - The 'Space Needle' is an observation tower in Seattle, Washington, a landmark of the Pacific Northwest, and a symbol of Seattle. It was built in the Seattle Center for the 1962 World's Fair, which drew over 2.3 million visitors. Nearly twenty-thousand people a day used its elevators.*

Walter was very much a part of this group of men that made sure that this happened.

Walter Schoenfeld: So now, the NBA wants to come to Seattle. Sam Schulman and Gene Klein are both from Los Angeles. The NBA gives them a list of five people they can talk to for a Seattle partner, and somehow my name got on that list. One of the guys that they were hiring as a GM; I knew him from the old USC days. I was the first they interviewed and they didn't want to interview anybody else. But they did; they interviewed the others then they called me to come down. Esther and I went down to San Diego and they offered me twenty-percent as the swing vote. It cost me, I think, four-hundred-thousand dollars, or something like that, for twenty-percent of the team. And that was how I got involved in sports, and believe me it was a nervous investment.

George Green: Were you always a sports fan?

Walter Schoenfeld: Oh yeah, I love sports. It was just fun to be involved because it was excitement. I love the city of Seattle. It's done everything for me and my family.

Esther Schoenfeld: It was very exciting for the city to have an NBA team.

Walter Schoenfeld: It was exciting for the city.

George Green: So now you've got sports and it wasn't long before you actually had both franchises, basketball (Supersonics) and baseball (Mariners).

Walter Schoenfeld: I was involved in both and, yeah, I had ownership in both for a while.

Esther Schoenfeld: Then we also had this soccer club, before the baseball.

Walter Schoenfeld: Ten of us, including the Nordstroms, were partners in the Seattle Sounders. But I had to drop out because both the Nordstroms and Sam Schulman wanted an NFL franchise.

Esther Schoenfeld: When we got the soccer franchise, we're back to the Century Twenty-One World's Fair because on those Fair grounds we built a stadium, a big memorial stadium. The high schools started playing their championship games at the Memorial Stadium which we built on those grounds.

George Green: Esther got very much involved in a big battle with Danny Kaye over who's going to have what kind of box.

Walter Schoenfeld: And she won, just like with our battles!

George Green: But tell me about the excitement of being an owner.

Walter Schoenfeld: Well, there's pluses and minuses. She (Esther) saw the minus side all the time. The plus side was the perks. People generally put you first all the time. With the neckwear business, I decided the only way I'm ever going to take this business and grow it is by building a plant in Europe, so that the Americans who will never buy from Seattle will love the company in Europe, they love that trip, they'll buy from us. We built a factory up in Scotland.

Esther Schoenfeld: We were going to Europe all the time. We would take the little children with us many times, especially in the summer time, which then led to moving to Europe to build this factory. We lived there for a year.

Walter Schoenfeld: How basketball helped... we're starting to build a factory in Scotland and the Americans are coming to buy from us. Marks & Spencer, the largest department store in all of Europe; I start talking to them wanting them to buy our ties. They were so price conscious. We're trying to be accepted as a new franchisee at Marks & Spencer, so we have a meeting. In order to be accepted you had to meet the chairman, Lord Sieff, whose family founded the Weitzman Institute. He's looked at my dossier; I'm the Vice-President of a basketball team, I've been a director of a railroad, I've been all this and that. So as we're sitting, he asks me, "With all this, why are you still in the neckwear business?" I tell him about my Father. He says, "You're doing this because of your Father? I'd like you to join me for lunch." To make a long story short he, like 'Scoop' Jackson, became our best friend. Our life down here (Palm Springs) was changed because of that.

George Green: You're also a trustee with the Barbara Sinatra Children's Center.

Walter Schoenfeld: Yeah! One night we're going to dinner with Kirk and Anne Douglas. They call and say, "We're going to the Sinatra's for dinner." I said, "Go right ahead!" She says, "No, we're always talking about you. Barbara wants you guys to come." Well, at the end of the evening Frank is walking us out with his arm around me. He says, "Now you're my friend, anybody tries to do anything to you, you have any problems, I want to know about it." We have been good friends with Barbara, and Frank, Sinatra for many years. Both Esther and I have been so proud of the work that Barbara Sinatra has done with the Barbara Sinatra Children's Center.

Author's note: *see interview with Barbara Sinatra.*

George Green: What turns you on today at your age, here in Palm Springs? You decided to turn the light off, get out of that spotlight and do something with your world and your body.

Esther Schoenfeld: If we can go back to 1970 when we're living in England... One day Walter walks on Carnaby Street and he saw shops that had faded blue jeans. The only blue jeans we had seen in our lives up until 1970 were dark blue Levis. So Walter started a company called Britannia Sportswear, and started going to China, to Hong Kong, and buying. And we're still in the neckwear business. He starts this jeans business and it becomes the biggest jeans company, probably in the world at that time. He was written up in Forbes Magazine; they called him the King of Jeans! The business was huge.

George Green: And you had that and sold it?

Esther Schoenfeld: Sold it, yes.

George Green: Did you sell everything?

Walter Schoenfeld: Well, yes. I sold everything, not perfectly, though. Back to turning the light off; I don't think I've shut it off.

Esther Schoenfeld: Never.

George Green: You haven't shut the light? It's a dimmer light, Walter, is it not?

Walter Schoenfeld: It's a different light. I'm not running a business anymore, and I miss that. The last business I ran was Vans, a public company that manufactures shoes. Back in 2004, Vans was a shoe company. What happened is I had a friend who had a lot of stock in it. My son was involved with them, and it was losing money. He asked me would I go down and help out, see if I could turn it around. Anyhow, going down to help out was like a three or four year project. We turned it around.

Esther Schoenfeld: Walter became the chairman.

Walter Schoenfeld: I became the chairman and it went from being worth nothing to... I think we sold it for about five-hundred-million dollars. So we really brought it back and got it working. So that was my last business, but I still have people that call, asking me to get involved or serve on their boards. Too late for that!

Esther Schoenfeld: Gary, our son, was the President of Vans while Walter was chairman, kind of teaching him and pushing him along. But then they sold it.

Walter Schoenfeld: I've never really 'thrown it in'. I think none of us really throw it in. I look at you, why are you sitting here? You haven't thrown in the towel. If you'd thrown in the towel, you wouldn't be doing this right now.

George Green: But look at all the things you've done in sports and businesses, and at this age, right now, close to eighty...

Walter Schoenfeld: Eighty-three...

George Green: Your body and mind don't really do what your head wants them to do anymore.

Walter Schoenfeld: That's correct.

George Green: You may say, "I wish I could do that, but I better start learning to be content within my own body, within my own head, and try to go at the pace that I'm physiologically capable of going at. I would die, literally, if I tried to do what I did when I was working sixteen hours a day."

Walter Schoenfeld: Absolutely, there's no question.

George Green: You've had a great life; you're still living a good life.

Walter Schoenfeld: Still living a good life, thanks to a fantastic family. But you're right; physiologically you can't do what you used to. Besides, I am battling my own medical problems. But I am not a complainer. I have nothing to complain about.

Esther Schoenfeld: He's still on a bank board in Seattle.

George Green: So the bottom-line on Walter and Esther Schoenfeld's life is that the light is pretty bright, even today at this age.

Esther Schoenfeld: Oh yeah! Especially to have three happily married children and eight fabulous grandchildren. We have the best times together.

George Green: What advice would you give young people that are ambitious; how do you get there?

Walter Schoenfeld: Young people, if you have a brain, use it and keep working. Just don't give up, and you'll get there. I schlepped suitcases in hundred-degree weather, and threw things that weighed forty pounds, to sell a two-hundred dollar order and make ten-percent on it. You know, all you've got to do is keep working, and if you work hard enough you'll get what you deserve.

Esther Schoenfeld: Take a chance.

Gone But Not Forgotten

John Robert Wooden

There's no bigger name in basketball. Period.

John Robert Wooden was born in October, 1910, in the town of Hall, Indiana. In 1918 his family moved to Centerton. As a young child, John's role-model was Fuzzy Vandiver from the Franklin Wonder Five, a well-respected basketball team that dominated Indiana High-School basketball for some time. When his family moved again, this time to Martinsville, John led the high-school team to the state championship three years in a row, and then won the tournament in 1927.

He graduated in 1928 and moved on to Purdue University. There he was coached by Ward 'Piggy' Lambert. After achieving a great deal there, he was given the name 'The Indiana Rubberman' for his 'suicidal' dives on the hard-court. He graduated from Purdue University with a degree in English in 1932.

After this he spent a number of years playing professionally with the Indianapolis Kautskys (now known as the Indianapolis Jets), the Hammond Ciesar All-Americans, the Whiting Ciesar All-Americans and was also added to the NBL's First Team in 1937. John also coached basketball during this time.

1942 saw the start of World War II, and John joined the US Navy. After serving for three years, he left as a lieutenant. He jumped straight back into basketball and resumed his career by coaching at the Indiana State Teacher's College (now known as Indiana State University).

In 1947 John's team was invited to the National Tournament in Kansas City, by the National Association of Intercollegiate Basketball. But John refused the invitation due to the NAIB's policy on African American players. Clarence Walker, one of John's top players, was an African American.

In 1948 John was signed as the head basketball coach at UCLA. He took the team to new heights and led them to excel dramatically. Despite John and his wife, Nellie Riley (his high-school sweetheart whom he married in 1932), being unhappy in Los Angeles, John kept his word and fulfilled his contract.

By 1955 John had sustained success at UCLA. However, things took a turn after a proposed scandal involving players in the football team being handed illegal payments. This resulted in the dismantling of the PCC (Pacific Coast Conference; a College Athletic Conference in the United States comprising of a collection of regional rivalries).

By 1962 this issue was resolved and John returned his team back to the top of the conference. The years that followed led to John Wooden being seen as having perhaps the greatest unrivaled impact on UCLA, and the game of basketball, in history. Due to this he was awarded numerous medals and awards, various schooling and athletic facilities were named in his honor, and a bronze statue made in his likeness was dedicated to him at the Pauley Pavilion in 2012. John also went on to publish a number of books related to coaching, UCLA, and basketball.

After his wife, Nellie, passed away in 1985, John chose to stay close to his Christian faith and visited her crypt on a monthly basis. Towards 2006 he began experiencing a number of health issues which rendered him hospitalized on occasion. In 2010 he was admitted to the Ronald Reagan UCLA Medical Center for dehydration, and sadly passed-away a week later, just ten days short of his one-hundredth birthday.

John Wooden is the only inductee in the National Basketball Hall of Fame as both a player and a coach. As a coach his record is unequal, including ten NCAA Championships, ten years consecutive victories, four full undefeated seasons and a remarkable win/loss lifetime record of over eighty-percent. He will always be remembered for his outstanding and innovative contributions to the one of the best-loved games in the United States; basketball.

Author's note: John Wooden is a perfect example of an individual who was thrust into the spotlight by what he accomplished, but did not need it nor particularly care for it. His basketball life was only the outside. His real life was always with his wife and family. For him, the spotlight really never mattered.

Interview with John Wooden

George Green: I would like to know about the popularity, what life was like and how you achieved your fame.

John Wooden: When I came to UCLA, basketball hadn't become very popular on the coast at all. Had I not signed for a three year contract, I would have left at the end of two because I wasn't at all happy with the things that occurred here. I was led to believe that by the end of my three year contract we would have a nice place to play on the UCLA campus. At the end of my second year I could see that it was not going to be. As a matter of fact, it didn't come about until after my seventeenth year. For seventeen years we practiced on the third floor of an old gym. During practice, most of the year, there would be gymnastics practicing on one side, wresting at the end; a couple of times a week there would be trampolines on the opposite side. It made it difficult for all coaches. I came to the conclusion after a number of years that we can never reach the peak that most people would like to, whatever the profession they're in, under those conditions. I was wrong, because we won our first two National Championships with those exact conditions! We had no Home Court for almost all those years. We played our Home Games in several different places, and each day before each practice I, with the Manager of the basketball team, would sweep and mop that area because the dust would accumulate on the floor during the day! And there were no private dressing rooms for either coaches or teams. There was just a large area of metal lockers. You would practice all week with just two baskets most of the time. Then you would pack up and go somewhere else to play a game. It was a very difficult situation through all those years. But, for every plus there is a minus. As time went by, I became adjusted to it and came closer to living what I should have tried to be living all the time, and that is; 'don't worry about the things over which you have no control and just make every effort to make the most of the things over which you do have control.' In `67 we had the new place to play and that was heaven! Pauley Pavilion! With six baskets, Home Court, it was the difference between night and day.

George Green: Did you have your eye on the National Championship from day one?

John Wooden: No. My aim at the beginning was to win the conference. As far as winning a National Championship, that didn't enter my head and I didn't want it to enter the heads of any of my players. We were concentrating on winning a Conference. If we won the Conference, then we were concentrating on winning the first round, then, hoping, you can get farther and go all the way.

George Green: You were coaching other places before you got to UCLA.

John Wooden: That's right. I coached in high-school for eleven years and coached two years at Indiana State University just prior to coming to UCLA.

George Green: As the most-winning basketball coach; what kind of a life is it when you are riding that kind of a wave?

John Wooden: If you permit yourself to get caught up in it, it would not be a very good life in my opinion. I never looked at myself in that way, shape or form. When people say you are a legend, I don't think of myself as a legend at all. I think I was fortunate that I was able to be a part of teams that did extremely well. As a player, I was fortunate to play in college and high school with outstanding coaches and outstanding players with me. The exposure and what you got from athletic competition and the game of basketball; so much depends upon the players with whom you are working. No coach ever had an outstanding winning percentage without outstanding players. You must never get caught up in the feeling that you are, sort of, an indispensable person because you're not.

George Green: When you are winning it attracts the big players, and everybody in the country wanted to play for Coach Wooden.

John Wooden: Winning attracts winning, of course. UCLA is a great university and I wanted youngsters to come to UCLA because it was a great university. If you want to just play basketball, go someplace else. My job was not to develop professional basketball players, my job is to try and develop the best basketball team possible with the youngsters I have under my supervision, and try to see that you get a good education; something that will be helpful to you all your life.

George Green: While the team was winning, and while you were winning and while the university was getting all this National acclaim, did you avoid the spotlight?

John Wooden: As much as possible. You can't avoid it completely. But when I got out of it, I wanted to avoid it. I stayed away from UCLA pretty much all the time, except to go to the basketball games, and I've gone to the various functions.

George Green: While you were staying away from that kind of spotlight, did you also stay away from the commercial guys?

John Wooden: Yes, I did.

George Green: Why?

John Wooden: Money was never my goal. Even before I retired, I was offered more money to make my players wear a certain basketball shoe than I was making in other ways at UCLA. I never did that. I have been asked, since I retired, to make certain commercials for products. That I just absolutely wouldn't do, and many things of that sort. But that doesn't mean that I didn't want to have an income. I had a very poor retirement for various reasons. But, since retirement I have done better than I ever did before I retired; primarily by motivational talks and things of that sort. I still get more requests. Even though I have been retired for twenty-one years, I get more requests to do that then I could possibly handle. Traveling is difficult for me now, but I take things more or less local where they pick me up and bring me home. I'm doing it as an obligation or for a friend, charity or something of that sort. Otherwise I won't do it. In other words, I'm not just doing it for money.

George Green: In 1975 when you won your last Championship; you decided to retire on that day.

John Wooden: I didn't plan it at all. I didn't know I was going to retire until ten minutes or less... I decided to do it... this was it. I had no plan. No one knew.

George Green: Not even Nel?

John Wooden: Nel didn't know it. I didn't know it myself! It was after the semi-final game; the NCAA Tournament. Both teams played very well. Now, the game is over and we're going to play for the Championship, Monday night. That was a Saturday night. But this time I didn't want to go in to the hundred people in the press and spotlight asking all sorts of questions, lights flashing in your face and all that. I didn't want to do it. On my way to the dressing room I thought, 'If I'm feeling this way about it, it's time for me to get out.' I congratulated my players and told them, "I am very proud because you are the last team that I will ever coach." They were stunned; my assistants were stunned; my trainer stunned. Nellie didn't know anything about it yet. Then I left there to the press room. I said much the same thing as I said to the players. My director got up immediately and said, "You don't mean this." I said, "Yes, I do." That's how it happened. There were reasons in back of that. My wife's health and some other little things that happened. It just seemed that it was time to get out. I've never regretted it. I've missed practices. That's all I ever missed. I never missed a game. I never missed all the falderal; the Tournaments and all the other things.

George Green: The next day you never had a second thought?

John Wooden: Never.

George Green: What did Nel say when you came home?

John Wooden: She was very happy!

George Green: How can you possibly stay out of the spotlight once you achieved the fame you did?

John Wooden: At the games you would go to at UCLA, there would be an awful lot of people wanting to get autographs and things to sign and all that. You can't avoid that and still be polite. It is an honor; don't get upset. They are really honoring you when they want this. I try to do it all, but I also try to avoid as many places that it will happen as possible. I don't go to places very much that it would happen. I would spend more time with my family or close personal friends. I have always said that the three F's are very important, that is; faith, family and friends. If you keep those in that order you are going to be in pretty good shape.

George Green: Did any of your children follow in your footsteps as far as playing basketball?

John Wooden: Most of them played through high school but none on into college.

George Green: When Nel passed-away, what were your feelings about getting more involved in the University?

John Wooden: When Nel passed away, I didn't have thoughts about getting involved in anything. I almost hibernated for a while and had my children a little bit worried. My children have said that it was the coming of the great grandchildren that got me back on track.

George Green: Was there any time during your retirement that perhaps you craved a little bit more action than you were getting in retirement?

John Wooden: Never. I made the statement that when you retire you really get busy. But the things you do after you retire are the things you want to do not have to do, and there is a world of difference there. With all my family being somewhat close, I was always busy and there is always something to do. I never have enough time! After retirement, it looks like you would have more time, but it hasn't worked out that way, at least in my case. I have tried to stay out of the spotlight as far as UCLA basketball is concerned, as much as possible. I didn't lose my interest. I wanted to stay close. I've missed very few home basketball games since I retired but would never go away to see one.

George Green: Do you still sit there and curl your program?

John Wooden: I had notes on that program is what people didn't realize! You would roll it up and you could hold it better. Then I would open it up and see my notes to myself as far as the game was concerned. No, when I sit in the stands now I don't do that!

George Green: When you won the National crown for the tenth time; that particular night you knew you were going to retire, was there something very special about that?

John Wooden: The special feeling would be because of the fact that this is your last game you are ever going to coach, not because it was the tenth National Championship. It was the last game I would ever coach and it did end with a National Championship. That made it very special, yes; one I consider among the most special.

George Green: Were you always such a positive happy person? Did you ever get down?

John Wooden: I have had my down moments, but I didn't want to be down around my wife. I was always that way. For example, when I was a high-school player, we lost a very, very important game one time. We lose it by one point, my teammates are all crying; I didn't feel like crying. Was I happy? No, I wasn't, but I did my best and played as hard as I could and they beat us. I see no reason to be down on that. I think that came from my Father who tried to teach that; 'Never get too high over anything, and never get too low. For every peak there is a valley.' Try to stay on an even keel and don't be the one who thinks that the glass is half empty. Think of the glass as being half full. Try to be positive. If I want my players to feel positive, when I working with other people, I better be positive.

George Green: People admire you as a person just as they admire you as a coach. I think that is the highest compliment that man can be paid; when they look upon the human qualities as much as they look upon your athletic qualities.

John Wooden: It's nice to be perceived in that manner. I have often placed my character before my reputation. My reputation is what you and others perceive me to be. My character is what I am, and you don't know that. You may have an idea but you don't know truly.

George Green: Perception is not necessarily reality.

John Wooden: No, and what I always tried to teach my players is that, at all times, be more concerned with your character than your reputation. But you can have both.

George Green: The age of sixty-five had no bearing on your decision to retire?

John Wooden: No, except that under the State of California I would have had to retire at sixty-seven.

George Green: How did you feel about the players after you retired?

John Wooden: Amos Alonso Stagg, a gentleman I had great admiration for said, "A coach can never tell if he is successful with players until twenty years after they've graduated." I had a birthday a few weeks ago and twelve of my ex-players came in here. I am proud that thirty-something of my players became attorneys. I am proud that eight of them became ministers. I am proud that several became doctors and dentists. They didn't all become professional basketball players. I am just proud that most of my players have done well after graduation in whatever profession they have chosen. If one hasn't, I wonder if I failed somewhere.

George Green: Emotionally, you always seem to be in control. Were you as calm on the inside as you appeared on the outside?

John Wooden: Probably not as calm, but I tried to teach my players that if you lose your temper you will be outplayed. I tried to give my players the feeling that I was always under control. I have said that one must keep their emotions under control to execute whatever they are doing. Can you do it one-hundred percent? Of course not. We are all imperfect. But we can all try and we are all equal as far as having the opportunity to try.

George Green: You seem to be a student of psychology. Did you have any formal training in that area?

John Wooden: I studied psychology quite a bit and took extra courses in psychology, because once I got into the teaching profession I felt it would be more important in coaching/teaching. I was working with my English students primarily from the mental, and to some degree emotional. In athletics, it's physical, more-so emotional, and mental. Emotional, because you are in the public eye, out in front. That becomes more emotional than the student taking the test because he is not in the public eye.

George Green: When you were coaching, did you spend time teaching your players how to be human beings?

John Wooden: I hope so.

George Green: During the actual sessions you would talk about how to become a human being and how to be more human.

John Wooden: There would be times when I thought the best way was by example. There is a poem that one of my players wrote to me and he said, "It's walkin' it, not talkin' it!" So, I think you do more by example.

George Green: I give my definition of leadership, but want to know if you have one.

John Wooden: I have many. I have read many, many definitions of leadership. I have a whole book of different peoples' ideas of leadership. I don't have any simple definition. A leader can be led. A leader is interested in finding the best way, not in having his own way. A leader must make sure that his followers understand that you are working together; they're not working for you. In business, if you have all the people under your supervision thinking they are working for you, they will punch the clock in and out. But if you have them feeling they are working with you, they will put in the extra time. They will go the extra mile. The leader is a people-person. He leads them, he doesn't drive them.

George Green: If your phone didn't ring, would you still be happy?

John Wooden: Sure. But at the same time I don't mind. I know it's friends calling.

George Green: What advice would you give others who have had the kind of personal achievements you have had; they reach retirement age and are out of the spotlight.

What would you tell them?

John Wooden: I don't like to give advice. I will give opinions. I would tell them to stay busy doing something that you really want to do. Stay active. You must do that. That is very important. Physically and mentally. You need to have something active to do, and a person needs to feel... in some way... that they are needed. If we don't feel needed in some way, there is not much purpose in being here.

George Green: You popularized the Wooden Pyramid of Success. How important was that in your coaching?

Author's note: John Wooden's Pyramid of Success:

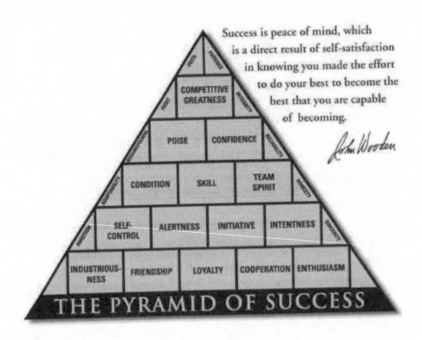

John Wooden: It was very important. It was just as important in my life as in my coaching. It wasn't designed primarily because of coaching. Primarily teaching English was what started me thinking about it. That's when I coined my own definition of success which is, 'peace of mind which can be attained only through self-satisfaction, knowing you made the effort to do the best of which you are capable.' That's all I tried to get those under my supervision to do. Never try to be better than somebody else; learn from others but never cease trying to be the best you can be. That's under your control. The other isn't, and when you have gotten too engrossed or involved in things over which you have no control, it is going to adversely affect the things over which you have control. I got the idea of a pyramid. I wanted success at the top, at the apex, that's where success is.

George Green: Why is loyalty at the bottom?

John Wooden: Because it is on the foundation. The cornerstones of the foundation are the most important parts of the foundation. That's hard work and enjoying what you are doing. Between the cornerstones, forming the foundation on the base, you have friendship, loyalty and cooperation. As you move up you have to maintain control, alert and alive, observing constantly (always learning). You have to have initiative (never be afraid to fail). You have to recognize that you are imperfect, you are going to fail on occasions and then you have to be determined and persistent. You have to persevere. I call that 'intentness'. Then you move up. You have to be conditioned for what you do mentally, physically, morally, emotionally, spiritually. You have to have the skills and you have to be able to do them. You have to be able to not only execute the skills; you have to be able to do them quickly. If you can't do them quickly, you may not get to them at all, and then you have to work with others. You have to have team spirit, and that's consideration for others. If you have these blocks that I have mentioned, they will make you poised and make you confident. So, they build up to that. You have to have confidence. You have to believe in yourself, and 'poised', to me, is just being yourself. When you have poise you are not acting, you are not pretending to be something you're not, therefore you will function to your own capability. Whatever we're doing we should do it to the best of our ability. But, the enjoyment comes from the difficult things. The last one is patience and faith. You have to have patience because good things take time. You have to have faith that things will work out as they should. I didn't say 'work out the way you want them to' because things don't always work out the way we want.

George Green: The Seven-point Creed is interesting because there, again, is a great deal of philosophy.

John Wooden: My Dad gave that to me when I graduated from grade school, on a little card. On the other side of the card there was a verse that said, "Four things a man must learn to do if he would make his life more true. To think without confusion clearly, to love his fellow man sincerely, to act from honest motives purely, to true in God and heaven securely". That was on one side of the card. On the other side was this Seven-point Creed. He said, "Son, try to live up to these."

Author's note: *John Wooden's Seven-point Creed:*

> **Be true to yourself.**
>
> **Make each day your masterpiece.**
>
> **Help others.**
>
> **Drink deeply from good books, especially the Bible.**
>
> **Make friendship a fine art.**
>
> **Build a shelter against a rainy day.**
>
> **Pray for guidance and give thanks for your blessings every day.**

John Wooden: Sometimes we pray for things but we fail to give thanks for the blessings we have.

George Green: Have you always been a religious man? Was your father religious?

John Wooden: I would say Mother and Dad were religious. Not because we went to Sunday school every Sunday. That doesn't make a person a good Christian at all. It might. It certainly isn't going to hurt them. In fact, it's bound to help you.

George Green: It seems that the older we get the more religious we become, perhaps.

John Wooden: I think that's because the older you get, you know you are approaching mortality. I'm writing a book of poems. Sometime after I lost Nel I wrote:

"The years have left their imprint on my hands and on my face.

Erect no longer is my walk and slower is my pace.

But there is no fear within my heart because I'm growing old.

I only wish I had more time to better serve my Lord.

When I have gone to Him in prayer, he's brought me inner peace.

And soon my cares and problems and other worries cease.

He has helped me in so many ways. He has never let me down.

Why should I fear the future when soon I could be near His crown?

Though I know down here my time is short, there is endless time up there

and he will forgive and keep me in his loving care."

George Green: You seem so happy with yourself. The gem is still as beautiful whether or not the spotlight is on it. There has to be an inner-serenity, calmness, a feeling of 'happy' within yourself; that's the way you seem.

John Wooden: I hope I am. I want to have serenity, and you get that through the life you lead. I don't think you can have it any other way. You get too involved in material things and they all get away from you. It's other things that are more lasting.

The Frank G. Wells Award 1995:

"The Frank G. Wells Award will be given every year at The American Teacher Awards to an individual whose life of civility, compassion, integrity, humility and respect for all humanity provides a compass for human behavior as Frank Wells did. In essence such an individual is a teacher by example. The American Teacher Awards is the ideal home for this award because the program honors outstanding teachers from across the country, in an attempt to provide recognition and appreciation for great teachers.

The first recipient of the Frank G. Wells is the perfect embodiment of the ideals set forth in the specifications for this honor. Our honoree this year has spent a lifetime working with young people. At UCLA he touched and transformed the lives of thousands of student athletes with his enduring values, discipline and academic achievement. His players, like the man himself, were always known for their good sportsmanship and poised demeanor. He is the only inductee in the National Basketball Hall of Fame as both a player and a coach. As a coach his record is unequal including ten NCAA Championships, ten years consecutive victories, four full undefeated seasons and a remarkable win/loss lifetime record of over eighty-percent. Here are a few comments from some of the people who were fortunate enough to come under the influence of the man affectionately known as 'The Wizard of Westwood', Mr. John Wooden.

"His presence at the bar was just commanding. Just commanding."
~ **Jamal Wilkes.**

"The thing that I respect him the most for is being a father in that he was so committed to his family."
~ **Mike Warren.**

"He taught us how to put our shoes and socks on properly so could we get our feet out of tight shoes."
~ **Marquis Johnson.**

"He taught us how to be good players, but more important, he taught us how to be good people. John Wooden gave me the greatest gift anyone could ever give and that is the ability to learn how to learn. He would have been one of the greatest teachers in whatever field he chose. Basketball, thank goodness for me, was what he chose."
~ **Bill Walton.**

This is the Frank G. Wells Award. It is made from a piece of Mt. Kilimanjaro which was Frank's first mountain conquest. I'm presenting this award to a man I have admired and whose players I have known for over thirty years, John Wooden."

Sid Caesar

That double talk could get you anywhere!

Isaac Sidney 'Sid' Caesar grew up performing short family sketches for those willing to watch. He also had another passion, the saxophone, and wanted to follow a musical career. But his talents as a performer ultimately paved his path.

He became one of the biggest names in show business; a movie star, a gigantic television personality who will always be remembered for his strong and strange sense of humor in the way he saw the world and, as importantly, for his 'double-talk' which left audiences around the world in hysterics.

Although he made it in the industry, he did so the hard way. Not every step he took up the ladder to success was straight up. He experienced a lot of difficulty in his life, along with a lot of disappointments and rejections. He was famous, yes, but the price of fame was high for Sid Ceaser, who passed away in his Beverley Hills home after failing to recover from a brief illness, in February, 2014.

Interview with Sid Caesar

George Green: Did you realize that you were the greatest superstar ever to hit this country in entertainment?

Sid Caesar: No, not at all.

George Green: You didn't. You thought you were just Sid Caesar, serviceman, hard-working guy makes good.

Sid Caesar: When I did 'Show of Shows' I was twenty-six-years-old.

George Green: And yet, you couldn't go anyplace without everyone knowing you, seeing you... and you never realized that you were a superstar?

Sid Caesar: No.

George Green: Never?

Sid Caesar: No, because I'm too busy. I didn't have time to do anything.

George Green: The ratings were coming in and breaking every record ever...

Sid Caesar: I was personally affected by it.

George Green: Certainly sometime during that four years you suddenly woke up and said, "I have really made it."

Sid Caesar: No.

George Green: Never! In four years, you never, even though you were the biggest thing that ever hit the entertainment business; you never realized who Sid Caesar was to the world?

Sid Caesar: No. I still don't.

George Green: You were enjoying a good life. Your family, children, entertainment, everything was going terrific.

Sid Caesar: I'm gettin' a little nuts, though, because of the pressure on doing a new show every week.

George Green: Let's go from 1954... tell me about the end of that show. How did that happen and why? How did you feel afterwards?

Sid Caesar: I came in this day and one of the guys from NBC says, "Sid, you're going to have your own show." I said, "Why, what's the matter." He says, "No, you're going to have your own show." I said, "What happened, what are you talkin' about?" He said, "Well, Imogine is going to have her own show, Max is going to have his own show, and you're going to have your own show." I said, "Why, what the hell is going on here, this is a great combination. Why are you breaking it up?" They told me it was already done. That was it. 'Hey, we got somethin' great that's sensational. Let's tear it apart.' With us, it was like... when I had the drinking problem, they said, "That's it, finish him."

George Green: Why were they treating you that way?

Sid Caesar: That's the way they treated people in those days. There was no anything. They didn't care. Use them up and then throw them away.

George Green: Did they think you were used up at that time?

Sid Caesar: Yeah, oh sure.

George Green: So, the fact is that you give this company seven years...

Sid Caesar: Eight!

George Green: Eight years of your life and they turn around and discard you like you were a piece of cheese... and what about the first eight years?

Sid Caesar: They didn't care. Nothing. I was shocked.

George Green: But how about the response from some of the people that you thought were your closest associates, allies, etc.

Sid Caesar: Nothing.

George Green: They abandoned you as well. So, you experienced the same thing I did when I walked out. It was like thirty-seven years I was never there.

Sid Caesar: You were never there.

George Green: That's what happened to me.

Sid Caesar: I never heard from NBC again.

George Green: How did you handle that particular situation?

Sid Caesar: The only ones who helped me, my brother and my wife.

George Green: David and your wife are your best friends, and they're the ones you know you can always depend upon.

Sid Caesar: Oh yes, they were always there. I was in tremendous turmoil. I was so disappointed. I thought, 'What the hell happened?' All of a sudden there was nothing. And they don't care. I said, "Can I get an explanation?" They said, "You're junk, that's all." I didn't do anything for about a year after that. I went to England and it was a tremendous success in England.

George Green: When you went there, were you starting to get control of your drinking?

Sid Caesar: Not really, no. It intensified it. Because you think you're not worth anything. You were a fake all these years, gettin' by on a pass. It was the only thing I had to turn to, my only friend. Have a couple of drinks and you forget about it.

George Green: When did you get hold of that?

Sid Caesar: Not until 1978. Twenty years I was just bump-a-bump-a-bump and I didn't care. I was so disappointed in mankind. In '78 I was in Canada and I was on the stage, opening night, and I couldn't remember one line. The first time that ever happened to me.

I was in absolute shock. I stood there and they were feeding me lines. The hotel said, "Let him go to the hospital for a week. Let him dry out. Let him take care of himself." That's what I did. I went into the dressing room and I looked in the mirror and I said, "Sid, you want to live or you want to die?" It's as simple as that. There's no uh... no gray area with this. We'll talk. No, that's it; give it up, or that's it. No other way. I called the doctor and I said, "Take care of me. I'm going to do it." Just like that, all those years of drinking, twenty years.

George Green: Then what happened?

Sid Caesar: What happened was that I got a part in a movie, a Peter Seller's movie, and it was going to be shot in Paris. I said, "Fine, we'll go there, we'll do this." I checked into the hospital and that's it. No pills, no booze, nothing and boy it was ... climbing the walls. But I did it.

George Green: So you actually helped yourself rather than the doctors or...

Sid Caesar: Well, I used to go to an analyst for twenty years, five times a weeks. But I didn't know what I was doing. What I did was learn the nomenclature. I can pick things up very fast if I want to. I didn't realize it, but I was using everything that I learned. I was my best psychiatrist. You can't lie to yourself.

George Green: Did some of those people start sniffing around at that time when they knew you were sober?

Sid Caesar: No. It was like it never happened. I did a show for CBS called the "Sid Caesar and Imogene Coca Cola Special". It won ten Emmys. They never replayed it. I said, "To hell with it. I'm not going to get mad at these people anymore."

George Green: Well at least you were able to deal with that portion of it, weren't you?

Sid Caesar: Because I went through it already. I said, "Who cares." I really didn't care. I was having a good life.

George Green: And you were fortunate that you were financially okay to be able to do that.

Sid Caesar: Oh, sure.

George Green: It took you a long time to get over the hurt, the rejection by friends, show people, associates. What advice would you give to some of the younger people who are encountering that kind of situation and they're going a little nutsy?

Sid Caesar: You gotta' live your own life. You have to find out if you're hurting yourself in any way or if you're the one who's at fault.

George Green: Even though you're happy today, content today, you're turning down opportunities that you wouldn't have turned down ten or fifteen years ago, you seem healthy, you seem relaxed, one thing is that you still love to entertain, don't you?

Sid Caesar: No, sir.

George Green: You don't.

Sid Caesar: No. I don't get a kick out of it anymore. It's too much. You gotta' be this; you gotta' do this. I'm not gonna' be proved that I'm better now than I was before. No way! Leave it alone. If you gotta' good reputation... don't. I don't have the energy. It's mostly energy and believing in yourself. You put something over and you go and get it. You have to go physically, and get it.

George Green: I don't care about how other people think about you, it's how you feel about what you're doing. The other night on the KCET thing, I thought you were marvelous. Everybody was hysterical. Don't you feel great after you did that?

Sid Caesar: I was in such pain. I gave it a shot because there is not that much pressure and that's the best thing about it. You keep yourself under pressure. Some guys can't let go. But, if you step back and look at life... You know I get a great kick out of it when I get up in the morning. The most insignificant things in life, I enjoy to the end.

George Green: You sound like you're enjoying life more now than you did before.

Sid Caesar: Much more, absolutely.

George Green: So you're saying that as intense as that spotlight was between 1950 and...

Sid Caesar: Between '50 and '58.

George Green: ...there's a different kind of spotlight on you today that's your own spotlight?

Sid Caesar: Nobody learns anything from success. All you learn from success is arrogance. You're so busy being 'me' and 'I' that you can't look and say, "Hey, wait a minute." The enjoyment of life is not you, it's the reaction to you. The people. I walk in the morning. It's clear, there's no noise, there's no traffic, no gas. You can walk and think. That, to me, I enjoy that... I really do. Just walking around the house and looking I say, "Gee, Sid, look what you got here. Boy, it's beautiful." And I appreciate it. The fact of getting up in the morning, and I'm not in pain, I'm not bleeding. I'm ahead of the game.

Gary Coleman

Different strokes for different folks!

Gary Wayne Coleman was born in February, 1968, and was best known for his role as Arnold Jackson in the American sitcom, Different Strokes. He suffered from focal segmental glomerulosclerosis, an autoimmune kidney disease. Due to this, and medication he received, his growth was limited and his facial structure retained its childlike appearance. As a child, working long hours along with complicated health issues ultimately led to his separating himself from the cast of Different Strokes. He continued as a performer, however, with smaller roles throughout his life. Gary also had a love for model trains and was noted for his 'Rio Grande' layout in 1990.

Life became financially difficult for Gary who put this turmoil down to the misappropriation of his trust fund. He consequently sued his adoptive parents and former business advisor over this issue. Having exceedingly high medical bills to pay, this course of action, he felt, was necessary. He won his case in 1993. In 2003 he became a candidate for governor in the California recall election. However, he chose instead to vote for Arnold Schwarzenegger. In 2007 he met Shannon Price and they were married months later, only to file for divorce in 2008.

Gary Colman faced countless challenges and struggles through life, which is sad considering his claim that all he ever wanted to do was 'make people laugh'. His life is an example of what fame can lead to for a young kid unable to make their own decisions. After a critical accident at his home that resulted in a severe head injuring during May, 2010, he passed away at the age of forty-two-years-old.

Interview with Gary Coleman

George Green: Tell me what life was like when that spotlight was intense?

Gary Coleman: Well, when you're a kid you don't notice those things. I was eight or nine-years-old when that spotlight hit me, but I didn't know. I'm just doin' the kid thing. I'm having fun. I'm thinking it's cool and having a ball. I didn't really get that recognition thing. That didn't happen right away.

George Green: Tell me about that.

Gary Coleman: I didn't understand it. I didn't know what it was about. I started to realize that this is a regular thing. I had to go to school, and people like what I do. I did get used to it. I was used to it up until the fourth year. The fourth year I was older.

George Green: So you are starting to realize that you are a superstar?

Gary Coleman: I wouldn't say that it went to my head.

George Green: Who was watching over you as you were doing this?

Gary Coleman: I had friends and there was this wonderful studio teacher, and one friend that I still have in my life, Dion Meall. They made sure that I did not turn into one of those kid actors who's spoiled rotten.

George Green: Where were your parents at this point?

Gary Coleman: My parents were, just kind of just sittin' back...

George Green: At the time the spotlight, and everything else, is heavy on you - you still feel that this didn't affect you as a child. The ego...

Gary Coleman: It really didn't affect me until I didn't want to do it anymore. I always was told that whenever I didn't want to do something, and whenever I got tired of something, all I had to do was say I wasn't interested and that would be it. Well, unfortunately, some issues of money and control took over and I was ignored pretty much by my parents and by business people.

George Green: When you're twelve-years-old, it's easy to be a victim.

Gary Coleman: People take advantage of children. That's what older people do, unfortunately. I'm not condemning older people. I was ignored because the money was too great. The fame, the fortune and power was too great.

George Green: Why didn't you want to do it anymore?

Gary Coleman: Because I wanted to go back to being a kid. I wanted to go back to my trains and my toys.

George Green: You realized that the real life was better than this artificial one.

Gary Coleman: Right. This is when the spoiling started. They figure 'okay, he's unhappy so give him anything he wants'. The parents were taken care of well.

George Green: And they don't want that money stream to stop.

Gary Coleman: You got it. Dion made me realize, 'your essence is suffering'.

George Green: You finally decided at that point that you are done? Is that what happened?

Gary Coleman: In year eight, ABC said they didn't want to do it anymore. That whole seventh - eighth season I was not into it; I was not driven.

George Green: You realize that the spotlight was about to dim.

Gary Coleman: Ultimately I chose to dim it myself. I just started living my life. I didn't want to be the lead. I just wanted to be involved.

George Green: Why were you depressed?

Gary Coleman: Because I could not go anywhere in the world and not be recognized.

George Green: You didn't want to be recognized?

Gary Coleman: I wanted that life without the spotlight.

George Green: Why did you come back to Hollywood?

Gary Coleman: Because I love to listen to people laugh. If I can do that and get some pleasure out of that, and get paid, then why not?

George Green: You've been gone twelve years, and you want to get back in the starring roles.

Gary Coleman: I can say, "Make an offer," and if everything is right something will happen.

George Green: How are you going to climb another mountain if the entertainment mountain isn't going to be open to you? Have you made a plan? Is there anybody who did step forward and say, "Come on and I'll give you work," because you never gave up?

Gary Coleman: I did give up. As of late, I have done some other little things.

George Green: What advice would you give to other young people who get subjected to that kind of pressure?

Gary Coleman: Be prepared for those up and downs. You're not always going to be the 'in' thing all the time. Learn some other thing to do when you're in the down mode.

George Green: When the light goes out, have something else to do.

Gary Coleman: Exactly. Take a hobby, for example.

George Green: So your advice to parents of a child star is...

Gary Coleman: Be a parent, don't be pushy. Let the kid grow up normal. Let the kid be a kid. You maintain your role as a parent. When the kid has to go to bed when it's bedtime, he can't be workin' past bedtime...

George Green: I don't think you have ever forgiven your parents for pushing you, have you?

Gary Coleman: Well, people don't like bitter people, so I try not to be bitter.

George Green: I wish you well. Climb that mountain. There are lots of mountains out there to climb.

Gary Colman: You say climb that mountain. Well, you know what; I'm on the easy slope. There aint no rocks on my side.

Jerry Dunphy

Shoot me, down I'll get back up

Jerry Dunphy was born in June, 1921, in Milwaukee, Wisconsin. After serving in World War II he found himself in radio, earning next to nothing which forced him to work as a salesman. After facing a few complications in radio, he began his television broadcasting career, in 1953. He started out as director and anchor at WXIX, owned then by CBS in Milwaukee, and also featured as a sports reporter on another CBS channel in Chicago. In 1960 he featured as anchor in LA's most popular newscast, 'The Big News' at KCBS-TV (channel two). He was later fired from this position, in 1975. He then went on to join KABC-TV (channel seven) until 1989. Shortly after this, he joined KCAL –TV (channel nine) and was one of the pioneering anchors of the news format 'Prime 9 News'. He subsequently returned to KCBS-TV (channel two) in 1995 and worked there until 1997 as anchorman. Then, in 1997, he rejoined KCAL-TV (channel nine) where he worked until his passing.

His career saw many changes as he moved back and forth between unknown and familiar faces. In 1983, Jerry was attacked and shot by would-be robbers, but fortunately made a full recovery. He suffered his first heart-attack in 1978, and then another in 1991. Sadly, in 2002, Jerry Dunphy experienced yet another heart-attack which ultimately led to his death. He is survived by six children.

His passing came as a shock to many. Hence, in the new CBS Studio Center, a newsroom was named in his honor. He was known for his catch phrase, "From the desert to the sea, to all of Southern California; a good evening." To this day, his phrase is still used by anchormen.

Interview with Jerry Dunphy

George Green: So, you were free of a contract and you accept the deal at channel two. And you say Goodbye, when?

Jerry Dunphy: In January 1995.

George Green: Now you're back working in the Network spotlight...

Jerry Dunphy: Working with Ann Martin, co-anchoring, etcetera... and I did that for five months. When I got over there I got a chance to smell things out and they were cutting instead of adding; in the editing rooms, on the street, they were cutting.

George Green: Five months goes by and then what happens?

Jerry Dunphy: They made the change. In front of me, here comes Westinghouse and buys CBS and they put their own show in there.

George Green: Westinghouse comes in, take over, five months later they come in to you and tell you what?

Jerry Dunphy: Not quite. First thing they have a meeting with Applegate, the guy that hired me. They fire him. We were waiting to see who the manager was going to be. They put an interim manager in. They say, "Jerry, we're going to move 'Day and Date' (the failure show that Westinghouse put on). We're going to move that into your slot, and... try as we might... we haven't come up with anything as an alternative for you. So, therefore, we're going to honor your contract, but we're taking you off the air." I looked at them and I said, "What? What you're saying to me is that you're firing me!"

"Well, your contract has a year and nine months to run, and we intend to honor every letter of it. We're going to pay you off."

George Green: They pay you off. They say you're gone although you can't go to work for anybody because it's a pay or play situation.

Jerry Dunphy: That's right.

George Green: This is the first time in your career that you, literally, were fired.

Jerry Dunphy: I guess - if you call it firing.

George Green: Now, what happens to Jerry Dunphy emotionally at that point? The transition, how you handle it? You had no clue and no warning. You never thought that the spotlight was dimming on Jerry Dunphy at any time up to that point. Never got a feeling...

Jerry Dunphy: Never! As a matter of fact, they said all of the nicest things.

George Green: Forty years go by with everything straight up. The spotlight is about as intense as it's ever been. It was like the switch went off right there?

Jerry Dunphy: And then after a while you start to think, 'Wait a minute... is there a way back?' That's what I'm working on right now; a way back.

George Green: What goes through your mind at that point?

Jerry Dunphy: At first you're convinced that the phone is going to ring. Then you begin to ask yourself, "Why it isn't?" But a funny thing is happening in the meantime; my closest friends felt around and think there is work for Dunphy in this marketplace. I began to wonder whether age was a factor and I certainly got concerned whether color was the factor. I would be unrealistic if I didn't, looking at the screen as I look at it today.

George Green: Have you had any moments when you thought, 'I may never be an anchor again, but I've got to do other things... or maybe not? Are you still hopeful? You haven't given any thought to the 'not' being that person that you were.

Jerry Dunphy: Why should I? I left on great terms.

George Green: You're very much like many of us who have turned the 'sixty' corner; do you like working?

Jerry Dunphy: I like working... feel good and I like the kind of work I was in. Every day was a new day and every day was a challenge.

George Green: So, the thought of retiring is not part of your vocabulary yet.

Jerry Dunphy: Nope. Nope.

George Green: Even though you're in a transitionary period...

Jerry Dunphy: I would be the most reluctant retirement guy you ever saw.

George Green: So, your goal is to get back in that spotlight as quickly as you can. In the meantime, what are you doing to mentally stay alive?

Jerry Dunphy: I'm listening to some positive voices.

George Green: What if you don't get that call, and have you thought about what's after this?

Jerry Dunphy: What's after is that you're forced into retirement against your will.

George Green: Have you thought of what you might do - because you're energetic, you look terrific.

Jerry Dunphy: I have one more agent on my behalf; George Green. I can't break the doors down and I don't own my own microphone, and I don't play golf. Never did. I do write lyrics and I have been published, and I'm working with some young kids now on country stuff... and we're putting stuff together... and I'm helping to produce the material.

Estelle Getty

The Golden Girl of Broadway

Estelle Scher-Gettleman (maiden name; Scher) was born in July, 1923, in New York City. After having attended Seward Park high school, she began her career as a performer in theater and on Broadway where she was first noted for her role in Torch Song Trilogy. In December, 1947, she married Arthur Gettleman and had two sons. She incorporated his name into her stage name, hence she became known as Estelle Getty. Arthur passed away in 2004.

In 1985, Estelle began her role as Sophia Petrillo in the award-winning comedy sitcom, 'The Golden Girls'. She won a Golden Globe award for best actress in a leading role in 1985, as well as an Emmy award for outstanding supporting actress in this show in 1988. She also featured in Empty Nest, a popular American sitcom, from 1993 to 1995. In 1993, Estelle compiled an exercise video for senior citizens and in 1998; an autobiography along with Steve Delsohn called, 'If I Knew Then What I Know Now... So What?' During this time Estelle was active in a number of AIDS related organizations, and even went on to take care of her twenty-nine-year-old nephew in his final stages of suffering from the AIDS virus.

In 2000, Estelle stopped making public appearances after revealing that she had Parkinson's disease and osteoporosis. It was later discovered that this diagnosis was incorrect and she, in fact, suffered from Lewy Body Dementia; classified as an underdiagnosed disease that resembles both Alzheimer's and Parkinson's. This came as no surprise to her crew as she was noted for often forgetting her lines.

In July, 2008, Estelle Getty passed away in her Hollywood Boulevard home in Los Angeles, due to her struggle with Lewy Body Dementia. On her birthday, July 25th, 2008, ten episodes of the Golden Girls featuring 'Sophia at her best' were aired in her honor. She would have turned eighty-five-years-old on this day. Estelle will always be fondly remembered as the wise-cracking Sicilian mother from Golden Girls, as well as a strong, motivated and caring woman.

Interview with Estelle Getty

George Green: How many years were you on the stage before you became Sophia in The Golden Girls?

Estelle Getty: All my life.

George Green: Before the Torch Song Trilogy? How many years before that?

Estelle Getty: I was a child until that point. Before Torch Song I was in New York, I did plays wherever I could. I worked when I could, if I could, where I could.

George Green: What was your life like when you were a star on the stage?

Estelle Getty: I knew no other life. I was always looking for work and very grateful when I got work. I loved the life.

George Green: Were there some periods in New York City where you were not in the spotlight?

Estelle Getty: Yes, there were times when I used to say, "How do I know I'm still an actor?" If you are an actor and you're not acting, what are you? Are you an actor? You have no credentials. You need credentials. I could have a letter saying that I'm a brilliant actress, but what is that going to mean?

George Green: So, there were periods where you weren't a star?

Estelle Getty: Yes. I remember calling up my telephone service once and said, "Did you put out the word that I died?"

George Green: How long of a stretch was that?

Estelle Getty: The longest was nine months. I did a lot of experimental theater. I was the one they called when they couldn't get somebody to do the job because it was like... really, really weird stuff. I did some really weird stuff and got great reviews, always.

George Green: Torch Song was the moment that the spotlight was the most intense?

Estelle Getty: Yeah.

George Green: But up until that time it was up and down?

Estelle Getty: Up and down. But, I was never without work. I studied with good people. I never stopped studying. I used to keep going to classes all the time.

George Green: What happened after Torch Song; you now start looking around and said, "My dreams have come true. I am what I was hoping to be my whole life, and suddenly I'm there."

Estelle Getty: I wasn't. The point is I never wanted it, nor thought about it.

George Green: But, it happened.

Estelle Getty: It happened and I thought, 'My God, so this is what they talk about.' I'm on good terms with big stars, and when I walk over and I say, "Hello," they say, "Estelle, how good to see you." And they hug me, and I think, 'They really think I'm one of them.'

George Green: So even through the stardom period, you haven't quite believed you were there.

Estelle Getty: That's right. To this very day, when Mickie Rooney came to work on the show, playing my boyfriend, I thought, 'Mickey Rooney.' I remember when I was a kid, I thought that if I went out to Hollywood and I met Mickey Rooney and he fell in love with me, we would be the biggest tiniest stars, height-wise, in this business. To this very day, when I meet a celebrity... I thought to myself, 'I'm standing here having lunch with Mickie Rooney.' We were laughing and talking about old days and I'm thinking, 'This is Mickey Rooney. He was the guy with Judy Garland. I mean, look who we're talking about!' I never felt as though I was one of these divas. I was very ready to recognize that I had a very limited talent, which was good; it was like having a good small car. I had no allusions that I would be a leading lady. It was never my intention to become a superstar.

George Green: When did you stop doing Torch Song? When did the Golden Girls happen?

Estelle Getty: Well, I went out on the road with the national company and I came back. Within a couple of weeks I had Golden Girls.

George Green: Then life really became super-stardom, did it not?

Estelle Getty: I never believed it. See, I always used to think that people were just saying it, but that it wasn't true. Until I went to Spain, or a foreign country, and people would see me in the street and stop me and call me 'Sophia'... and talk to me in Spanish. I had no idea... Somebody said, "International star, Estelle Getty."

George Green: Then you believed it, didn't you?

Estelle Getty: No, I didn't believe it then.

George Green: Even at the height of the popularity? Why is that?

Estelle Getty: I don't know.

George Green: Some people believe they are superstars and they are not, but you were.

Estelle Getty: I was a superstar and I did not... I still don't know. I mean, when I go any place and people start pandering me, I think to myself, 'What do they think I am? Who do they think I am?' I mean, this should be held for people who really do something in this life. I remember one incident, which gave me insight as to what could happen, I was walking with Charlotte Rainey to one of the awards affairs. The photographer turned to her and he said, "Miss Ray, do you mind?" And I realized that he was telling her to step out of the picture. So I had this rather insightful way of seeing things, more so than most people because I didn't believe it was going to last; I didn't believe any of the hype. When I first came to Golden Girls I had my name on my spot and it said 'Estelle Getty'. That was my spot for my car. I drove around the block, turned off the key and walked over to the wall. I realized that those were 'stick-ons'. They peel right off. Why would they have that? These were spots allocated only to stars. I thought to myself, 'It's that simple'. They take off your name, and you're nobody. But I never had that problem.

George Green: Was that a protective device, so that you are not going to be as disappointed as most of the superstars become?

Estelle Getty: I was always very realistic about it. I didn't feel that, 'How could they take this all away from me.' I had a good run. I left when I was on top. There isn't a day that goes by in my life that somebody doesn't say, "I love you."

George Green: I love you.

Estelle Getty: See how simple it is! I didn't program myself to feel that way. I had it good.

George Green: After the producers and everybody said, "This is going to be our last season," what were the emotions?

Estelle Getty: Well, considering my age, too, it was more relief than anything.

George Green: Looking back, you don't miss the spotlight?

Estelle Getty: I still have that. Here I am. You came to interview me. So, I still get invited to everything and I'm very active in many organizations.

George Green: And keeping you busy...

Estelle Getty: Yeah, not so busy, but it's good enough. And when I get bored, I'll find something else to do.

George Green: Do you want to work?

Estelle Getty: I want to work and I don't want to work.

George Green: You would like the telephone to ring tomorrow and say, "Estelle, we got grandmother part for you?"

Estelle Getty: I have had a dozen of those. I just turned down probably three sitcoms, three movies, and I've done about three different things since I'm out. But what's going to happen to me when I can't do this, when I'm too old or something like that?

George Green: Do you think about that?

Estelle Getty: Oh, sure.

George Green: You obviously feel that working and show business is the way to keep being healthy, and have a happy life.

Estelle Getty: Yeah, but I like not being busy. I like the fact that I've given so much time to everyone and everything. This is the first time in my life I have said 'no'. I would say, "No, I can't do it." Then it would become, "Oh well, maybe I will." Then I would think, 'Why am I being so unreasonable?' I always thought being reasonable was a very important thing in my life.

George Green: Age has never been a factor it seems, in your life. Yet most other people in show business; age becomes a factor, yet as you age you are still being called upon to do things indicative of the age group.

Estelle Getty: My best friends are all in their thirties. I have a lot of friends my own age, but the people that I run with are kids; very talented writers, conductors, musicians, actors, lawyers.

George Green: What advice would you give to others, to win that spotlight when theirs starts dimming? What should they do?

Estelle Getty: You can't become seduced by this. You go into this business having made a normal living and all of a sudden you are making fifty-thousand dollars a week, which is a ridiculous sum of money. Depend on no one for your sustenance. Don't turn your life over to anyone who can ruin it. Depend upon yourself because in the final analysis that's all you've got. It's not the spotlight that kills you. What kills you is that you have to send the car back; you have to send the horses back, the private school back, and the new swimming pool back. You either pay for them as though you were working, or you don't have them, which is why some of them go into debt by the millions. They don't want to change their lifestyle. If you are not prepared to pay the piper, don't act on it. Don't act like it's going to stay here forever. The hardest thing is to know that this is not reality. This is not the reality of life. It can be taken from you just like that.

George Green: You've felt like that your whole career; it could be here today and gone tomorrow.

Estelle Getty: Except when I was doing Golden Girls. After a while I became very comfortable because there was never any time that our fame and our fortune was going downhill. We were top notch. There was never a point that we knew we might be slipping, because we never slipped.

George Green: It also has to do a little bit with your heritage, which is somewhat like mine; we were raised that you put money away and you always prepare yourself.

Estelle Getty: I understand that's difficult to do when you're young. They live like... you see a sweater for four-hundred dollars. "Come on," they say, "so what? You don't have four-hundred dollars?" I say, "Yeah, I have four-hundred dollars, but I'm not going to spend it on a sweater." And I was thinking, 'where do they get these ideas from?' The more you live spending four-hundred dollars a sweater, the harder it is for you to give up.

George Green: You get accustomed to four-hundred dollar sweaters.

Estelle Getty: You become addicted to four-hundred dollar sweaters.

George Green: I think that what you're saying is, 'Live within your means.'

Estelle Getty: I still live within my means, because there is no way for me to make up if all the money dissipated, there's no way I could exist for however long I'm going to live. So, I still have trepidation spending large amounts of money. I never stop being grateful to all the people who have helped me.

George Green: Was there anybody particularly that helped you with that wonderful philosophy of life that you have?

Estelle Getty: It's only a wonderful philosophy of life because I've learned it the hard way through therapy and curiosity. Of course, I keep thinking about what I would have done with my life if this hadn't happened. What would I have done? I would have become a secretary, which I did during my slack periods. I would always have a job.

George Green: If the spotlight really went out, if show business played the 'show biz' game and disappeared on you totally, then what? Would you be the same?

Estelle Getty: No.

George Green: So you are dependent upon having that light?

Estelle Getty: I don't know if I'm dependent upon it, but I sure like it.

George Green: You've done so many comedy things, but you have done some serious roles in your life, too. How do you feel about that?

Estelle Getty: I'm comedic, you know, and high-drama does not come easily to me. Can I do it? Yes! Like I can play a five-year-old girl, I can play an eighty-five-year-old. That's my business. That's what I do for a living.

Art Linkletter

Do what you like to do and enjoy doing it

Art Linkletter was born Gorden Arthur Kelly, in Canada, July, 1912. Abandoned at only a few weeks old, he was adopted by Mary and Fulton John Linkletter. Art graduated from San Diego high school when he was sixteen-years-old. After working odd jobs on passenger trains he went on to earn his bachelor's degree from San Diego State Teachers College, now known as San Diego State University.

In 1935, Art met Lois Foerster whom he married, and together they had five children. Their marriage is noted as one of the longest-lasting among American celebrities. He began working in radio during this time then later moved to San Francisco, and then on to Hollywood where he continued his career in radio. 'People Are Funny' was his first major radio show which he put together with John Geudel. This show later went on to become a television show.

Art performed in other shows after this time, too, like 'Hollywood Talent Scouts', and he also worked on a show with his son, Jack Linkletter, known as 'Life With Linkletter'.

Art was good friends with Walt Disney who asked him to build and operate the new Disney Hotel. But, mistakenly seeing no prospects in such an endeavor, Art showed no interest in the position. However, due to their friendship, Art offered to cover the opening ceremony on ABC radio with co-hosts Ronald Reagen and Bob Cummings. The opening was a success and Walt believed it to be due to Art's exclusive coverage via radio. He became known as a Disney Legend.

Aside from also becoming a spokesman for the National Home Life insurance company, he also involved himself with political institutions. In 1969 his daughter, Diane, took her own life which Art believed to be a drug-induced decision. Before her passing he recorded a discussion about permissiveness in modern society. Diane featured in this recording called, 'We Love You, Call Collect'. The recording won a Grammy Award in 1970 for 'best spoken-word recording'. In 2003 he won a lifetime achievement Daytime Emmy award and was added to the National Speakers Hall Of Fame.

In 2008, Art Linkletter suffered a mild stroke. Sadly, in May 2010, he passed away in his home in Bel Air, Los Angeles, California. Art was noted as 'having a full life of fun and goodness; an orphan who made it to the top'.

Interview with Art Linkletter

George Green: Everybody knows this marvelous wonderful career that you've enjoyed and still enjoy. Can you highlight some of that career?

Art Linkletter: I look back over eighty-five years and, in a way, my life is divided into thirds. I was a poor kid, abandoned as an orphan with older, adoptive parents. I had a very small vision of life, what the world could be. I never remembered getting anything that I didn't work for, including my clothes. So I scrambled through life. I wanted to be big and play basketball. I went out on the road and started hitchhiking. Then I started riding the freight trains then the passenger trains and doing jobs everywhere; was on Wall Street as a typist... and two months later I got a job as a sailor on a ship to South America. I was eighteen and getting street smart and learning how important work and attitude is, to get by. Then I was in college studying to be an English professor. My junior year I wrote a musical comedy for San Diego State College which attracted the attention of a local radio station manager. He asked me if I would like to have a part-time job as a radio announcer. In the midst of a depression you don't ask what the work is! So, I became a radio announcer and I graduated from college a year and a half later. I'd been studying the radio business, trying to figure out where I could go in it. They didn't pay any money for sports announcements or news, and I couldn't do any of those things so I thought, 'Well, I'll go back to teaching.' In June, 1934, CBS started a program that I happened to hear in the afternoon. It was a 'Man-on-the-street' program in Texas. When I heard that my whole life changed. I said, "That's what I can do! I'm not a performer, I'm not a comedian or a storyteller, but I'm curious and I'm a good speaker." So I decided to stay on those grounds in radio, if I could do my own 'Man-on-the-street' show. And that began my introduction. By 1942 I'd met John Geudel, a bright young radio guy, working for the Dan B. Minor advertising agency in L.A. I had an idea for a show called 'Meet Yourself,' based on my minor in psychology, where we get people up on the stage and we do stunts with them and then we'd have a psychology professor tell what kind of a person they are. He had a program called 'People Are Funny,' with exactly the same thing. We put ourselves together and I wrote and he wrote, and we did an audition and sold the show.

George Green: When was the first airing of 'People Are Funny' in radio?

Art Linkletter: About 1943.

George Green: Right during the war.

Art Linkletter: Yeah, during the war. We went to Chicago and sold it to Russell Seeds. Three years later I had a show on the Pacific Coast called 'What's Doing, Ladies?' John and I had an idea for a show called 'Under 21'; all kids, and GE said, "We would like to take the little kids part of your 'Under 21' but we want more of the housewives.

George Green: That was 'Kids Say the Darndest Things?'

Art Linkletter: That was 'House Party.' There was never a show called 'Kids Say The Darndest Things.' It was a book that I wrote. The last thing on the show was 'What's In The Purse?' and stunts in the audience. That show lasted for twenty-six years. That was really my introduction to being a nationally known person.

George Green: That had to be the highlight as far as the intensity of spotlight.

Art Linkletter: Here I'm on all the networks, radio and television, riding all of these shows while the radio drifted off. I had moved my family down here from San Francisco, then I went back to Dallas, Texas to the Texas centennial where I was radio director. Then to San Francisco, and while I was up there I did a lot of things in radio. I've never had an agent you know, in my life.

George Green: You never have?

Art Linkletter: Never, because I'm an independent guy; don't want anyone telling me what I can do before I even hear about it.

George Green: In 1953 you were on every network, radio, television. There were some cancellations. Did cancellations ever get to you?

Art Linkletter: Never bothered me.

George Green: Tell me what you mentally did to accept that kind of thing.

Art Linkletter: My nature is to be hugely optimistic.

George Green: So your confidence and your self-esteem, and belief in yourself was so strong that you had no doubt.

Art Linkletter: I had no doubt. I have never had any... any fears.

George Green: So you felt no ill feelings about the cancellations?

Art Linkletter: I thought they were making wrong choices at times. In the meantime I had gotten into the lecture field. The death of my daughter, Diane, who took her life, was before I was off the air. Norman Vincent Peale called me and suggested that I make a memorial to her life by leading my own personal crusade against drug abuse. So I started lecturing. I wrote a book 'Drugs at my Doorstep.' Dick Nixon called me back to Washington and I became a member of the President's Commission on Drug Abuse. I suddenly realized I'd rather be a lecturer than be on the air. I'd get up, I'd speak for an hour and all of a sudden, I looked at myself and I said, "This is what I was born for. All the rest of it is preparation, becoming famous, so I could command audiences. Now I'm ready to do what I was intended to do."

George Green: Climb another mountain.

Art Linkletter: That's another whole mountain. I went out on the positive thinking rallies. I became one of the national speakers. I speak on drug abuse, positive thinking, salesmanship, business, an evening with Art Linkletter - anything I want to talk about. I love it!

George Green: You enjoy that as much as you did when you were on the air?

Art Linkletter: More. I have an audience who's concentrated. They're there. They're not people that tune you in or walk into the studio. Now I've got an audience of people who have come to see me. In the meantime, I was in many businesses, fifty-five different businesses.

George Green: So, you went through a transition then back up into another spotlight, and into another spotlight and into another spotlight, and it just kept going ahead.

Art Linkletter: That's right.

George Green: The intensity of the spotlight... different kind of intensity, right?

Art Linkletter: That's right!

George Green: How do you do all this? You're eighty-five years old?

Art Linkletter: I'm well organized. I know my priorities. I'm good at inspiring people to do more than they should. I've a very good ability to shrug off very tough things. Businesswise I've lost on occasion; million, two million dollars. I bet on the wrong guy or something went wrong. And it stuns me for about... twelve seconds, no more. I say I'm healthy. I have a wonderful family. I have a gorgeous home. I have a few million dollars left. So, let's go somewhere else. That's my attitude.

George Green: The key to it is keeping busy, keeping your mind active and occupied, and being involved.

Art Linkletter: Being involved.

George Green: Isn't that the secret to retirement? Isn't that the secret to transitionary periods?

Art Linkletter: That's right. I don't ask how old you are. I ask you how are you old? Some people are old in their attitudes at forty. Some are young in their attitudes when they're eighty-five.

George Green: And to those people who say, "Art, why don't you just go play golf. Just travel around the world. Why are you doing this?"

Art Linkletter: I'd rather do this, what I'm doing, than anything else. I have vacations. I ski four weeks every winter. I spend a lot of time with my eleven great grandchildren, nine grandchildren and my children and wife. We take over a whole bed and breakfast. This is great fun for me. The whole thing is. At these family gatherings we formed a family corporation and each member of the family had stock in the family corporation. I would report back to them on how their stock was doing which correlated with how I was doing. And we would issue actual money dividends to each family member. If they need money they can make a loan. I share dividends. They all get dividends each year from me. I probably give out a couple hundred thousand a year just to the kids, so that they can learn how to handle money. They get five thousand here and ten thousand here, and learn what it's going to be like to have money.

George Green: If you had to give advice to other people...

Art Linkletter: Do what you like to do, and enjoy doing. Don't do it because you're gonna' get rich or famous or have power. Do it because you like it.

George Green: You're a happy man.

Art Linkletter: I am.

Ed McMahon

And now... here's Johnny!

Edward Leo Peter (Ed) McMahon Jr. was born in Detroit, Michigan, in March, 1923. Throughout his earlier years he worked on various jobs, from the carnival to the bingo hall to the Atlantic City Boardwalk where he sold vegetable slicers.

Ed always wanted to be a U.S. Marine Corps fighter pilot. After Pearl Harbor, when the college requirements for entering the U.S. Marine Corps were dropped, Ed enrolled for flight training and then fighter training. Throughout this time he flew a total of eighty-five combat missions, and earned six Air Medals. After the Korean War he stayed with the Marines as a reserve officer and retired in 1966 as a colonel. In 1982 he received an honorific to recognize his support for the National Guard and Reserves.

During this time he also majored in speech and drama, which led him to a career in show business. He became most famous for his position alongside Johnny Carson on 'The Tonight Show' from 1962 to 1992. Prior to this, from 1957 to 1962, Ed and Johnny worked together on another show known as 'Who Do You Trust?' From 1983 to 1995 he hosted a talent show known as 'Star Search'. Then, from 1982 to 1998, he co-hosted the show,

'TV's Bloopers and Practical Jokes' alongside Dick Clark.

Having almost lost his home, in 2008, and his life after a serious fall which resulted in a severe neck injury, Ed's journey was not always on the up-and-up. After being hospitalized and operated on, he went on to sue the hospital for fraud, battery, elderly abuse and emotional distress.

Aside from the star-studded roles (and many others) mentioned above, Ed McMahon also went on to publish as many as five books. Ed married three times in his life. His third marriage lasted until 2009, when he passed away. Unknown to many, Ed had been admitted to hospital for pneumonia almost a month before he passed-on there, in June, 2009.

Tribute was paid to Ed by Conan O'Brien who stated on air, "It's impossible, I think, for anyone to imagine The Tonight Show with Johnny Carson, without Ed McMahon. Ed's laugh was really the soundtrack to that show. There will never be anything like that again."

Interview with Ed McMahon

George Green: I don't want to rewrite the bio I have, but why don't you give it a shot.

Ed McMahon: In the early days, I would play radio in my grandmother's parlor every afternoon. My little dog, Valiant Prince, would sit there with me, and he was my audience. When I was very young I got a job working on a sound truck; a panel truck that went around the neighborhood that had advertisements on the outside and two big bullhorns on the roof. Then they had an audition at the Lowell High School where I was attending, for an announcer to get a job on the radio. I audition and I come in second. Anyway, the guy who beat me was so good that they lured him to Boston. But they remembered that I came in second, and I got his job. I was about seventeen and I was a broadcaster; greatest training in the world. I also had signed up for the United States Marine Corps because I wanted to become a Marine fighter pilot. I became a naval cadet and was signed, but I had to wait until they called me. While I was waiting I worked in radio at night. I worked for the war effort during the day and at night. I was a disc jockey. Finally I got called into the service. Then when I got my wings (I got my wings in `44). I went to a fighter base in Florida.

There I ran the Bingo game, I announced. Whatever it was, I was on a microphone all the time I was in the service. I got out in `46, went to New York and at NBC I took an audition called the 'Welcome Home Audition.' I took the audition and I got offers of two jobs. Then I debated; should I take those jobs or get a little more training in college. I decided to go back to college. I was accepted at Yale. They had a very good drama school. But I needed a job to support a wife and child. Somebody told me about Catholic University in Washington. It had a great drama department. I went down there. There was a Priest and he said, "No, my son, you'll come here." I knew in Washington I could do something. So I got in, majored in speech and drama and went there for three years. Great training, but, again, I wasn't interested in plays, I was interested in variety. So I formed my own variety troop. We went around and entertained at all of the Marine, Army and Navy bases around the Washington area. I was very good at selling and at night, in Washington, I sold pots and pans, door-to-door. Three years of going to school, getting a degree in speech and drama; three summers at being a pitch-man on the Boardwalk in Atlantic City; three years of selling pots and pans at night was incredible training for what I was about to do. I got out in June of `49. I worked that summer in Atlantic City, and September, 1949, I started as the co-host of a three hour daily variety show, and I was also the producer. That only lasted for about three months. But out of that I got my own hour show. It was a variety show. I have worked in television every single day since then, except a stint in the Korean War for a year and a half when I went back into the Marine Corps.

George Green: The Tonight Show; where you met Carson - how did that happen?

Ed McMahon: When I got back from Korea, Dan Kelly says, "I got your apartment." I move in and who's my next door neighbor? Dick Clark! We're both aspiring performers in this world of broadcasting. Edward R. Murrow used to do a style of interview, like; the cameras went to somebody's home. They did Dick Clark; CBS cameras all over the place. The owner of the apartments invited all of the CBS people down to a party. He said, "You come down." I was there. He said, "Get up and entertain these people." I get up, I entertain them, and when I finished Dick Clark's producer said, "You're pretty good. You ever thought about going to New York." I said, "Only every second..." His office was right next to Johnny Carson's dressing room. He heard the producer talking to Johnny that they gotta' replace the announcer and Chuck Reeves yells from his desk, "I got the guy. I'll have him here tomorrow morning." I came up, met Johnny Carson. We were both looking out two windows in his dressing room because they were changing a marquee across the street for 'Bells Are Ringing'. We talked about what was going on outside the window.

We looked at that for about seven minutes. He turned to me and said, "Where did you go to school?" I told him. He said, "What are you doing now?" I told him. He shook my hand and said, "Ed, it's nice meeting you. Thank you for coming up from Philadelphia." I figured that's over. I blew that one. Three weeks went by. I was supposed to go to Europe. I didn't go. The morning of the day I was supposed to leave, I get a phone call and it's Art Stark, the producer of 'Who Do You Trust.' He said, "We'd like you to wear suits." I said, "What?" He said, "Well, Johnny, he wears sports clothes and we want you to wear suits." I said, "What are you talking about?" He said, "Didn't my secretary call you? You got the job. You start Monday." What I didn't know, until many, many years later was that the minute Carson saw me, he'd made his decision.

George Green: '62 to '92, the show is about to end. What were some of the emotions going through your mind?

Ed McMahon: That was the most intense shining of the spotlight on me.

George Green: You were the number one, number two guy in America.

Ed McMahon: That's exactly right. I would walk down the street and a car or truck would go by, and I would hear, "Yo, Ed!" I was 'Ed' to a lot of people. I would get special treatment. It was wonderful. I couldn't go anywhere, where I wouldn't get special treatment. If you don't expect everything, you get a lot because it just happens if you do it right.

George Green: You had a marvelous thirty years with John. Were you guys close friends as well?

Ed McMahon: Oh yes. We hung out together. We kind of gravitated to each other whenever there was a disturbance in our life. We got very, very close. It's unusual. I've heard stories about other couplings, where they did their job and that was the end of it. We were lucky that we have a friendship as well as a career together.

George Green: The show was about to end. Did you think about the future?

Ed McMahon: No. I found there was a big thing in my contract that I had to stay six more months after Johnny Carson said goodbye. I didn't want that, I didn't want to stay one day after Johnny Carson. But NBC had that thread and they wanted me to stay on with whoever the new guy was, to just bridge that gap and get him started. I finally got that out. I really had to fight.

George Green: What was life like during that transitionary period? Did you have any down moments?

Ed McMahon: Not really, no. I had 'Star Search' and I've always had other things.

George Green: You've acknowledged the fact that there was no spotlight that was ever as intense as that thirty years. You were in the other spotlight in 'Star Search' and you went into other things. But you're still able to not compare one spotlight to another. You never look back and say, "Those were the good old days?"

Ed McMahon: Well, a lot will say, "I thought you retired." I said, "No, I finished a show. I didn't retire. I never said anything about retiring."

George Green: For you, retirement is not a word in your vocabulary.

Ed McMahon: No, I'm never going to retire.

George Green: Why?

Ed McMahon: I don't know. I just feel... maybe it was my father. I mean, my father worked until the day he died.

George Green: When your friends say, "Ed, doggone it, why don't you just learn how to play golf; take it easy. Why are you workin'?"

Ed McMahon: I love it. I love to get to this desk; working hard, but I love it. I would feel funny if I woke up in the morning and all I had to look forward to was reading the paper and playing golf. I would be bored to death.

George Green: It's interesting about show business people. Almost all of you have an endless desire to just want to continue. What is it about show people versus business people?

Ed McMahon: I don't know.

George Green: You're over sixty-five and you look so terrific. How do you do that?

Ed McMahon: Well, I walk three miles on the treadmill. I lift weights. When I don't do it I feel funny. Sometimes my wife and I will take a walk in the evening. I drink red wine at night, that's all I drink. Red wine is supposed to be good for you! I think it's having a positive attitude. They'll have to get me out of this business at gun point!

George Green: What's your advice to people who are searching for the look of Ed McMahon, the attitude of Ed McMahon, and obviously the desire to go on and on and on?

Ed McMahon: Don't ever stop. Don't ever shut it off. I think it starts in the outlook. For advice, I say, you never give up, you never lose your curiosity to learn new things and you always have a positive pleasant outlook. Keep going. That's it. Die at the desk. I would like to die on the air, broadcasting.

Fess Parker

Davy Crockett... the winemaker?

Fess Elisha Parker Jr. was born in August ,1924, in Texas. He was raised on a farm in Tom Green County near San Angelo.

Toward the end of World War II, Fess joined the Marine Corps as a radio operator in the South Pacific, not long before the atomic bomb ended the war.

In 1947 he enrolled in Hardin-Simmons University on the GI Bill (a law that provided a range of benefits to returning World War II veterans). In 1947 he was transferred to the University of Texas. There he majored in history and continued to remain active in drama. After graduating in 1950, he still had another year left on his GI Bill, so chose to study drama at the University of Southern California.

In 1951, Fess began his career in show business, earning little for his role as an extra in a play called 'Mister Roberts'. It wasn't long before he found himself on location playing a minor role in a motion picture called 'Untamed Frontier'.

Then came his big break, when Walt Disney noticed him and believed he would be the best actor to portray the character 'Davy Crockett'. During his time with Walt Disney, Fess was not permitted to take on other roles that did not portray the same character-type as Davy Crockett. Ultimately he developed another character very similar to Crockett, known as Daniel Boone. This show also became a huge success on NBC. In 1991, Fess Parker was declared a Disney Legend.

In 1960 he married Marcella Belle Rinehart and together they had two children. During this time he perused a number of real-estate ventures and discovered his place in this industry. As his career in show business ended, so Fess followed another dream; to open a winery in California. The Fess Parker Winery, one-thousand-five-hundred acres of vineyard, still operates today and is managed by the Parker family.

Sadly, Fess passed away in his home in Santa Ynez, California, in March, 2010. He will always be remembered for his 'coonskin cap', and later his passions for real-estate and wine-making.

Interview with Fess Parker

George Green: Tell me about the highlights of your career and those intensity years.

Fess Parker: I was two years in the Navy. I knew I wanted to be a film actor. I got my degree in American History at the University of Texas. I had a brief reading with Adolphe Menjou who asked me if I'd like to work films. One thing led to another; I came to Hollywood. 1950 was a difficult time in the movie business. I went to USC for a year, worked on my Masters. I completed all the course work; didn't write the thesis. Three years later, Walt Disney saw me in a film and cast me as Davy Crockett. Now, Davy Crockett put ABC on the map. I was totally exploited. I did all of that for five-hundred dollars a week. At any rate, that was the high point. Then I left Disney in '58 and I went to Paramount, made two or three pictures there. In 1964, NBC and 20th Century Fox wanted me to do 'Further Adventures of Davy Crockett'. Walt Disney at NBC didn't like that idea, thought it might compromise his shows. After working in films for twenty years, I lost touch with the industry. I was exploring opportunities to become involved in business. I started out developing real-estate.

George Green: Were you disenchanted to any degree with show business? Were you going through any kind of transitions?

Fess Parker: I was just a kid. I now know that I was exploited to the nth degree. John Ford wanted me to do 'The Searchers'. But the studio didn't even tell me. I realized that I was not getting film opportunities, and it took me a long time to come to terms with that.

George Green: You were characterized; they positioned you in a corner.

Fess Parker: Pretty much.

George Green: In those days you had no personal life, did you?

Fess Parker: None at all. I began to think of the future, trying to do something with whatever money I was making. It wasn't that much. However, Walt Disney did in fact give me ten-percent of the Walt Disney Davey Crockett merchandise.

George Green: Did you love what you did as an actor?

Fess Parker: No, I didn't love it. I was somewhat disappointed in it.

George Green: You weren't achieving the goals that you wanted to achieve as an actor, so you had some new goals in business. You pursued that with all your independent vigor and accomplished that.

Fess Parker: It wasn't so much that I was a smart businessman. I found out that I had this knack of looking at a piece of ground and saying, "You know, I think that a certain kind of project will be successful here." That's basically as simple as it is.

George Green: That transitionary period, what was that like?

Fess Parker: I really wanted to have a more universal kind of respect. I needed to do something on my own, for my own account. I just found real-estate to be the medium.

George Green: Tell me about the real-estate business and getting into the winery.

Fess Parker: I started, in 1961, to build a mobile-home park. We built one of the finest mobile-home parks in the United States. I stumbled along on various things, taking land from agricultural zoning and turning into industrial and commercial land. All of this growth was taking place along with my family life. So I was able to have a very good life. I found this beautiful little ranch in the Santa Ynez Valley, so we bought it. From 1989 to this date, we have accomplished a great deal.

George Green: Compare the two spotlights of your film career and your business career.

Fess Parker: I've had a greater satisfaction out of the wine business!

George Green: The spotlight is as intense now as it ever was in the fifties when you were on the screen.

Fess Parker: I wouldn't say it's as intense. But it's still there. I'm a natural optimist. If I had to say who Fess Parker is in terms of a profession, I would say that my first major suit is selling. I think that's what actors do; they sell a personality. In developing real-estate you must be able to communicate your goals; persuade the public. I think you have to be persistent. It's not a casual thing.

George Green: What lessons can you pass on to people, in order to survive and be happy like you are?

Fess Parker: I guess two things. One, believe in yourself. Two, you have to find something that you believe in. Listen to what people tell you; research things.

George Green: How important is loving your job and loving what you're doing?

Fess Parker: I don't think you can succeed without an enthusiasm for what it is that you're about to undertake.

John Raitt

Ooklahoma here we come!

John Emmett Raitt was born in Santa Ana, California, in January, 1917. He attended Fullerton Union high school, and during his time there performed in several drama productions at the Plummer Auditorium. He also enjoyed football and won the 'football throw' at the California State high school Track and Field Championship in 1935. He was named 'athlete of the meet'.

He was best-known for his onstage appearances in Broadway musicals such as 'Oklahoma', 'Carousel', 'A Joyful Noise', 'Carnival In Flanders' and others. In 1957 he was featured opposite Doris Day in the movie, 'The Pajama Game'. After that he teamed up alongside Mary Martin for the national touring version of 'Annie Get Your Gun'.

During his life he made a few appearances in television, too. However, his forte was theatre. He was married three times in his life. His daughter, Bonnie Raitt, also went on to succeed as a singer.

Sadly, John Raitt passed away in February, 2005, at his home in Pacific Palisades, California, after experiencing complications with pneumonia. He was eighty-eight-years-old at the time. John's contributions to live-theater will always be remembered, especially through his star on the Hollywood Walk Of Fame.

Interview with John Raitt

George Green: When the spotlight was the most intense on you, what was life like?

John Raitt: The first time was 'Carousel' in 1945, because I won every award you could win back in those days, and it was tremendously exciting. I was very fortunate to have, like, two and a half years with two different shows, without an empty seat in the house. The next one was 'Pajama Game' in Chicago in the mid-fifties. Then I got an opportunity to recreate the role for the film with Doris Day. Right after that same year, I was able to perform 'Annie Get Your Gun' with Mary Martin, and we did a two-hour live television show of that with NBC. I spent five years of life on 44th Street in New York, which has been a very lucky street for me!

George Green: What was life like when you were a superstar?

John Raitt: Just work. They would get all these interviews, and television was just coming in, so I did a lot of Ed Sullivan Shows, and all that. But you do eight shows a week, for two and a half years; that's about it. Then I started the Chevy Show on NBC...

George Green: Your wife and family at that time kind of basked in your glory.

John Raitt:. Yeah, I think so.

George Green: I'm sure you were offered a lot of television opportunities at that time, or motion pictures?

John Raitt: Well, I got the 'Pajama Game' picture and won a couple of awards for that, but somehow nothing else was forthcoming. I just continued to do theatre because I started out as a concert singer.

George Green: Why didn't you continue in the opera field?

John Raitt: I don't think I could put up with them! I'm so schooled in singing like you talk...

George Green: Was there a time when you realized that perhaps the spotlight on your career was beginning to dim?

John Raitt: Why sure, of course. But mine never got really terribly bright anyway. I wasn't pushing it either. The only time I had a bad year was right after I left 'Carousel'. I turned down 'Guys and Dolls'. I only worked three weeks that year. That was not too good because I had three kids to support and everything. I actually saved a little money, so I was dipping into the savings.

George Green: You were concerned about your career then?

John Raitt: Sort of, as to which way we were going or what was going to happen.

George Green: You actually opened a show and closed, maybe a week or two later?

John Raitt: It's the nature of this business. You never know. It looks pretty good at the beginning, but as it starts to go; if it isn't produced well, at least it isn't that big a shock to ya'.

George Green: Business people consider that a failure. Show people think that's 'just part of what you do'.

John Raitt: We used to call it 'a flop'!

George Green: Flops are part of stage peoples' lives?

John Raitt: Everybody has them... everybody. I have friends who have eight flops in row! It takes two years out of your life, and then you're never sure. You never know about the numbers.

George Green: Most of the show business people I've met, they never feel that there's an end.

John Raitt: No, no. You always have to keep on going. I learned, a long time ago, where my limitations were vocally and physically, and also to just enjoy the moment.

George Green: Emotionally you sound like a very healthy man.

John Raitt: Yeah. I got great shock absorbers!

George Green: Would you say that you've had this attitude your whole life?

John Raitt: Whole life. Never drank. Never smoked. Don't drink coffee. The adrenalin level is tremendous in me.

George Green: Do you wish you were fifty years younger?

John Raitt: Not really. No. Just as long as I can get along... I think I hold my age pretty well.

George Green: After the cheering stops, what now?

John Raitt: I don't know. I just take these things. I've got my star on the Hollywood Walk of Fame. I've been inducted in the Theater Hall of Fame, in New York. I get plaques all the time that people want to honor me. I say that's fine.

George Green: What advice would you give other show people who are going through transitions?

John Raitt: I say that you've got to know what you have; what your equipment is. You gotta' know your limitations and when anybody asks you to perform, singing especially, sing. Under any conditions, just don't say, "I can't sing." Just sing, because you don't know. Everything changes. The whole business is changed so much. You have to be smart enough to say, "Look, I'm going to go audition." I tried to write a book about how to audition. Never put it out. I may have to do that sometime, because that's so important. You have to realize that the people you are auditioning for want you to be good. Those are your two minutes and you must grab the moment. You go out there and say that 'I want to get this job'.

In Conclusion

Almost all forty-five interviewees from *OUT OF THE SPOTLIGHT* were asked, "What advice would you give to younger people or others who are out of work; those who are trying to climb the ladder of success?"

Their answers varied.

I remember Monty Hall walked the streets of New York and sent memos, every day, to all of his prospects. Finally, his memos paid off and he was hired by NBC Network to play his first major role as a cowboy in 'Cowboy Theatre'.

Then I remember Pat Boone. He did extremely well until he decided to mimic Axel Rose, coming out on stage dressed as a Goth or Heavy-metal Rock Star. Moving in religious circles and being deeply spiritual himself, others believed he'd turned 'dark' which, of course, he hadn't. He had to do a lot of explaining to get his career back on track!

Fess Parker almost had his spotlight put out when he was told he would never be allowed to portray another character other than a 'coonskin-wearing' frontiersman. He was stuck; all that talent held back. But he simply created another character that Disney would approve of, and onward he went!

Then, Steve Garvey; he started out in a small town with parents who had very little. His father, a driver for Greyhound bus services, was assigned to transport the Dodgers Baseball Team. Steve enjoyed being batboy at the games they played in his hometown, and through practicing with their discarded bats and balls, he grew up and went on to become the National League's Most Valuable Player in 1974 and again in 1978, with 1727 games played.

When interviewed, it seems to me that every one of the interviewees responded with advice that included dealing with rejection. One person might say 'no' to you when you're looking for a job, but if you ask enough people eventually someone will say 'yes'.

Indeed there is another word for this; *PERSISTENCE*. I also believe that another important bit of advice was '*not to look back at what was*' but rather to '*take a look at what is*'.

Looking at our past lives with all the good memories of our days in the sun is okay, as long as we don't dwell on the past. There is 'today' and we hope tomorrow will be there when we open our eyes in the morning.

As they say... *yesterday is history, tomorrow is a mystery, and today is a gift. Enjoy today!*

There is nothing that replaces hard work. Employers enjoy working with people who do not look at the clock. Besides; work is not 'work' if you're truly enjoying your job!

Show people are in a category of their own. Their Egos often have a way of destroying them. What a shock it is to our system when the spotlight goes out.

But then we see someone like Estelle Getty. She was eloquent in her remarks when she was at the top of her game in the famous TV series 'Golden Girls'. She knew that someday that light would go out, and it did... but she was mentally prepared for it and knew in her heart that it would. She personally chose to enjoy every moment in her Spotlight and never took her fame for granted.

Each of our interviewees has a different attitude and opinion regarding their present and future. Sometimes expectations lead to frustration. That's what happened frequently, to many of our interviewees.

Arte Johnson had his moments of fame each time he said, "Very interesting, but stupid!" as he played his role in 'Laugh In'. Life was never the same for Arte when his spotlight went out. NBC never called him again for twenty-five years. He had to deal with rejection... and he did.

There are so many conclusions to this book that it is difficult to single any of them out.

I hope that your reading experience has been enjoyable, interesting and that you've learned a little something. Feel free to share the advice given, and always remember... *our world has many mountains waiting to be climbed!*